C000221323

Between

Two Fires

What really happened in the Forgotten War? Though the events recounted in this book took place more than half a century ago, they have never been more relevant than today as Spain struggles to come to terms with its recent history. Years of research were necessary to dig out long-concealed information about that desperate conflict.

Journalist and author David Baird has been based in Spain for many years and has an intimate knowledge of the area where the anti-Franco guerrillas operated. His reports have appeared in leading publications worldwide, including The Economist, Maclean's Magazine, The Scotsman, the Sydney Morning Herald and the International Herald Tribune. He has twice been awarded Spain's national prize for non-Spanish travel writers. His other books range from travel guides to fiction.

"David Baird has painstakingly recreated the tragic yet heroic story of one small group of guerrillas. At a time when Spain is wracked by bitter dispute over what happened during and after the Civil War, this superbly written book could not be more timely. As exciting as any thriller, yet deeply moving, it deserves to be read by everyone concerned with the history of contemporary Spain."

— Paul Preston (author of *Franco - A Biography* and *The Spanish Civil War*)

By the same author

Sunny Side Up

Don't Miss the Fiesta!

Typhoon Season

Inside Andalusia

Back Roads of Southern Spain

East of Málaga

Spain - The Versatile Guide

The Incredible Gulf

Between Two Fires

Guerrilla war in the Spanish sierras

by

David Baird

Maroma Press

Copyright © David Baird 2008

First published February, 2008, in conjunction with the Cañada Blanch Centre for Contemporary Spanish Studies, London School of Economics.
Reprinted May, 2008.
Second edition, 2011.

Depósito Legal: MA-175/2008
ISBN: 978-84-612-2053-3

Published in Spain by Maroma Press
Calle Real, 76
29788 Frigiliana (Málaga)
http://maromapress.wordpress.com/
Spanish edition published by Editorial Almuzara, Córdoba.

All rights reserved. No part of this book may be reproduced, stored in a retrieval system, or transmitted, in any form or by any means, without the prior written permission of the publishers.

Front cover: guerrilla leaflet from Spanish Communist Party archives, Venta Panaderos photo by the author

Back cover: image courtesy of Civil Guard archives

Photographs of interviewees, Santiago Carrillo, Dolores Ibárruri and sierra scenes are by the author. Historic photographs and documents are from official archives (see list of sources) or have been kindly loaned by many individuals.

**To the village of Frigiliana
and its people**

And to those who never came home

CONTENTS

ACKNOWLEDGEMENTS

RESEARCH for this book would not have been possible without the cooperation of many people. Most of all I owe a debt of gratitude to the men and women of Frigiliana whose personal reminiscences are printed here. They answered my questions with exceptional patience, even when dealing with events which must have been painful to recall.

Many others aided my researches. I am particularly grateful to Sebastián Martín Iranzo for invaluable background information. Others helped with information and photographs, including Dolores García Platero, Rosario Platero Martín, Antonio Rodríguez Santisteban and his wife Carmelita, Manuel Rodríguez Santisteban, Ana Sánchez Santisteban, Adolfo Moyano Jaime, Antonio Acosta Cerezo, Manolo Ortega Rosa, Antonio García Sánchez, Federico Martín Requena, Antonio Urbano González, José Padial and Sebastián Orihuela Herrero.

Antonio Sánchez Sánchez generously shared with me the results of his many years' researching Frigiliana's history and his daughter Rita Sánchez Ruiz saved my life with her transcriptions of many hours of taped interviews. I wish to thank three friends who spent long hours checking the text, José Manuel Cabezas, Aníbal Alfaro and Antonio Martín Rodríguez. If errors have sneaked in, I alone am responsible.

J.E.Taylor (OSS archivist, National Archives, Washington), Vicki Ramos (Historical Archives of the Spanish Communist Party) and José T. Olea (secretary of the Association of Republican Army Veterans) furnished essential aid in tracking down documents and information, as did military archivist Eusebio Rodríguez in Almería and Granada.

This book would have been much more difficult to research but for the work of three local historians who have spent many years investigating the guerrilla war in the Axarquía. I am especially grateful to José Aurelio Romero Navas for sharing his knowledge and am also indebted to José María Azuaga Rico and Juan Fernández Olmo.

Acknowledgements

Ian Gibson and Paul Preston played an important part in bringing this book to press and I truly appreciate their help.

Frigiliana's parish priests, Damián Ramírez Lozano and Juan Manuel Báez Zambrana, obligingly allowed me to consult the parish records and the Frigiliana town hall opened its municipal archives to me.

I am deeply indebted to Charles and Carole Snyder for their help and hospitality in Washington. Others who aided my researches include former guerrilla (Comandante) José Murillo, Luis Domingo Ruiz (Foro por la Memoria, Granada), Almería researcher Juan Hidalgo, Pedro Peinado (La Gavilla Verde), Txema Prada and Pepe Narváez (Torrox Civil Registry).

Thanks too to Rob Stokes, Chris Fajardo, Edward Owen, Ken Brown, Mark Williams, Alan Roberts and Bruce Kaplan for all their practical advice and encouragement.

Above all, my thanks to my wife, Thea, for her patient support.

David Baird
Frigiliana
January, 2008

PROLOGUE

THE FOREIGN TOURISTS who flock every summer to the pretty village of Frigiliana, situated in the hills behind Spain's Málaga coast, cannot be expected to know what happened in this region (known as the Axarquía) during the 1936-1939 Civil War and during the subsequent years of the Franco dictatorship. Nor to be aware of the movement now afoot in Spain, after the long silence imposed by the regime, which favours investigating in the greatest possible depth every aspect of those agonising years.

For such visitors this book will come as a revelation, for Frigiliana and its surroundings were the scene of an epic, bloody struggle between the Civil Guard and the guerrilla. A struggle hardly mentioned in the official press, almost unreported outside Spain and today, so long afterwards, difficult to research in sufficient detail.

The experienced British writer and journalist David Baird has been living for years in Frigiliana and knows its people well. There could be nobody better suited to tell this story, and he has done so magnificently, devoting years to interviewing survivors and their families and burrowing into the archives. Local history? Yes, but local history that sheds intense and necessary light on the larger issues.

When the rising against the Republic began in July, 1936, the "Reds" of Frigiliana killed nobody. Nor did they do so during the following months. On the contrary, many right-wing people were afforded generous protection. It did the Republicans no good, however. When the Fascists entered the village in February, 1937, they established the same system of terror imposed in those that had already fallen, and the executions began at once, with the mayor as first victim.

It was inevitable, in such circumstances, that numerous villagers should flee to the high mountains behind Frigiliana and join the guerrilla movement. Baird's accounts of their exploits makes gripping reading. When what was to be the Second World War began in September, 1939, only a few months after Franco defeated the Republican army, the losers thought that the Allies, if they prevailed, would depose the dictator. This was believed particularly by the Spanish guerrillas who, with great bravery, were then harassing Hitler and the Vichy régime in France. How could the Allies fail to recognise the contribution made to their victory by the Spanish opponents of Fascism at home and in Europe, and thus do away with the execrable dictator responsible for the destruction of democracy south of the Pyrenees? The conviction that they would act accordingly increased the determination of the Maquis to continue the struggle in Spain, not least of those operating in the Axarquía. To accuse them of naivety, it seems to me, would be grossly unfair.

They were encouraged in their belief, moreover, by the Allies themselves. In 1942, after the latter's victory over Rommel at El Alamein on October 23 and the invasion of French Morocco and Algeria (Operation Torch), secret agents of the OSS (Office of Strategic Services) of the United States began to train Spaniards liberated from Vichy concentration camps in the north of Africa in guerrilla tactics, men desperate to return to their country and join the resistance.

At this point David Baird's narrative generates the excitement of the best Graham Greene. Take Carleton S. Coon, for example. What a character, expert in the tactics of subversion and in explosive devices who, having provisionally relinquished his prestigious university chair of anthropology, became involved in training Spanish *guerrilleros*! And his colleague and successor Donald Downes, the brain behind Operation Banana, whose mission was to plant spies in Spain, and who fell foul of the British Secret Service (SIS)!

The Allies' great worry at this time was that a machiavellian Franco might open the doors of Spain to Hitler, allowing him to hurry south and to take over Gibraltar. Allied espionage had to continue behind the scenes in Spain, of course, but the secret services were not always in agreement about how this should be done.

Such was the situation when, in October, 1943, the first landing of Spanish maquis trained in Africa took place on the beaches of the Axarquía. Baird reports that the men were armed with American and French weapons, machine-guns, pistols and bombs, plus a portable radio. When the Franco authorities learned of the operation, arrests followed and the US Embassy in Madrid found itself in serious difficulties with the regime, whose continued neutrality in the war was a major priority for Washington. It was Santiago Carrillo, the Spanish Communist leader, however, who was mainly responsible for cutting the American link and ensuring that his party was the only body responsible for the organisation of the guerrillas.

When a little later it became apparent that further resistance was useless, given the evident fact that the victorious Allies had now abandoned all intention of deposing Franco — these were the initial days of the Cold War — and that Stalin himself was recommending a different tactical approach in Spain (Communist infiltration of Franco's "vertical syndicates"), the Maquis, uninformed of the real situation, continued to operate in the Axarquía.

The dissident Communist Enrique Líster would later blame Carrillo, perhaps unjustly, of having betrayed the Maquis by not informing them of what was taking place and facilitating their escape. Their leader was the enigmatic "Roberto" (José Muñoz Lozano), whose bravery and discipline were such that he commanded the respect of his arch-enemies, the Civil Guard. An almost Romantic figure reminiscent of "El Tempranillo" and other colourful 19th-century Spanish bandits, as well as of the *guerrilleros* who opposed the forces of Napoleon, "Roberto" was finally captured and executed in Granada in 1953. His death spelt the end of the guerrilla movement, to the intense satisfaction of a regime which could now boast that Spain was genuinely at peace.

There are families in Frigiliana today who continue to wait for justice to be done to the memory of the villagers who died and suffered for the cause of democracy under the Franco dictatorship, some of whom still lie in unmarked graves in the Sierras Tejeda y Almijara. It is to be hoped that the so-called "Law of Historical Memory", recently passed by the Spanish Parliament, will help their cause. This book should certainly do so. By focusing public attention on those events and the courageous men and women involved, David Baird has done a great service, not only to Frigiliana but to Spain.

Ian Gibson
Madrid
January 18, 2008

INTRODUCTION

FROM TIME to time a stray hiker wandering about the ravines and crags of the Sierras Tejeda y Almijara nature park in southern Spain stumbles across splinters of human bone bleached by the sun. These forgotten fragments, and little else, exist as reminders of a pitiless war which many Spaniards were hardly aware of and which was ignored by the world beyond the Pyrenees. More than half a century has passed since that conflict which destroyed and exiled whole families, most of the protagonists have passed on, and one by one the witnesses are disappearing.

By chance — its geographical position and the effects of particularly harsh repression — in the 1940s the village of Frigiliana in the Axarquía region of Málaga province found itself in the front line of that war to the death. From a community of just over 2,000 inhabitants, 21 men fled to the mountains and joined the band led by Roberto, the nom de guerre of a legendary chief of the anti-Franco guerrilla movement.

Poor and isolated, Frigiliana lived through an inferno. Something hard to imagine when one looks at the village today. Avocadoes, custard apples, tomatoes and strawberries flourish in well-watered, terraced fields warmed by the Mediterranean sun, but few inhabitants continue to live from the land. They have discovered that there are more profitable fruits than those from the soil, fruits ripe for the picking.

A wave of fugitives from the grey skies of northern Europe have settled here, some to start a new life, others to enjoy their retirement years. Houses on the point of collapse sell for astronomic prices as do precipitous building plots, without water or electricity but with sea views. Scores of tumbledown farmhouses dotting the hills have been converted into luxury villas, each with barbecue and swimming pool, to shelter the new residents or to let at a juicy profit. Bulky four-wheel-drive vehicles squeeze though the village's narrow streets where tourists and residents rub shoulders and where it's hard to make out any Spanish amid so many tongues, English, German, French, Danish, Swedish, Russian, Chinese… Every day buses discharge groups of visitors eager to take photos of the picturesque Moorish quarter, try the local wine and make a purchase in one of the numerous souvenir shops.

Where until recently there were only mules, donkeys and goats, a multi-storey car park rises. The community of peasant farmers has become a part of the Costa del Sol and construction proceeds at a frenetic pace. In summer, when the houses, apartments and hotels are full, the population quadruples. Thanks to tourism, Frigiliana has been converted into one of the most prosperous villages in the province.

Few of the visitors are aware of this area's turbulent recent history. In the 1940s it was the sombre footsteps of troops and Civil Guards which echoed along the village's main street. Cars, heating, toilets and telephones were part of an unknown world. Here poverty and the curfew ruled. A state of war existed.

Although, officially, the Spanish Civil War ended on April 1, 1939, armed resistance against Franco and his Regime was not over. In the 1940s groups of guerrillas slipped out of their sierra hideaways to harass the dictatorship and try to create a climate of rebellion throughout the peninsula. The authorities regarded them as "bandits", "outlaws", "thieves" and "fugitives". These were not words picked haphazardly. The Regime did not want to dignify the rebels by admitting they had any ideology or any political objectives.

To the Spanish Communist Party, which set out to organise the anti-Franco rebellion from 1944, they were "heroic *guerrilleros* fighting against Fascism". The rebels were also known as "the Maquis", a name imported from France by Republican ex-combatants who had taken part in the underground resistance against the Nazis. In Frigiliana, where scores of families had some connection with the guerrillas, they simply refer to them as "the people of the sierra".

At first the rebels had some success and for a few years they kept the forces of the Regime on edge. Little news filtered through to the public inside or outside Spain of that war which in Málaga and Granada provinces reached a peak in 1948 and 1949 and where the last fighters continued in the mountains until 1952. The rebels fought against

Franco and Fascism, they fought against a brutal repression and for their own survival. But they were engaged in a war they could not win. They sacrificed themselves for an impossible dream, finally betrayed by all. As in all wars, especially in one where there are no clearly defined fronts and the enemy can be a neighbour, the struggle became dirty. There were acts of courage and of cowardice, of egoism and of selflessness, of tragedy and of treachery. And those who suffered for the sins of others were, as always, the innocent ones.

In this book the survivors (fewer every day) speak, those who lived through that brutal era and remember how it was. They include farmers, housewives, Civil Guards, rightwingers and leftwingers. Inevitably, as they represent a wide range of views, the opinions of some contradict those of others. Let the reader decide where the truth lies.

Most of those who speak are from the village, many of whom never had the opportunity to attend school. Country people, humble, without pretensions, people who don't appear on television, who don't write books or letters to the newspapers, people without a voice. They relate how a community found itself in the centre of a whirlwind over which it had no control. It is the history of what passed in one *pueblo* among many, a small part of the history of Spain. It's the story of how Frigiliana found itself trapped *"entre la espada y la pared"*, literally "between the sword and the wall".

CHRONOLOGY
A century in the life of a village

1900: Frigiliana population: 2,519.

1904: First street lighting installed.

1905: Hundreds of men and their families demonstrate, demanding food and work.

1916: Work begins on construction of a road between the village and the coast.

1921: New Civil Guard barracks, built at the expense of the Duchess of Fernán Núñez, owner of the Frigiliana mountains and El Ingenio sugar mill.

1929: Duke of Fernán Núñez, Count of Frigiliana, sells all his property in the municipality to the de la Torre Herrero family for 138,000 pesetas.

1933: Frigiliana's mayor and councillors flee the council chamber via windows and rooftops when it is invaded by members of a socialist trade union demanding help for the unemployed.

1936, February 26: Following general elections Popular Front members take control of the town hall.

1936, July 18: Urgent council meeting to discuss news of the uprising by a "subversive military-fascist movement", referring to the rebellion led by Franco.

1936, July 25: Parish church altarpiece destroyed and sacred images burned. A "people's committee" occupies the church and opens a market there.

1937, February 9: Málaga falls and Nationalist troops enter Nerja and Frigiliana while thousands flee along the coast towards Almería.

1937, May 21: Eight Frigiliana men, including the Republican mayor, are executed by a military firing squad at the Torrox cemetery.

1937-39: Guerrillas known as Los Niños de la Noche (Kids of the Night) make sabotage attacks in the Nerja-Motril area.

1939, April 1: The Spanish Civil War officially ends.

1943-44: Agents of the OSS (Washington's Office of Strategic Services) train and arm Spanish Communists in North Africa.

Chronology

1943, October: Joaquín Centurión Centurión (Juanito) arrives by boat from Algeria with men and arms, disembarking near Río de la Miel.

1944, February: Communist groups with American weapons and radios arrested in Málaga, Madrid, Melilla and other towns.

1944, September-October: 7,000 Spanish guerrillas under Communist command invade Spain through the Pyrenees but the attempt to foment an uprising fails and they quickly withdraw.

1944, October: Ramón Vías Fernández disembarks with nine comrades near Nerja to launch a guerrilla movement in Málaga.

1945, July: Moorish troops are posted to Málaga to combat the "delinquents".

1946, April 9: Frustrated attempt to kidnap Justo López Navas in his house in Calle Generalísimo Franco, Frigiliana. Nine villagers arrested.

1946, May 1: Ramón Vías and 25 other prisoners escape from Málaga prison. Vías is shot and killed by Civil Guards on May 25.

1946, summer: José Muñoz Lozano (Roberto), picked by the Communist Party to head the Málaga guerrillas, sets about uniting the fugitives in the sierras.

1946, September 2: Guerrillas kill Miguel Ángel Herrero, vice-president of

A hunting party at the Venta Panaderos, an inn on the busy mule track between the Málaga coast and Granada province. The picture was taken in 1919. In the 1940s the inn was frequented by both guerrillas and Civil Guards.

Málaga's Juvenile Court, at his farm, Los Almendros, and his foreman Antonio Lomas Orihuela when Herrero tries to resist being kidnapped.

1946, November 16: Confidential police report declares that "Málaga is the cradle of Spanish Communism and a breeding ground for common delinquents".

1947: Twelve Frigiliana men flee to the sierra and join Roberto's group.

1947, February 1: Four persons attack a Nerja electricity plant, leading to the detention of Antonio Ruiz Cerezo (Yelo).

1947, February 27: Ángel Sánchez García kidnapped at Cortijo Morea, freed after a ransom of 75.000 pesetas is paid.

1947: Four Frigiliana residents disappear, allegedly eliminated by the Civil Guard: Sebastián Platero Navas, 37, Manuel García Herrero, 40, and his dumb son Manulillo García Platero, 15, and Manuel Santisteban Gutiérrez, aged about 20.

1947, August 22: Paulino Fernández Ortega, aged 50, kidnapped by five armed men at his Frigiliana farm. A ransom of 150,000 pesetas is demanded, but he is found dead.

1947, November: Nerja-Frigiliana-Torrox is declared a war zone.

1948, February 21: Guerrillas steal 950 kilos of flour from the mill at La Molineta, Frigiliana.

1948, March 29: Seven infantry soldiers are killed and five wounded in an ambush in the Sierra de Cázulas (Otívar, Granada).

1948, June 30: Francisco Cecilia Cecilia (Porrete) is killed at Los Caños farm, Frigiliana, in a Civil Guard ambush.

1948, July 10: Joaquín Centurión Centurión (Juanito) dies in a confrontation with the Civil Guard at Los Peñoncillos, near Acebuchal.

1948, August: The Civil Guard orders all the inhabitants of Acebuchal to leave their homes.

1948, September 14: At the Cortijo Los Caños the guerrillas kill three villagers, Miguel Orihuela Moreno, aged 46, Rafael Orihuela García (El Zorro), 33, and José Lomas Orihuela (Narri), 36, accusing them of informing.

1948, September: Meeting in Moscow of Santiago Carrillo and La Pasionaria (Dolores Ibárruri) with Stalin who suggests a change in tactics, including using the guerrillas to protect Communist leaders in Spain.

1948, October: The Spanish Communist Party decides to dissolve the guerrilla movement.

1948, December 6: Hundreds of Civil Guards and soldiers try to wipe out Roberto's group on the Lucero mountain but the attack fails.

Chronology

1949, April 16: Miguel Moreno González is kidnapped by the guerrillas at a Frigiliana farm and executed as an informer.

1949, July 27: A shootout in the Cómpeta area results in the death of a guerrilla and a Moorish soldier and the wounding of two soldiers and two Guards.

1949, August 9: The terribly mutilated bodies of Francisco Iranzo Herrero (Paco Bendita) and José López Jurado (El Terrible) are found hanging in the Frigiliana riverbed. They are accused by the Maquis of being informers.

1949, September 17: Fierce battle at Cerro Verde. Two guerrillas are killed, Miguel Ángel García Platero (Espartero) of Frigiliana and Rafael Jurado Martín (Nico) of Torrox, and two Civil Guards, Antonio Toribio Tejada and Antonio García Reyes.

1949, November 2: Francisco López Centurión (Lucas) is executed by his fellow guerrillas after a court-martial in the sierra.

1950, April 20: Mohamed ben Abdela, a Moorish soldier, suffers an axe attack in Frigiliana by Antonio Platero Martín, El Moreno (Silverio), who flees to the sierra with José Castillo Moreno (Mocha) and Antonio Sánchez Martín, Lomas (Manuel).

1950, April 22: Three villagers, Antonio García Martín, 25, Antonio Triviño Cerezo, 26, and Manuel Martín Ruiz, 18, are arrested and taken to La Loma de las Vacas. Later their bodies are delivered to the cemetery, all "shot by the Civil Guard" according to the parish registry.

1950, July 17: Mocha, of Frigiliana, is among six guerrillas killed in a Civil Guard ambush at a farmhouse near Alhama de Granada.

1951, January 17: Blas Martín Vozmediano of Frigiliana and Gerardo Molina Cardeñas (Claudio) of Salar are shot and two other guerrillas taken prisoner in the Barranco Cordero off the Higuerón river valley.

1951, February 8: Blas Martín Navas (Gonzalo) and José Sánchez Martín (Domingo), both from Frigiliana, shot by the Civil Guard on the Contraviesa mountain (Granada).

1951, March 15: Vicente Martín Vozmediano, one of the Artabús brothers, surrenders with El Jacinto and cooperates in hunting down his former comrades.

1951, April 16: José Rojas Álvarez (Arturo), of Frigiliana, dies in a skirmish with Civil Guards on El Cisne mountain.

1951, July 5: Trapped in a shootout with the Civil Guard near Torrox, Antonio García Martín (Gaspar), of Frigiliana, commits suicide.

1951, August 16: Antonio Rojas Álvarez (Carlillos), of Frigiliana, is shot at the Alhama de Granada cemetery.

Chronology

1951, August 26: Bautista Acosta Urdiales (Tomarroque), of Frigiliana, dies in a confrontation with the Civil Guard at Cerro Gitano, Sierra de Cázulas (Granada).

1951, September 26: Roberto is arrested in Madrid with Francisco Sánchez Girón (Paquillo) and Ana Gutiérrez Rodríguez (La Tangerina).

1951, December: José Martín Navas (Tomás) and Sebastián Martín Vozmediano of Frigiliana are among the guerrillas detained in Málaga.

1952, January 20: The last of Frigiliana's guerrillas at liberty, Antonio Sánchez Martín (Lomas), is shot at the Ángel Rojas farmhouse.

1953, January 22 : Roberto is executed in Granada.

1953, May 6: Sebastián Martín Vozmediano (Artabús) executed in Granada.

1954, April 3: Antonio Platero Martín (El Moreno) and Manuel Triviño Cerezo (Valeriano) are executed in Málaga.

1958: The first telephone lines are installed in Frigiliana.

1964: The Frigiliana-Nerja road is paved. Television reception begins. The first foreigner settles in the village.

1975, November 20: General Franco dies and Spain begins a transition to democracy.

1979: In the first municipal elections since before the Civil War, the Unión del Centro Democrático becomes the ruling party.

1981: The town hall decides to establish a public library.

1983: The Partido Andalucista (Andalusian Socialist Party) wins municipal elections.

1986: Names of streets and squares are changed — Calle Generalísimo Franco becomes Calle Real and Plaza de José Antonio is renamed Plaza de la Iglesia.

1988: Frigiliana is awarded first prize in a competition for most improved and embellished Andalusia village.

21st century: The tourism boom and the surge of foreign settlers in rural areas introduce a new era of prosperity and frenetic construction in Frigiliana. Summer population: more than 8,000.

2001, May 16: The Spanish Congress agrees to eliminate the descriptions "delinquents" and "bandits" in official records relating to the guerrillas, but refuses to recognise them as Republican combatants.

2007: The Spanish parliament approves the Law of Historic Memory, intended to help "heal wounds still open among the Spanish and satisfy the citizens who suffered, directly or through their families, the consequences of the Civil War tragedy or the repression of the Dictatorship".

PART ONE

From the Phoenicians to Franco

GLOSSARY

AGL: Agrupación Guerrillera de Levante y Aragón. Guerrilla group operating in the Aragón and Valencia regions.
Brigada Político-Social: Franco's anti-subversion police.
CNT: Confederación Nacional del Trabajo. Anarchist trade union.
Civiles: members of the Civil Guard, a para-military police force.
FAI: Federación Anarquista Ibérica. Anarchist federation.
Falange: Fascist party, founded by José Antonio Primo de Rivera
Movimiento Nacional: ruling party, incorporating the Falange, during the Franco era
OSS: Office of Strategic Services. US intelligence agency.
PCE: Partido Comunista de España. Spanish Communist Party.
PSOE: Partido Socialista Obrero Español. Socialist Party.
Regulares: Moorish troops.
SIS: Secret Intelligence Service. British intelligence.
SOE: Special Operations Executive. British sabotage and subversion unit.
UGT: Unión General de Trabajadores. Socialist trade union.

San Sebastián's Day

JANUARY 20, 1952: San Sebastián's Day fell on a cold and wintry Sunday that year but the weather did not deter anybody from enjoying the festivities. Merry-go-rounds had been set up and children thronged around the stalls selling nougat and other delights. Forgetting about work for a day, the men chatted over drinks in the village's Casino bar while their womenfolk, preening in dresses bought with months of savings, gossiped as they strolled through the streets. Tradition ruled in this age-old fiesta and soon — as custom demanded — the saint's image would be borne through the streets in solemn procession. In the parish church, the faithful were attending mass. Civic dignitaries were seated in the front pews, including the Civil Guard chief, the mayor and the justice of the peace.

Then a Civil Guard slipped into the church, approached his superior and spoke to him in a low tone. Abruptly the officer rose to his feet, crossed himself, put on his tricorn hat and strode from the building. There was a murmur of comment among the congregation; something important had happened. And so it was, something which took everybody's breath away. When the people came out of church, they were in time to witness the arrival of an unscheduled procession. A squad of Civil Guards tramped into the plaza, escorting a mule. Sprawled across its back, face down, was a man's body. Behind came a woman and her small daughters, weeping. Amid a stunned silence, the macabre cortege crossed the Plaza de José Antonio and continued along the narrow, winding main street, the Calle del Generalísimo Franco.

The procession proceeded past the Casino bar and the candy stalls and merry-go-rounds and halted before the Civil Guard barracks. The guards entered to make their report and, shortly afterwards, began transmitting triumphant messages to Málaga and Madrid, while the mule and its cargo remained outside in view of a hypnotised public. There it stayed for hours, blood dripping steadily on to the cobbles. The villagers looked on, repelled but fascinated. Everybody knew whose body it was and everybody understood the significance of that scene. Lomas, the last man in the sierra, one of the village's own, was dead. It was all over.

Lomas, full name Antonio Sánchez Martín, was one of 21 men from the Andalusian village of Frigiliana who had fled to the mountains to join the guerrillas waging war against the Franco regime. He met his death at the age of 31. By then all his comrades had fallen: shot, detained, betrayed, executed by their own people. Now there was nobody left in the wild Sierra Almijara which rises behind the village. The sierra was empty, unless you counted the wild goats and the vultures. And the bones...

The Sierra Almijara and the village of Frigiliana as it is today

1. If God wills it

HIGH ON A ROCKY hillside 300 metres above sea-level, Frigiliana is one of the villages of the Axarquía, the easternmost corner of Spain's Málaga province. Springs of crystal water gush from many points in these foothills of the Sierra Almijara, accounting — or so it is said — for the villagers' nickname, "*los aguanosos*" ("the watery ones"). Man has scratched a living here from the time of the first Iberians and the Phoenicians. Water was not the only attraction: the lofty position allowed intruders to be easily spotted as they approached from the coast where in the past waves of invaders disembarked, from Romans and Vikings to Moors and Turkish corsairs.

For most of its existence Frigiliana was one more *pueblo* (village), forgotten and unknown, except for a 16th-century battle which earned it a brief mention in the history books. It occurred during the War of Granada when, following continued persistent persecution, the Moriscos (Moslem converts to Christianity) of the Alpujarras and the Axarquía rebelled against King Phillip II. The area was already suffering from the marauding *monfíes*, Morisco outlaws who sometimes made joint raids with the corsairs landing on the coast. The Moriscos of the Axarquía named as their leader Hernando el Darra, descendant of a family which had governed "Frexiliana" when the Moors ruled the whole of southern Spain. Respected for his intelligence and good judgment, he selected the Peñon

Frigiliana during the 1950s with El Fuerte mountain to the rear

de Frigiliana, the crag above the village, as the place where his people would make a stand. Thousands of Morisco families entrenched themselves in a desperate act of defiance in the Frigiliana fortress and on the sides of the adjacent El Fuerte mountain.

In 1569, with reinforcements shipped from Italy, a vastly superior Christian army crushed the Moriscos, killing 2,000. Some Morisco women leaped off clifftops when they saw the battle was lost, "preferring to die smashed to pieces rather than to fall into Christian hands", according to the historian Mármol de Carvajal. Their fears were probably justified for both sides committed horrific massacres. El Darra fled to the Frigiliana sierra, a formidable barrier of bare, grey peaks eroded by the elements and riven by aprupt chasms. From this refuge, he continued fighting for some time but his campaign could not succeed against the large number of opposing forces. Centuries later, that first guerrilla movement would have its parallel in this same zone of the Axarquía. There would be another echo of the past too. The first Christian soldier to raise the flag on the summit of El Fuerte was rewarded with land and settled in Frigiliana. He was called Gonzalo Vozmediano. Three of the guerrillas who fought in the sierra in the 1940s, the Artabús brothers, bore the same surname.

After ejecting the last Moriscos from their land in the Sierras de Almijara y

Tejeda, the Christians repopulated the area. Life went on with few major changes during centuries. The years passed: good years, bad years, bad harvests, good harvests, the typical history of an agricultural community. From time to time there were natural disasters, epidemics which devastated the population, storms which desroyed crops, and frightening earth tremors. God's anger. The villagers took the saints out in procession and prayed the rosary. Away from the world, isolated by poor communications, Frigiliana had no strategic importance and life, hard but peaceful, continued without much incident. The men worked the land, the women fulfilled their duty, the Counts of Frigiliana directed, the priests preached.

"If God wills it" was the solace of the *aguanoso*s. Fatalism sustained them in the face of privation. The community of small-time farmers always lived at the mercy of others, of rapacious pirates, unscrupulous politicians, distant monarchs, careless bureaucrats, absent aristocrats, high-handed administrators, inflexible clergy. They were chained to their small plots of land carved from the steep hillsides, their horizons cruelly limited by the need to gain their daily bread. Only their stoicism and their patience sustained them. Only a lucky accident or perhaps a miraculous connection with somebody of influence could rescue them from their ignorance and a predestined fate.

The invasion of the peninsula by Napoleon's forces at the beginning of the 19th century did have an impact. There were skirmishes with guerrilla bands, shootouts, fugitives, executions. When some French soldiers mysteriously disappeared and their bodies were found buried in Frigiliana basements and corrals, the furious invaders punished the village by hanging several men. To this day the place where they died is known as La Horca (the gallows). The violent incidents were a foretaste of another guerrilla conflict which would assail the area 130 years later.

Wars, political and social instability and the growth of anarchism among landless Andalusian peasants characterised the 19th century and had their repercussions in the Axarquía. Yellow fever and cholera accounted for the deaths of thousands, in 1884 earthquakes desolated parts of Málaga and Granada provinces (in Frigiliana several houses collapsed but there were no serious injuries), and then came an economic crisis provoked by the *phylloxera* plague which wiped out whole vineyards.

Guerrilla groups formed in the Axarquía during the War of Independence later developed into outlaws. Poverty, injustice and *caciquismo* (dominance by local tyrants, usually wealthy landowners) contributed towards the continuing growth of this phenomenon until the 1880s. Bandits terrorised the countryside and some became allies of the local bosses. In exchange for impunity guaranteed by these *caciques*, the outlaws offered their services at key moments, particularly during elections when bribes and menaces proliferated.

El Ingenio, biggest of the village's four water-powered mills, formerly belonged to the Dukes of Fernán Núñez (Photo: Padial de Nerja)

To battle against the increase in banditry, the Civil Guard was formed in 1844 and in the 1880s this paramilitary force confronted one of the most notorious outlaw bands. It was headed by three brutal Axarquía criminals: El Bizco of El Borge, El Melgares of Algarrobo and Frasco Antonio of Vélez-Málaga. Popular legend has it that El Melgares committed one of his most daring crimes in Frigiliana. He slipped into the village disguised as a priest and entered the Ingenio, the mansion of the Counts of Frigiliana, where at the point of a pistol he stole 20,000 *duros* (equivalent to 100,000 pesetas, a fortune at the time) from the manager before coolly making his exit.

Apart from delinquency, poverty and corruption, the Axarquía suffered from a serious lack of health and education facilities. At the start of the 20th century the expectation of life was little more than 30 years. One old-timer recalled that of 41 Frigiliana youngsters who went to the Cuban War only three knew how to write their names. More than 80 per cent of the village inhabitants were illiterate, a figure that was not to be reduced significantly until the second half of the century. Even so, with the new century some traces of the modern age arrived. Electric street lighting came to the village and in 1916 work began on building the first proper road from Frigiliana to the coast. But the change of most significance for the *pueblo* came in the year 1929. The Dukes of Fernán Núñez, grandees of Spain, who numbered among their titles that of Count of Frigiliana, sold all their holdings in the village to a local family. The purchase included a large area of forested mountains, the Ingenio (a rambling 16th-century structure which sheltered a sugar factory and the estate manager's residence), the Civil Guard barracks and hundreds of hectares of irrigated terraces and unirrigated hillsides. The total price was 138,000 pesetas.

On the new company, formed by the numerous members of the de la Torre family, depended the life of the village. The sierra, a source of resources for almost everybody, was theirs and the Ingenio, with its countless halls, cellars, stables, doors and balconies, symbolised power. The Company produced molasses (today it continues to do so and is the only such factory in Europe), bought honey, esparto and timber collected and transported from the sierra by the peasants, and levied a charge on the goatherds whose flocks grazed on the mountain slopes. While the Company complied with its inherited paternalistic obligations, the peasant farmers worked from dawn to dusk in the olive groves, the vineyards and the tiny terraced fields sown with sugar cane, potatoes and tomatoes. The Church was where it had always been. Tradition, custom, ritual. Life continued as always, unchanging. In 1929 the village, with 2,238 inhabitants, boasted four olive oil mills, three flour mills, one perfume factory, four apiarists, one sugar refinery, one electricity works, one vet, two barbers, one shoemaker and one doctor.

Rural life changed little over the centuries. This family, pictured in 1945, scraped an existence at the remote Cortijo del Imán — a perilous location during the years of the guerrilla campaign.

2. The Republic and the war

IN THE EARLY 1930s, a distant rumble indicated that things would not always continue the same. The king of Spain abdicated, the Republic came into existence, and amid demands for "Bread and work!" Anarchists, Socialists, Communists and scores of other groups manoeuvred to take advantage of the new situation. Even in Frigiliana there were signs of the incipient revolution. In 1933, when the mayor and councillors were holding a meeting, members of the Sociedad Obrera de la Vegetación, a Socialist union, erupted in the chamber demanding help for the unemployed. Matters became so heated that the councillors fled, escaping from the council chamber via windows and rooftops.

The year 1936 began peacefully enough with the customary seasonal rites. In January Frigiliana celebrated the fiesta of its patron saint, San Sebastián. The saint's blood-stained image, skewered by arrows, was carried in procession as usual. That year the fiesta was better than ever with hundreds of visitors present, reported the Diario de Málaga. "This year's attractions were unbeatable: good music, stupendous fireworks, popular and fashionable dancing, beautiful religious ceremony, election of Miss Frigiliana." The *pueblo* gossiped, danced, drank, enjoyed itself and went to bed as usual. It was the lull before the storm.

The triumph of the Frente Popular (Popular Front), a leftwing coalition, in February's general elections provoked a mixture of delight, alarm and turmoil across the country, with some provinces declaring a state of war and workers' strikes in Málaga. Amid popular fervour, members of the Popular Front seized control of the Frigiliana town hall. The two Spains confronted one another, one outrage succeeded another and the country tumbled into the abyss. Military revolt broke out on July 18 and the voices of reason fell silent.

In Frigiliana, as in many villages, there was a violent reaction. Anarchists and others broke into the parish church and burned the sacred images and, in an act of rebellion against all the traditional values, the Communists set up a meat market there. Although initially the commander of the Civil Guard post put himself "unconditionally on the side of the legal government", the barracks was sacked and the town council decided to install two classrooms in it. Some individuals amused themselves by walking through the village in guards' uni-

Canadian doctor
Norman Bethune

forms with tricorns on their heads, while residents considered to be "*los ricos*", the wealthy, were besieged in their houses and harassed by armed men demanding money. Their cows were confiscated and taken to the church where the "Reds" butchered them and prepared a banquet, inviting everybody to eat free of charge. The priest, Miguel Martín García, fled and spent some months in hiding until the arrival of the Nationalist troops. He served in Frigiliana and the neighbouring coastal town of Nerja between 1935 and 1949 and, though regarded as a right-winger, he interceded with the authorities on several occasions to help people under suspicion during the time of the guerrilla.

Local inhabitants insist there were no barbaric acts in Frigiliana such as those that occurred in other villages and certainly no deaths. When extremists from other places arrived to try to take vengeance on the Falangists (Fascist party members), village leftwingers saved their lives. Unfortunately, the Nationalist forces did not show the same compassion when they entered Nerja and Frigiliana on February 9, 1937. Aided by Mussolini's soldiers and air force, the rebels had taken Málaga the day before and the coastal highway was blocked by militia units and thousands of families fleeing before the advancing Fascists. The fugitives, mostly on foot, were mercilessly bombarded by planes and warships. The highway passed six kilometres from Frigiliana and a number of villagers joined the flood of refugees heading for Motril and Almería in the Republican zone.

Norman Bethune, the heroic Canadian doctor who organised a mobile blood transfusion service for the Republican army, encountered shocking scenes when he arrived at the coast to give help. He observed "a silent, haggard, tortured flood of men and animals" tottering along the Málaga road. "Dying burros had been pushed on to the beaches below, where people lay stretched in exhaustion, their swollen tongues hanging from puckered mouths. More children, more militiamen, more deserted villages. Stopped momentarily by an obstruction on the road, we were engulfed by shouted pleas, hands reaching out towards us, people begging for water, for transport to Almería." Planes swept overhead, Italian fighters and German Heinkels, "their machine-guns weaving intricate geometric patterns about the fleeing refugees." An estimated 3,000 to 5,000 people died on the highway to Almería.

In the village, amid cries of "Arriba España! (Up with Spain!)", a Carabineros captain announced the new order: the formation of a militia of Falangistas, all arms to be handed in, refugees to return to their homes so that their conduct could be investigated. On February 19 the streets were given new names, Generalísimo Franco, Queipo de Llano, José Antonio, 8 de Febrero... The rebels rounded up all those in any way connected with the Republic. For the "Reds" there was no mercy. Many women had their heads shaved and a number of men were forced to swallow castor oil until they vomited. Some residents were hauled off to jail, others to the firing squad.

When trucks carried off the detained men to Torrox, a neighbouring village, their womenfolk threw themselves in front of the wheels. In vain. Courts martial delivered their sentences on the "Reds", Socialists, union members, all those accused of being "rebels". Life sentences were doled out to the more fortunate ones. Manuel Martín Cortés, a member of the Socialist UGT (Unión General de Trabajadores), was spared the death penalty because he had hidden, he claimed, the chalice when the church's sacred images were burned. Others had no escape. The Torrox Registry records that on May 21, 1937, 14 men died at the cemetery "due to the discharge of firearms". Among those shot were eight inhabitants of Frigiliana: the Republican mayor Baldomero Cerezo Iranzo, aged 37, the deputy mayor Sebastián Conejero Espada, 27, an official of the Communist Party, and the councillors Eduardo García Platero, 43, and Antonio Gutiérrez García, 44, along with Francisco García Martín, 26, José García Ramírez, 32, José Pérez Castillo, 27, and Francisco Rojas Ramírez, 30. On August 12 another Frigiliana man, Antonio Cerezo Moreno (el Zocato), trying to hide in the sierra, was shot by a Nationalist patrol.

Sebastián Conejero, pictured with his wife, reportedly interceded to save the lives of local rightwingers when he was Frigiliana's Republican deputy mayor. Even so, he was not spared when eight villagers were executed at Torrox.

3. Franco's peace

IN THE CIVIL WAR, a number of villagers fought with the Republicans, others with the Nationalists. Sometimes political conviction led them to serve on a particular side, more often it was decided by sheer chance. When the war ended in 1939, those who had fought on the losing side or were accused of collaborating with "the Reds" were tried for "military rebellion" by the actual rebels. Some were sentenced to years in prison, others were sent to forced labour camps in such projects as the Lower Guadalquivir Canal. Frigiliana men (see the recollections of Francisco Martín Triviño) were among the thousands of prisoners who built that waterway which helped transform the Guadalquivir marshes into ricefields. All manner of public works including dams, new settlements and the Valley of the Fallen, a colossal shrine to Civil War victims, were constructed by the slave labour of luckless opponents of the Regime.

In these circumstances, it is hardly surprising that a good number of Axarquía men, finding themselves always under suspicion and treated as second-class citizens, decided to run off to the mountains.

In the 1940s global attention was fixed on the events of World War Two. Spain, deep in misery after the horrors of its own war, was forgotten. On their knees amid the ruins of their country, the Spanish people struggled to recover, watched over by an implacable regime.

Compared with city residents, the Frigiliana community was fortunate because most families were lucky enough to cultivate their own land, small though their holdings were. Some 2,120 plots were divided among 500 owners, a system of *minifundismo* which allowed subsistence farming but little more. The soil was exhausted and there was no money to invest in fertilisers or in improving the irrigation channels or the quality of the seeds. But at least there was almost always something to eat, *migas* (fried semolina), sweet potatoes, figs, potatoes, tomatoes, beans, a piece of bread spread with olive oil or molasses.

Nerja, the nearby coastal town, was not so lucky. Almost all the land around that poor fishing community belonged to the Marqués de Larios and was sown with sugar cane to supply his many mills. There, every morning the men lined up before a bar hoping to be rewarded with a day's work. Hungry people from Nerja trudged up to Frigiliana to beg for food.

A network of paths crisscrossed the countryside and along these moved the farmers and their mules and donkeys. Only 300 hectares of the Frigiliana municipality was irrigated, through a system of waterways that had existed since Moorish times. The commonest crop was sugar cane, another legacy of the Moors. The 1,200 hectares of unirrigated land produced moscatel grapes, olives and almonds. Each family proudly prepared its own wine in its *cortijo*, or farmhouse, using methods that weren't much different from those employed by the Romans. To obtain stronger wine, they trod a mixture of grapes and raisins which had been dried under the sun. The sweet golden liquid, with an alcoholic content of about 17 degrees, was no luxury. It was a necessity, something to help them endure life's hardships.

Behind the village rose the sierra, a source of wealth covering 2,300 hectares. All belonged to the Company and a good part of the population depended on it. Every day they would rise at 3 or 4am and hike into the mountains to cut firewood or collect esparto grass and then, if they didn't own a mule or donkey, they carried back the fruit of their endeavours on their backs.

Towards the end of the 1940s labourers earned 12 pesetas a day, working from dawn to dusk. But a loaf of bread cost 15 pesetas, a kilo of sardines or octopus four or five pesetas, and a light bulb six pesetas. A litre of brandy from Jerez could be bought for nine pesetas — but who had the cash for such luxuries? To obtain basic foodstuffs (and tobacco), ration cards were needed, but the amounts distributed from time to time, such as a quarter litre of oil and 200 grams of rice per person, were clearly insufficient.

Under these conditions, the black market (the *"estraperlo"* as it was known) flourished. The continual movement of men and animals between the Málaga and Granada provinces was nothing new. The fastest muleteers, the elite, transported fresh fish. In the afternoon they loaded their mules on the beaches and climbed up into the sierra at a run along a narrow, winding, rocky path. In darkness they traversed El Puerto, the Frigiliana pass 1,200 metres above sea-level, and began the long descent to reach the villages of Granada by the following morning. En route, they would pause only for a few seconds to take a drink in one of the wayside inns. Also via the Puerto, passed loads of raisins, molasses, fruit and tobacco heading for Granada and flour, lentils, chick peas and other basics bound for the coast. Some inhabitants regularly made the exhausting trip to buy bread in Granada villages, carrying it back to sell for a few pesetas in the streets of Frigiliana. The postwar scarcity of so many commodities made the business of the muleteers extra profitable. It was difficult to control the black market and inevitably the guerrillas sought to benefit from this traffic through the sierra. In 1949 the town hall annual budget totalled only 123,600 pesetas. In

1952, when the budget rose to 144,000 pesetas, the secretary's annual pay was 17,500 and the municipal policeman's 5,500. Frigiliana had no library and no football pitch, and neither a doctor nor a dentist.

The villagers, except for the handful of so-called *"ricos"* (a very relative description), lived in dwellings of extreme simplicity. The style had not changed in centuries: thick walls made of mud and rocks sealed by innumerable coats of whitewash, roofs of pine beams covered with cane and tiles, windows with shutters but no glass, floors of compacted clay or earthenware tiles, furniture of poplar and pine with rush seats. The women cooked over wood fires in the chimney place and carried water from the fountains in earthenware vessels. As in many houses the stable was at the rear, an esparto mat had to be spread over the floor to allow the mule to enter and leave. Each family's goat, which also slept in the stable, went out every day with the village flock, a service for which the town hall received a fee. As flush toilets were virtually unknown, the stable also served as a bathroom.

Malta fever was endemic and ridding the fleas from their children's hair presented mothers with a never-ending challenge. Outbreaks of typhus, tuberculosis, diarrhoea, enteritis, smallpox and diphtheria wreaked havoc all over the country, infant mortality reaching 142 deaths per 1,000 births.

Every day the bakers, on foot or leading a mule or donkey, passed through the village, delivering bread from house to house. In more peaceful times they carried it to the farmhouses too. From Nerja fish-sellers trekked up on foot, selling their wares and haggling over the price with the housewives at the top of their voices. From time to time there passed through the *pueblo* blacksmiths, knife-sharpeners, chair-repairers, tinsmiths and pedlars with their donkeys, loaded with used clothing, goat cheese, rustic pots.

In the evenings entertainment was strictly limited: a glass of aguardiente or the local wine or ersatz coffee (prepared with roasted barley), a stroll, a Celta or Ideal cigarette of black tobacco lit with a flint lighter, a game of dominoes or cards in the Casino cafe, gossiping in one of the tiny bars installed in neighbours' living rooms. Then the conversation would be enlivened by spicy jokes, popular sayings, retailing of amusing anecdotes, verses composed on the spur of the moment. Even in the most difficult times the innate humour of the *aguanosos* emerged. But not for long. From 10 o'clock every night a curfew ruled. It was wisest to return home early, especially for those living in the Barrio Alto (considered a nest of subversion), because the Civil Guard patrols suspected anybody walking through the streets without a very good reason.

In winter, under the feeble light of a 10-watt bulb, the family gathered around the *mesa camilla* (a round table draped with a large cloth that covered everybody's knees). Under the table a brazier filled with hot ashes, the only heating in the house, toasted all, but only up to the waist. As no girl of good reputation

Franco proclama la verdad, el derecho y la razón

PATRIA

sagrados e indiscutibles DE ESPAÑA

DIARIO DE FALANGE ESPAÑOLA TRADICIONALISTA Y DE LAS J.O.N.S.

frente a la suicida y loca cobardía del mundo

"TODOS SABEN QUIEN AMENAZA DE VERAS A LA PAZ Y QUIEN CONSPIRA CONTRA ELLA, Y SIN EMBARGO, NADIE SE ATREVE A PRONUNCIAR EL NOMBRE"

La actitud gallarda, noble, caballerosa e inmaculada de España durante la guerra está muy por encima de todas las calumnias e infamias del comunismo y sus inconscientes servidores

"ES INMORAL QUE LOS MISMOS QUE SE BENEFICIARON DE NUESTRA NEUTRALIDAD PERMITAN QUE SE DISCUTAN LOS MEDIOS QUE EMPLEAMOS PARA ALCANZARLA"

EL CAUDILLO HIZO ANTE LAS CORTES UNA LARGA, MINUCIOSISIMA Y MAGISTRAL EXPOSICION DE LO QUE NUESTRO REGIMEN ES Y SIGNIFICA PARA ESPAÑA EN TODOS LOS ASPECTOS DE LA POLITICA INTERIOR Y EXTERIOR

LAS CORTES PRIMERO Y EL PUEBLO MADRILEÑO EN MASA DESPUES, RINDIERON A S. E. EL MAS FERVOROSO Y EMOCIONANTE HOMENAJE DE INQUEBRANTABLE ADHESION

Cien minutos duró el sensacional discurso del Jefe del Estado

Cuarenta y seis veces fué interrumpido por los frenéticos aplausos de la Asamblea

DETALLES DE LA SOLEMNISIMA SESION INAUGURAL DE LAS CORTES

¡NUESTRO REGIMEN NO LO ES DE DICTADURA!

"Sensational speech by the Chief of State" — *Patria* of Granada dutifully reported Franco's declarations

was allowed out alone with her boy-friend, this was one of the few opportunities for an engaged couple to flirt with one another. On the three or four radios in the village one could listen to the programmes of Radio Nacional, the soap operas, the soccer commentaries of the popular broadcaster Matías Prat, the latest songs of Concha Piquer, Juanito Valderrama and Imperio Argentina, or the music of Glenn Miller. Only the most daring, or most imprudent, tried to tune in to the anti-Franco transmissions of Radio España Independiente, known as *La Pirenaica*, a weak, crackling signal from a distant world.

On Sundays there were film shows for those who could pay the six *reales* entrance (a *real* was one quarter of a peseta) although, as blackouts were frequent, you were never sure of seeing the end of the film. The forces were among the best clients, trying to relax alongside the countryfolk they were policing. Besides the No-Do, the Regime's news service, the audiences could enjoy such films as *The Sign of Zorro*, with Tyrone Power and Linda Darnell or *Lady Hamilton*, with Vivien Leigh and Laurence Olivier. Of course, any morally dangerous scenes had been removed by the censors, implacable during that era when kissing in public was forbidden and the scandalous works of Alberti, Balzac, Gide, Hemingway, Lorca, Moravia, Sartre and many more were prohib-

Frigiliana street around 1950

ited either by the Church or the Regime, or by both.

The Church, one of the pillars of the Regime, played a particularly important role. School tuition left no doubt about the superiority of the Roman Catholic religion and the moral rectitude of the glorious "national crusade". Every year on November 20, the anniversary of the execution by the Republicans of José Antonio Primo de Rivera, founder of the Fascist Falange party, a ceremony was held to renew the inhabitants' patriotic fervour and, at the same time, to underline who had won the war. The whole village walked in procession from the church to the large cross erected in front of the Ingenio. The priest and the mayor, a government-appointed Falangist, presided over a homage to the fallen, in the presence of the third pillar of the Regime, the military, represented by the Civil Guard.

One by one the mayor called out the names of the villagers who had died in the Guerra Civil: Antonio Julio Jiménez Navas, Antonio Cañedo Sánchez, Antonio Rodríguez Sánchez, Plácido Ramos Platero, Manuel Agudo Martín, José Jaime Castillo, Bautista Cerezo Álvarez, followed by the name of José Antonio. After each name the people responded: "¡Presente!" Then, arms raised in the Fascist salute, they sang the Falangist anthem, "*Cara al sol (Face to the sun)*". The seven men honoured had fought in the Nationalist army. Nobody had the nerve to ask about the fate of the other combatants, the men who had served in the Republican ranks and had never returned home. About them there was only silence, which continues to this day.

One Republican war veteran did return, Francisco Ruiz García. Very ill, he died shortly afterwards. But the families of the others still do not know what happened to them. Such is the case of Sebastián González González. His son, Sebastián, a retired municipal policeman, recalls: "His comrades told us they had seen him fatally wounded in the battle of Teruel. But we have never found out where he was buried." The others who never came home were two brothers,

Miguel and Javier Retamero Peralta, and Baldomero Ruiz Cerezo and Eduardo Platero López. Their names do not figure on any commemorative monument. Nor do those of the Nationalist side, united in death though they are. Even today the matter is too fraught with emotion.

The Church guarded over the faithful and, when a couple wished to marry, the Church's blessing was essential. But, as there was little money for elaborate celebrations, the bride and groom had to think carefully about the details. For this reason some couples elected to have their weddings at four in the morning. As Don Domingo Campillo Gascón, one of the village's more memorable priests, explained to them, he followed the fee system set by the Church and the ceremony was cheaper in the hours of darkness. There was another obvious advantage: it was the custom at wedding celebrations to offer food and drink to all and sundry, which could cost a family a small fortune, but few neighbours were going to rise before dawn to attend a reception. Thus, more than one wedding was solemnified in darkness. And, as in those days honeymoons were something one saw only in the films on Sundays, the groom could always, if he felt so inclined, take advantage of his early rising and go out to the fields to earn a day's pay. Poverty ruled in the *pueblo.*

Frigiliana's communications with the rest of the world were very limited. There was no way of communicating by telephone nor by telegram, although there was a telegraph office in Nerja (the telephone did not reach Frigiliana until 1958, six years after Nerja). A visit to the "capital", Málaga, was not something one undertook without good reason. As there was no public transport, the villagers had to walk to Nerja where they caught one of the three daily buses of the Alsina Graells company. Only in the 1950s did the village acquire its first "bus", a large, green Chevrolet saloon belonging to Vicente Ruiz.

The 60-kilometre journey along a winding road full of potholes was lengthy and tiring. And Málaga was like another planet. There were the offices of the tax collectors and all those other bureaucrats whose only interest, it seemed, was to create problems for humble country folk. There too was the only hospital and everybody knew that one could pray the rosary and recite a thousand Lord's Prayers but, when the sick returned from the capital, it was most likely that they arrived in coffins. Everywhere one noticed the yoke-and-arrows insignia and the photos of the Generalísimo and José Antonio. From official cars alighted well-dressed men, their hair glistening with Brillantine. There in the capital were the residences of the big landlords and the businessmen who moved like fish in the waters of the Francoist system.

Pedlars, war-disabled, blackmarketeers, beggars, boot-blacks, gypsies, legionnaires, sailors, smugglers, wheeler-dealers swarmed through the streets. In the dry, dusty Guadalmedina riverbed, barefoot, half-naked children played amid the rubbish and the rats. Long queues indicated when it was a day for distribution of flour, oil or other food rations. For the well-off, naturally, there were no shortages. Everything was for sale in the city: women, liquor, coffee, contraband of all sorts. You could even buy cigarettes with blond tobacco like those they smoked in the movies, although these tasted of damp straw.

Members of high society could attend tea-dances in the Hotel Miramar or enjoy "Spain's best spectacle of Andalusian art", a performance by Lola Flores and Manolo Caracol in the Teatro Cervantes. In better-class establishments, white-shirted waiters served immaculate, dark-suited clients, who scanned the daily papers, the Falangist *Sur de Málaga* and *ABC* (traditionally monarchist), when not engaged in interminable conversation. In order to assure oneself that all was well with the world one had to read the tightly controlled press. This was slow to wake up from its love affair with Fascism. Thus, in January, 1945, nobody questioned a headline in *Sur* which reported: "Enthusiasm of the German people for Hitler's speech".

Apart from Hitler, sport, bullfighting and the Church also received favourable treatment in the pages of *Sur*. And also Falangist rituals, as in this typical report: "Reaching Vélez-Málaga at an advanced hour, the Cardenal Cisnero Centuria (Youth Front) proceeded to the cross of the fallen, where they pronounced the customary prayers and sang *Cara al Sol*, giving the ritual responses to the Centuria chief, comrade José Utrera." José Utrera Molina was a staunch follower of José Antonio Primo de Rivera and eventually became secretary of the Movimiento (the Falange's national organisation). He was a familiar figure in the Axarquía, acquiring a luxurious residence in Nerja with views of the sea.

In the press the pronouncements of the Caudillo were sacred. On January 19, 1945, he warned the Falange's National Council: "We cannot rest in our work for the battle is not yet over." So hard was the battle that about 80,000 political prisoners languished in Spain's jails and executions continued without pause. In the month of October, 1944, alone 1,647 prisoners were executed. The figure was not mentioned in the media but in a confidential report of the United States ambassador.

Sur did reveal something of what was going on. In the February 27, 1945, issue, you could read: "Sentence fulfilled – At dawn today the sentence ordered by the courts against 16 Communist terrorists was carried out. Among them were several chiefs of action groups infiltrated via the Pyrenees frontier who had committed crimes and other terrorist acts." The paper also reported that 300,000 persons had rendered "the ultimate homage to the Falangist comrades assassinated by the Communists in Madrid".

However, the world knew little or nothing of the anti-Francoism resistance in the sierras. Only the inhabitants of villages like Frigiliana were about to discover exactly what a struggle of this type signified. For the *aguanoso*s it was not necessary to read any newspaper. Because, between the years 1945 and 1952, they would experience guerrilla war at first hand.

4. War in the sierras

ON MOONLESS NIGHTS in 1943 and 1944 small craft cruised stealthily into the remoter coves along Spain's southern coast to deposit armed men trained in guerrilla warfare. It was the start of a Communist-inspired attempt to create a nationwide movement that would coincide with Allied victory in northern Europe and result in the ousting of the Franco regime.

The base selected for this enterprise in southern Andalusia was a range of dolomitic limestone as spectacular as it is difficult to penetrate. The Almijara and Tejeda sierras present a tormented landscape of narrow gorges, wild valleys, extensive caves and sharp ridges, perfect for mountain goats and for guerrillas. Only a few stony paths, steep and sinuous, crossed the mountains, winding below abrupt ridges. Up there were the Cortijo del Imán, Cerro Verde, Puerto Blanquillo, Cueva del Daire, Venta Panaderos, El Cisne and Collado de los Civiles, places lost in the sierra but with names etched for ever in the history of the Axarquía and its people. The paths linked small villages, such as Frigiliana, Torrox, Cómpeta and Canillas de Albaida in Málaga province with Arenas, Fornes, Játar and Jayena in Granada. Formerly, there was a constant coming and going

Armed rebels landed on this beach near Nerja

of loaded mule trains along these routes, as well as the movement of smugglers, black-marketeers and all manner of travelling salesmen. The traffic never ceased day and night, and at dawn others arrived, timber-cutters, quarrymen, lime-kiln workers, charcoal-burners, and collectors of esparto grass and pine resin.

Today, due to the ravages of man and particularly a series of devastating forest fires, where once there were pines, oaks, wild olives, carobs, yews and other trees, you find stunted bushes and scrub. In the past, when forests offered more shelter and only paths and mule trails penetrated the Sierra Almijara, it was much easier to hide up there. Taking to the mountains is an old tradition in Andalusia. For centuries fugitives from repression and justice have found refuge in the sierra. So it was in the years following the Spanish Civil War.

The first anti-Franco guerrilla movement was organised between 1937 and 1939 when the battle line between Republican and Nationalist forces was situated to the east of Motril in Granada province. Guerrillas gathered information and attempted sabotage along the Granada coast and in the Axarquía, the easternmost corner of Málaga province, where Frigiliana lies. Because they often went into action at night, they were known as Los Niños de la Noche (kids of the night). In the spring of 1938 the Niños took part in an unprecedented rescue. They freed 300 Asturias Republicans, officers and men, held in the Carchuna fort on the coast and escorted them to the Republican lines, all without firing a shot.

After the war, while the country endured fierce repression, thousands of exiles spread across the world, from the Soviet Union to Mexico, from Algeria to England, from the ranks of the French Foreign Legion to Mauthausen concentration camp (of 7,000 Spaniards who died in German camps, about 1,100 were from Andalusia and 148 from Málaga province). The exiles dreamed of reconquering Spain, but the opposition to the Franco regime was scattered, disorganised and riven by discord, incapable of working together. In a bid to unite these groups, in 1942 the Spanish Communist Party forged the Unión Nacional Española, an anti-Franco alliance. But many Republicans, recalling events in the Civil War, were suspicious of Communist intentions. Anarchists, Socialists and Republicans plus Basque and Catalan nationalists formed their own organisation, the Alianza Democrática Española.

While the Socialists did not support the idea of armed struggle, pinning their hopes on the Allies, who would surely cross the Pyrenees to expel Franco, the Communists prepared to act. Thousands of ex-Civil War combatants were fighting in the Maquis, the French Resistance, and it occurred to the Unión Nacional leaders that the same guerrilla tactics could be exported to Spain. The aim: a national rising in preparation for the arrival of the Allies once they had crushed the Germans. As the Spaniards had fought the Nazis both inside and outside their country, they believed the Allies would repay the debt. And the Communists would have a head start in forming a new government. Within Spain there was no attempt at reconciliation. Republican sympathisers or those who had joined any leftwing party or trade union found themselves, if not executed or imprisoned, continually harassed. Many jobs were denied to them and their families. Even after years in jail, those with what were considered subversive backgrounds had to report frequently to police stations. Many fled to the sierras, some fearing for their lives, others sick of being persecuted. Some had blood on their hands, others were common delinquents, but others had simply fought on the losing side. An unpardonable error in the Francoist empire. These, the fugitives, were to form the nucleus of the guerrilla, but it was the Communists who undertook to supply them with arms and organise them in disciplined groups.

After the ill-advised attempt to invade Spain en masse across the Pyrenees in October, 1944, resulted in failure, the Communists concentrated on creating a guerrilla force. Experienced combatants began infiltrating into Spain and made contact with fugitives and Republican sympathisers. Eventually six guerrilla groups were formed, those of Galicia-León, Asturias-Santander, Central Spain, Extremadura, the AGLA (Agrupación Guerrillera de Levante y Aragón) and Andalusia.

Although the AGLA (operating in Teruel, Cuenca and Valencia) had the closest contact with leaders in exile and was considered the strongest and most active group, the one created in Málaga and Granada provinces distinguished itself for various reasons. When the other formations had already succumbed to tough repression, the group in the Almijara and Tejeda sierras was approaching its maximum effectiveness. Because of its distance from the French frontier, it was impossible to send arms and men by land. Instead, they came from North Africa.

On the other side of the Mediterranean, only 200 kilometres or so from the Andalusia coast, Algeria in 1943 and 1945 was a hotbed of intrigue, of the military, spies, refugees, conspirators, blackmarketeers. The Spanish exiles dreamed of returning to their country and United States agents offered them help in one of the strangest clandestine operations of World War Two: American instructors trained and supplied arms to the Spanish Communists with the aim of infiltrating them into the peninsula. Once in Spain, besides creating a security problem for the dictator and his pro-German regime, they had to report on the coastal defences. Allied plans were fermenting to invade Europe, including — who knew? — Spain.

When a tip-off exposed the American infiltration, it created an embarrassing situation for Washington in an especially critical moment just before the Normandy landings. The affair enraged the Communist Party hierarchy as much as it did the US ambassador in Madrid. Neither one nor the other approved of such a collaboration between Reds and capitalists.

5. Comrades — the OSS and the Communists

ALTHOUGH SPAIN had kept out of World War Two, the protagonists mounted clandestine operations throughout the peninsula. Scores of agents were engaged in espionage, deception, sabotage and misinformation from Madrid to Gibraltar, Lisbon to Casablanca, Algiers to Tangier. The Abwehr (German intelligence) chief in Spain, Wilhelm Leissner (pseudonym Gustav Lenz), commanded a network of 1,300 people, of whom more than 700 were full-time officers and agents. The Third Reich representatives enjoyed special privileges from the Franco regime, which shipped war material to Germany and turned a blind eye to German U-boats receiving supplies in Vigo and the Canaries.

Britain's MI6 ran a network of agents from Madrid and Gibraltar. The United States only established its intelligence agency, the Office of Strategic Services (OSS), the forerunner of the Central Intelligence Agency, in 1942. It was founded and headed by Colonel William A. (Wild Bill) Donovan, a World War One hero, successful lawyer and friend of President Roosevelt. The OSS created at least two networks in Spain, one consisting of 14 agents and 75 "sub-agents" (presumably part-timers). It also ran a shipping company, with three vessels totalling 540 tons, whose true business was the transport across the Mediterranean of refugees, escaped POWs, arms and other clandestine cargo.

In 1942 intelligence work intensified. Dozens of American diplomatic officials with unusual skills were posted to North African ports as part of the OSS's first major mission. Supervising North Africa was Colonel William A. Eddy, who set up shop in the international port of Tangier, liaising with the Special Operations Executive (SOE), the secret British organisation created to arm and train armies in Axis-occupied territories, and also members of the Cinquième Bureau, French military intelligence.

Tangier was handy for French and Spanish Morocco and, just across the water, Gibraltar. Spies virtually tripped over one another in such locations as the stately Hotel Reina Cristina in Algeciras, where Abwehr and MI6 agents eyed one another over the tea-cups between scanning the Straits for shipping movements. The Abwehr had worked with the Spanish navy to construct a sonic detection system in the Straits and 14 infra-red surveillance stations, nine on the Spanish coast and five in Morocco. The Germans suspected that sooner or later the Allies would launch an attack on Europe. The only point was: where? The guessing game was in full swing in the autumn of 1942 when thousands of Allied troops in the US and in Britain prepared for action and tons of equipment were being assembled in Gibraltar. On October 23 General Erwin Rommel's Afrika Korps, which had scored notable victories in the desert sands of Libya and Tunisia, was sent reeling by a huge British assault commanded by General Montgomery. German hopes of controlling the Suez Canal were blasted by the decisive battle of El Alamein. Then, on November 8, came Operation Torch. Germany's High Command was stunned as Anglo-American forces, monitored by General Eisenhower in Gibraltar, streamed ashore in Morocco and Algeria, French possessions controlled by the pro-Nazi Vichy regime.

The Allies were acutely concerned about how Spain would react. Franco had incorporated the internationally administered city of Tangier into Spanish Morocco in 1940 and dreamed of extending his empire by absorbing French Morocco. It was feared that launching Torch might provoke Franco to discard his neutrality, either throwing in his own men — said to number 150,000 in Spanish Morocco — or permitting German troops to pass through Spain to attack Gibraltar and cross the Straits. To keep Franco onside, Sir Samuel Hoare, the British Ambassador to Madrid, assured him shortly before Torch that Britain would not intervene in Spain's internal affairs during or after the war, nor would it invade the mainland or any Spanish overseas territory. And President Roosevelt sent Franco a message declaring: "I hope you will accept my full assurance that these moves are in no shape, manner or form directed against the government or people of Spain or Spanish Morocco."

Such assurances must have been music in Franco's ears. He was playing a risky game. His phoney neutrality was a constant provocation to the Allies who had debated the wisdom of an attack on Spain. Indeed, OSS files show that in April, 1942, an official named Edward Dodd suggested that the Spanish peninsula was "the slickest of all places to attack". His top-secret memo proposed an invasion direct from the USA, entering all Spanish and Portuguese ports but chiefly Santander and Bilbao. Specialised troops would ensure the Pyrenees was an insurmountable barricade against the Germans while Spain was converted into a gigantic base for a future offensive.

Dodd claimed: "The populace is still about 70 per cent anti-Franco. It is also pro-American because the U.S. has been feeding it right along and because Spanish America has some influence on the mother country. It would probably be the least-difficult country in Europe to conquer because its fighting strength and resources are exhausted, and because it is not reinforced as much by Germans as are the occupied countries." He added (ironically considering the

Allies' postwar hands-off policy): "Spain is the one neutral in Europe which we could jump on saying we were liberating the country from Fascist oppression." Although OSS chief Donovan received the memo, described by an aide as a "grand idea", there is no record that he took any action on it.

Following the successful Torch landings, Rommel's forces in Libya were squeezed between US soldiers pushing eastwards into Tunisia and Montgomery's victorious Eighth Army. Algiers became a military command post and the base of Allied intelligence operations. Colonel Eddy moved into the Villa Rose, a stone's throw from General Eisenhower's headquarters, the St George Hotel. His growing band of OSS operatives worked from a splendid mansion named the Villa Magniol. Among them was Carleton S. Coon, a noted Arabic-speaking anthropologist and university professor. Daring, resourceful, with a ruthless streak and a taste for adventure, Coon could have been the model for Indiana Jones.

Carleton S. Coon

In Algeria were thousands of potential anti-fascist activists, many of them Spaniards who had fled into exile in 1939. In his autobiography, Coon records that at Aîn-Taya on Cap Matifou, about 30 miles west of Algiers, a British army colonel named Crawford ran a training school for anti-Vichy volunteers of mixed origin, French colonists, Arabs, Jews, Spaniards and others. "They were young, enthusiastic, and eager to learn," recalled Coon. "My job was to teach them all sorts of paramilitary activities, including tossing hand grenades and tying up prisoners."

Coon was not a man to hesitate before a violent solution, as a memo he later wrote to Donovan indicated. Advocating the creation of an elite corps of assassins, he declared: "There must be a body of men whose task it is to throw out the rotten apples as soon as the first spots of decay appear." With such sentiments it is logical to suspect Coon's involvement in the assassination in Algiers of Admiral François Darlan, a Vichy leader and Nazi collaborator whom the Allies had reluctantly recognised as Algeria's commander. Darlan's killer, a fanatical young Frenchman, was one of Coon's trainees and he used a .22 long-barrelled Colt Woodsman. Just such an unusual weapon, which was not part of the US or British forces' armoury, had been brought from the US by Coon. In addition, at the time of the killing, Coon was in the immediate vicinity. Several instructors working for the Americans were arrested but not Coon; Eddy abruptly despatched him to a SOE unit well away from Algiers.

Later, as an expert in subversion and setting booby traps, Coon was posted to Oujda, close to the border with Spanish Morocco, where he liaised with G-2, US army intelligence. His prewar studies of the people of the Rif mountains came in useful for he had many friends among their chieftains. One mission was to check the best route across the mountains for General Mark Clark's Fifth Army armour to confront German troops should they indeed have rushed south through Spain. Another task was to liaise with rebellious tribesmen and guard against German spies and saboteurs infiltrating from the Spanish-controlled zone. "We laid elaborate plans to capture or kill the Germans and presented these to General Clark," reported Coon. "He said that we could not step foot in Spanish territory, nor shoot over it; we would have to get the Germans on to French territory before we could touch them."

In addition, a programme was mounted to recruit and train anti-fascist guerrillas for infiltration into Spain and elsewhere. In Vichy-controlled Africa thousands of prisoners were held in concentration camps. An OSS agent named Donald C. Downes set out to find men who were tough, able and willing. He reported to Washington that with Major Godfrey Paulson of the British Army he had visited camps in Algeria and Morocco seeking recruits for "special services" of the OSS and the SOE. Bou Arfa and Beni Oukil in Morocco and Colomb Bechar, Kenadsa, Djelfa, Bogar, Boghari and Barroughia in Algeria were among the camps. Downes noted that the inmates were being wretchedly treated by the French and the slowness in releasing political prisoners was resented.

The prisoners fell into five categories: veterans of the Spanish Civil War including men of the Republican army and of the International Brigades; volunteers of all nationalities who joined the French Foreign Legion in 1939-40 to fight against Fascism and Nazism; interned enemy aliens, mostly Italians; individuals stranded in North Africa by the war; and foreign residents who opposed the Vichy regime. "If even a weak imitation of the magnificent pre-D-Day job done in North Africa is to be repeated elsewhere, we must be able to recruit resolute anti-fascists and anti-Nazis of the various occupied and enemy nationalities to do the ground work," insisted Downes.

Some of the first Spanish recruits proved over-enthusiastic. They created a scandal when they turned up at US army quarters in Oujda and loudly demanded pistols, bicycles and money. Downes was away but Coon realised they were some of his recruits when they started talking about "Ricardo", officially a parachute corporal but actually a secret agent. To calm down the unruly Spaniards, Ricardo rushed from Algiers and paid the trio off.

Several of the Communists later smuggled into Spain recalled that they had been recruited by a "Captain Ricardo". According to the memoirs of Desmond Bristow, an MI6 agent who served in Algeria, Gibraltar and Spain, Ricardo Sickler (or Sicre) was the son of a Catalan doctor and had fought for the Republicans in the Spanish Civil War before deserting and escaping to England. After working for the OSS in North Africa, he was dropped behind the German lines in France, survived to tell the tale and later returned to Spain.

Coon did not speak Spanish and admitted that he could not handle the Spaniards who "always seem to me like a separate biological creation. They are small, sternly chiselled men, intent on their own interests and with ideals and preocupations that I cannot easily understand". Downes, who took over the clandestine Spanish connection when Coon was posted elsewhere, had a better understanding of Spanish ways. He had already worked with Spaniards when he organised a series of daring burglaries at the Spanish Embassy in Washington. After Downes enlisted the help of a Jewish expert from New York to crack the embassy safe's combination, a team led by a Spanish Republican named José Aranda entered the building several times by night. By examining the embassy cipher machine and code books, the Americans were able to read coded messages passing between Madrid and its diplomats.

A portly, larger-than-life figure bearing some resemblance to Winston Churchill, Downes smoked cigars in a long holder and was driven around by a sinister-looking, wall-eyed Arab. In a confidential OSS report, he recalled: "Using the Spanish organization I had brought with me from the USA, exploiting the Spanish Republican underground in North Africa, and employing the best of the Spaniards recruited in the concentration camps in February 1943, we established an espionage training camp at Rasasfour, 20 miles from the nearest village, on the top of a mountain overlooking the desert. Here we had found an abandoned Chantier de la Jeunesse camp for which the Fifth Army G-2 most amply supplied us with all the necessary equipment to make it into a model camp. Lassowski, Goff, Sickler and the others gave the courses to 35 picked Spanish students."

According to Coon, Sergeant Goff was "a small, wiry idealist. A former tap dancer and vaudeville trouper, who fought in the Spanish wars for his ideas of freedom and became one of the world's most accomplished and renowned guerrillas." Sergeant Lassowski, he said, was made of similar stuff, "a man of complete confidence". Downes infiltrated agents into military camps in Spanish Morocco and into the Spanish engineers' corps in Melilla to spy on defensive measures. To reach Melilla, the men disguised themselves as Arabs and were smuggled from the Molouya river border across the Spanish zone by friendly Moroccan tribesmen. Those who were escorted in this way invariably made it, but half of those who tried the trip alone were detained or killed. Meanwhile, two other OSS agents, Sergeant Michael Jiménez and his brother, trained 16 radio operators at a school near Algiers. The men were sent to Melilla, Málaga, the south of France and Italy.

By May, 1943, after the Allies had finally crushed Axis resistance in North Africa, taking 275,000 prisoners of war, they prepared to use Algeria as a stepping stone for the next landing, somewhere in Europe. Plans went ahead for subversive operations in the Iberian Peninsula and Operation Banana was launched.

6. Operation Banana

IN THE SECOND WEEK of July, 1943, an innocent-looking Portuguese sardine boat slipped out of harbour in Algeria and headed for the Málaga coast. The battered, salt-scoured vessel was actually under the command of the British Secret Intelligence Service (SIS), which had renamed it HMS Prodigal. Aboard were four men with radio equipment from the Rasasfour school. A rendezvous was arranged in Spain and the landing was successful. Soon vital information about Spanish and German military preparedness was being transmitted back to the US Fifth Army.

But not for long. Mechanical problems arose and the SIS agreed to mount Banana Number 2, taking a replacement man to Spain with spare radio parts. At 2pm on the day of the operation, however, the British phoned Colonel Eddy to inform him that they were cancelling Banana 2 on instructions from the Foreign Office in London. Downes was enraged at the way the reception committee on the Málaga beach had been left stranded. This, he said, "has imperilled if not killed an American chain with radio in Spain. They are now without money, supply, and with a broken receiver so we cannot talk to them."

Downes claimed it was impossible to cooperate with the British because of "a long series of evasions, knifings, broken agreements". He went on: "American officers are again and again reporting to me that the British services are out for the skin of the OSS...what I am really charging is that SIS is putting Empire Building ahead of Cooperation for Victory in their schedule of priorities." Such friction was not uncommon between the two secret services, the gung-ho Americans finding the SIS, an intelligence-gathering organisation with close ties to the Foreign Office, stuffy and patronising while the British deemed the Americans naive and clumsy. However, the OSS men generally had good relations with the SOE, a like-minded group specialising in sabotage and subversion.

Whatever the difficulties, the Allies continued infiltrating men into Spain, and not only radio operators. Training in guerrilla warfare went ahead and, with the cooperation of Spanish Communists in Algeria, the first boatloads of volunteers disembarked in the coves of La Caleta, Cantarriján and Cerro Gordo, between Nerja and Almuñécar. Some recruits later claimed the Americans had offered them salaries of up to $2,000 a month, but they had never received the cash.

The first significant disembarkation took place in October, 1943. The group came from Algeria, bearing French and American arms, machineguns, pistols and grenades, and a radio transmitter. Almost certainly among them was Joaquín Centurión Centurión (Juanito), a native of Río de la Miel. This former fighter with the Niños de la Noche made several under-cover trips from Africa and played an important part in the guerrilla movement because of his knowledge of the Axarquía. In fact, the name Centurión is inseparable from the anti-Franco struggle. Descendants of a noble family, the Marquises of Estepa, many of the family suffered from the Francoist repression. A number were jailed or shot. In the 18th century one of the Centurions built a paper mill on the coast near the mouth of the Río de la Miel. There, 200 years later, the Civil Guard interrogated those who were suspected to have relations with the guerrilla.

The guerrillas found shelter in the Río de la Miel valley, a little to the east of Nerja. The valley gave access to the sierra and allowed them to filter westwards through the mountains. Traditionally a refuge for smugglers, the Río de la Miel became a breeding ground of resistance, to the point where it was called "Little Russia". The inhabitants lived in isolated farmhouses, away from the world. Their isolation and the lack of health services, in fact of all services, are indicated by the incidence of leprosy, one of the highest in Europe (in the 1990s there were still about 100 cases in the zone). Once ashore, the guerrillas were guided by local men with knowledge of the sierras. Among these was Antonio Urbano Muñoz, a larger-than-life character nicknamed El Duende (the imp). Near his house at the Río de la Miel was a tower built by the Moors where arms were concealed (though on the point of disappearing, the ruins can still be seen). It was a dangerous game and El Duende, a former *carabinero* (border guard), finally joined the guerrillas.

The guerrilla movement was barely launched when disaster struck. On February 11, 1944, a man was arrested in Madrid for distributing Communist propaganda and found to be carrying 500 US dollars. At first the detainee, named Antonio Rodríguez López and known as Antonio de Amo, claimed to be Mexican. Under interrogation, however, he admitted to being Spanish and to distributing propaganda for a group in Málaga which received supplies from North Africa by means of an American launch. Using Rodríguez and a code obtained from detained radio operators, one named Antonio Ortiz, the police tried to lure the boat to a rendezvous on the Málaga coast on February 17. The boat failed to appear.

Members of the political police arrived in Málaga to investigate and reported that the Americans in North Africa had made use of a Communist fugitive from

Old paper mill at Río de la Miel manned by the Civil Guard

Nerja called "Maromo" (clearly a reference to Joaquín Centurión). He had organised local liaison and made several trips to bring in "parachutists", the name given to the invaders.

About 90 men were arrested in Málaga province, one of whom had notes on the military positions along the coast from Málaga to Maro, and a machine-gun, nine submachine-guns, automatic pistols and hand grenades, all of American manufacture, were seized. Also unearthed were two US Army portable radio transmitters concealed in suitcases. A major crackdown on anti-Franco elements was mounted across the country and there were further arrests in Almería, Granada, Córdoba, Madrid, Santa Pola and Valencia. In a raid on a house in Melilla, a shootout occurred in which two suspects and a police inspector died. More firearms and a radio were discovered there. American diplomats learned that detainees had named a Señor Peláez as the chief recruiting agent in North Africa, particularly for the schools at Oujda and Algiers, for under-cover operations in Spain. The head of the Málaga ring was "Carmen", real name Victor Moreno Cristóbal.

As wild rumours circulated, Carlton J.H. Hayes, the US Ambassador to Madrid, sought information from the American Consul General in Málaga, Harold B. Quarton. This official seemed poorly informed to judge by his vague response, suggesting that the local authorities were "making a mountain out of a molehill". He had heard a rumour that British submarines had landed American guns and ammunition near Torre del Mar, a fishing village to the east of Málaga, but doubted this as the water there was too shallow for submarines to approach the coast. There had been a large number of arrests following the seizure of a boat loaded with arms. But, wrote Quarton, the so-called "Communist plot" may really have been nothing more than a small smuggling operation.

The burgeoning scandal came closer to home on March 13 when a young man named Luis Pérez Tapia called at the US Embassy in Madrid seeking help for his brother Jaime, who had been arrested and charged with smuggling an American transmitter from Algiers into Spain via Nerja. The embassy disclaimed all knowledge of his brother. In fact, Jaime, an ex-Republican officer, had been recruited from a concentration camp by none other than "Ricardo". After training in espionage at Oujda, he was despatched to Spain following instructions from a US army lieutenant-colonel. Apparently he was accompanied by two others, Moreno and Gonzalo, and in Spain had contacted another Oujda graduate, Ignacio López Domínguez, also known as "Ricardo".

Ambassador Hayes informed Washington that Lisardo Álvarez Pérez, chief of the Brigada Político-Social (Spain's brutal police force responsible for investigating political subversion), had reported the alleged American connection to the Interior Ministry. General Franco himself was "greatly exercised" over the report.

Hayes, a history professor for 32 years with no diplomatic experience before being posted to Madrid in 1942, was outraged because he considered that uncoordinated OSS activities were sabotaging all his careful diplomacy. He had previously complained that the OSS was incompetent and providing poor intelligence. It was, he considered, "the weakest and worst conducted of all our manifold activities in Spain". He claimed one leading agent showed signs of mental instability, was dangerously indiscreet and "distributes money like a drunken sailor". His hostility was amply returned by the OSS. They complained that he did not allow them to use their radio in the embassy, refused to transmit OSS cables through State Department channels and was revealing agents' proper names in his cables. According to Frank Ryan in an internal history: "Ambassador Hayes gave the local OSS agents the feeling that he lacked a realization that the Allies were engaged in a total war and that every means within our power be utilized to gather every available scrap of information on our enemies."

Hayes, the scholarly academic, was appalled by the indiscreet OSS "cowboys" and this latest scandal was the last straw. It was time, he recommended to the Secretary of State, Cordell Hull, to insist that American agencies outside Spain did not engage in activities directed against the country or involving clandestine penetration. "The chance that such amateurish and bungling efforts... will result in any advantage to our war effort is greatly overbalanced by the chance that they will continue to place impediments in the way of achieving objectives which the Embassy is seeking," he charged.

Intent on maintaining Spanish neutrality, Hayes was engaged in delicate ne-

EMBASSY OF THE
UNITED STATES OF AMERICA

No. 2211 Madrid, March 22, 1944

Subject: Alleged communist activities in Spanish territory and possible implication of an American agency.

~~Strictly Confidential~~

The Honorable
The Secretary of State,
Washington.

Sir:

I have the honor to submit the following report on developments in the uncovering of espionage activity and the distribution of subversive propaganda in Spanish territory by a ring which has allegedly been receiving assistance from American sources in North Africa. The highlights of these developments have already been reported in the Embassy's telegram No. 991 of March 22, 1 p.m. and several previous messages.

As was indicated in the above mentioned telegram, the situation has now reached a point where it is receiving the attention of the head of the Spanish state, at a time when we are pressing for the elimination of clandestine German operations. Apparently the actual intervention of the Spanish authorities in this matter and their discovery of its ramifications resulted from the confession of one Antonio Rodriguez Lopez, also known as Antonio de Amo, who, according to information reaching the local OSS from a police source, was arrested in Madrid during the second week of February with "communistic" propaganda and $500 in American currency in his possession. This individual, who claimed that he was a Mexican but was later reported to be of Spanish nationality, is supposed to have told the police that he was distributing propaganda on behalf of a group in Malaga which was being supplied from North Africa by means of an American launch.

On the basis of his confession, the police took Rodriguez to Malaga as a decoy to uncover the group with which he had been operating. The American launch was expected on February 17 but failed to appear; however, a few days later, apparently on February 23, the police rounded up a considerable number of persons in Malaga and discovered supplies of American firearms, allegedly ranging from a machine gun and several submachine guns to automatic pistols, all of American manufacture. Some types were of American government issue. About a dozen American hand grenades of the Mills type were also said to have been seized, as was likewise a portable radio transmitter of an American army type built into a suitcase.

DECLASSIFIED
E.O. 11652, Sec. 3(E) and 5(D) or (E)

At

Ambassador Carlton Hayes reports to Washington on the scandal involving the OSS and clandestine anti-Franco operations gotiations with the Franco government on several fronts. Assuring the Regime that the US would not interfere in domestic affairs, he was pushing for German clandestine operations to be eliminated. Spain had cooperated with the Allies in allowing hundreds of downed airmen to escape Nazi clutches by way of Gibraltar and the Allies were pressing Madrid to permit the evacuation of thousands of French patriots in Spain (many finally went to North Africa where they joined the Allied forces).

In addition, negotiations over Spanish exports of wolfram were at a highly critical juncture. Spain was one of the few sources in the world of this ore from which is derived tungsten, essential for hardening steel in armour-plating and armour-piercing projectiles. The Allies had applied heavy pressure to stop or reduce exports of any strategic materials that could help the Nazi war effort. Even so, Germany still managed to obtain from Spain vital supplies of wolfram for their war machine.

In late 1943, Washington decided to tighten the screws. Its demand for a total embargo on wolfram exports having failed, it blocked petroleum supplies to Spain. The US had only agreed to allow oil shipments to Spain on condition that a Petroleum Commission supervised its use and ensured that none ended up in German hands. This allowed a team of inspectors to be placed at strategic points around the peninsula and, at one time, of 15 inspectors 14 were US secret service agents. Now, a full-blown crisis erupted. A national oil shortage halted taxis, trucks, buses and fishing craft.

The revelation that the US was actively aiding Communist subversion in the peninsula caused Hayes unwanted complications in dealing with the touchy Franco regime at the worst possible moment. He fired off urgent messages to Washington and Algiers insisting that any further shipments of US arms for Communists be halted. In response, the OSS assured the Secretary of State that similar incidents would not recur and agents still in Spain were being removed. In addition, the Chief of Staff for US forces in North Africa claimed no organisation under his control had infiltrated agents since October 15, 1943, and no further agents would be introduced without the approval of the US Ambassador in Madrid. No organisation under headquarters control had made any unauthorised arms shipments to Spain, nor had headquarters any knowledge of the British or French shipping arms and ammunition to that country.

No doubt all these assurances placated Hayes, but they did not mean that the OSS actually scrapped its training and infiltration programme. In fact, combat training of Spaniards by its agents at desert locations in Algeria continued. The intelligence organisation saw no need to ask the US military for permission to mount operations, nor to report what it was up to. The OSS went its own way, as rival intelligence chiefs in Washington frequently complained. Not only Hayes believed Bill Donovan and his men were a loose cannon.

Many Communists later blamed the scores of arrests by the Spanish authorities on a tip-off emanating from the US consulate in Málaga. No indication of such a betrayal exists in the confidential US records now available for public scrutiny and it is difficult to see what the consulate would have gained by embarrassing its own embassy and secret service. Even so, it was a particularly critical moment and somebody in the devious netherworld of realpolitik and intrigue may have deemed it expedient, in a Machiavellian twist, to throw the Communists to the wolves to reassure the Franco regime about US intentions.

In the spring the wolfram crisis finally abated. Madrid agreed to certain concessions in exchange for the Allies allowing very limited wolfram exports. Soon came the D-Day landings in Normandy and even Franco could see the writing was on the wall for Hitler. Communists in exile from Moscow to Buenos Aires prepared for action.

7. The man from Uruguay

"Spanish Communists are establishing military headquarters at Algiers, North Africa, and are building up an expeditionary force or secret action group whose ultimate aim is to assume control of the government in Spain by creating discord and unrest through measures which include a sabotage program. It is reported that, in the event that the present conflict comes to a sudden end, Spanish Communists hope to take advantage of a postwar period of indecision and crisis in Spain to accomplish their ends." — **J. Edgar Hoover, FBI director, reporting to the US State Department in July, 1944.**

HOOVER KNEW at least part of the story. Another player from Latin America had entered the scene. In June, 1944, a short, bespectacled, moustached individual posing as a business executive departed from Buenos Aires, briefly visited Montevideo and arrived in Lisbon. His Uruguyan passport named him as Hipólito López de Asís and he claimed to be studying the organisation of the fish-canning business. But soon he was on a plane to Casablanca and then, hitching a lift aboard a US military aircraft, he flew to the port of Oran in French Algeria. He was, in fact, Santiago Carrillo, high on the Franco regime's list of most wanted men. Astute and ruthless, he had been the Communist youth leader and responsible for public order in Madrid at the start of the Civil War, a time when in murky circumstances summary justice was dealt out to hundreds of rightwingers. Escaping Spain by the skin of his teeth, he had since led a clandestine existence, adopting a variety of disguises and false identities as he flitted between countries.

In Algeria, he was stunned to find that at least 30 party members were participating in guerrilla training at a secret US camp. Local leaders had ignored party instructions from Mexico that they should have nothing to do with the Americans. Among them was Argüelles (pseudonym of Ricardo Beneyto Sapena), who was later to become the guerrilla supremo for all Andalusia. Carrillo pointed out that one group which had disembarked in Spain had already fallen,

Santiago Carrillo in Madrid, 1978

referring to the February detentions, and took it upon himself to replace the local leadership immediately. He appointed a new ruling committee, which included Argüelles and Ramón Vías Fernández, using the opportunity to demote comrades associated with his powerful rival, Jesús Monzón, the clandestine Communist leader in Spain. All contact with the Americans was broken. Or almost all contact. The Communists needed the US supplies that were flooding occupied Oran. On the black market everything was for sale in the chaotic city, from cigarettes and liquor to bombs and machine-guns.

"Entire ships' cargoes were disappearing without anybody knowing how or where they had gone…anarchy and disorganisation reigned in that city where more than one American soldier must have made himself rich," Carrillo recalled in his memoirs. Party members working as drivers and dockers diverted military trucks to Communist storage places. Tons of food, medicine and gun boats – were accumulated ready for a rising against Franco. And several motor launches were acquired to make the trip across the Mediterranean.

About 60 ex-Civil War fighters were picked for landings on the Málaga coast. They were given instruction in politics and guerrilla warfare, including the handling of explosives and using camouflage. Forced marches with little or no food and water were part of the ordeal to prepare them for the rigours of the Spanish sierras. Carrillo consulted comrades who knew the terrain and carefully studied maps of southern Spain.

Everything was prepared for the expedition to "liberate Spain". Carrillo planned to land in Málaga with a trusted colleague, Ramón Ormazábal, and 20 of his best men. He sent a message explaining the plan to the party secretary-general exiled in Moscow, Dolores Ibárruri (known as La Pasionaria, whose cry of defiance "They shall not pass" during the Civil War had converted her into a legendary figure). Back came her reply: "Ok to the plan. But you must go to France." Carrillo recalled: "I was looking forward to what we could organise from Andalusia. With bitterness, I had to renounce forming part of the guerrilla group."

La Pasionaria wanted him to travel immediately to France to try to avert a massacre: in an ill-advised invasion attempt, 7,000 Spanish veterans of the

French resistance had marched over the frontier into the Arán valley in the Pyrenees. They would have almost certainly suffered crushing defeat from Franco's far superior forces had the decision not been taken to retreat before a major confrontation occurred. Monzón's role in inspiring the invasion led to his political liquidation in the ruthless struggle for power within the Spanish Communist Party.

Dolores Ibárruri

If Carrillo had headed the guerrilla, he almost certainly would not have survived. As it was, more than 30 years were to pass before his return to Spain. After Franco's death, the Marxist revolutionary and would-be guerrilla leader entered parliament at the head of the (newly legalised) Communist Party, endorsed a constitutional monarchy and shook hands with King Juan Carlos.

The man who took his place was not so lucky. Shortly after Carrillo's departure (he reached Toulon hidden under a bunk in a French man-of-war), Communist-led commandos began infiltrating Andalusia. Their leader, Ramón Vías, had only a few months to live when he and his tiny group launched the quixotic crusade to save Spain from fascism. World War Two was nearing its end but the Cold War was soon to start, converting any thought of American collaboration with Spanish Communists into an unreal dream.

8. Night landing

THE DISEMBARKING of 10 armed men on the Andalusia coast in October, 1944, signalled a new phase in the anti-Franco struggle and the start of eight brutal years in the Málaga and Granada mountains. They landed after midnight in a cove near the hamlet of La Herradura, a poor fishing village in Granada province. According to police files, the boat was French but steered by two Spaniards. Ramón Vías was the leader and with him came Joaquín Centurión, Antonio Pascual, Enrique Lozano, Luis Aguayo, Arturo Moreira, Eugenio Navarro, Manuel Joya Gallego, Alfonso Armenta and a man named Perico. They brought four sub-machineguns, six pistols and a Colt revolver, all of American manufacture, and five hand grenades, plus a transmitter in the charge of Moreira.

Vías, a cutler by trade and a member of the Socialist trade union, UGT, had helped defend Madrid during the siege by Nationalist troops. At the end of the Civil War he went into exile in Algeria where he was forced to work in the construction of a trans-Sahara railway. He escaped from a refugee camp and joined the resistance in France. At one point the Vichy government condemned him to death. Returning to Algeria, he joined the Unión Nacional, like many exiles.

Ramón Vías, in Málaga prison

Once ashore, Vías and his group marched to the Río de la Miel and then penetrated further into the Sierra Almijara. They set up camp in the Cueva de la Montés, near Cerro Verde, a hill close to the hamlet of Acebuchal, and not far from the Venta Panaderos, an inn renowned in the Axarquía as a rest stop for muleteers, Civil Guards and guerrillas. Behind the inn rises the Cerro Lucero, at 1,779 metres the highest peak in the Frigiliana sierra. From his bolt-

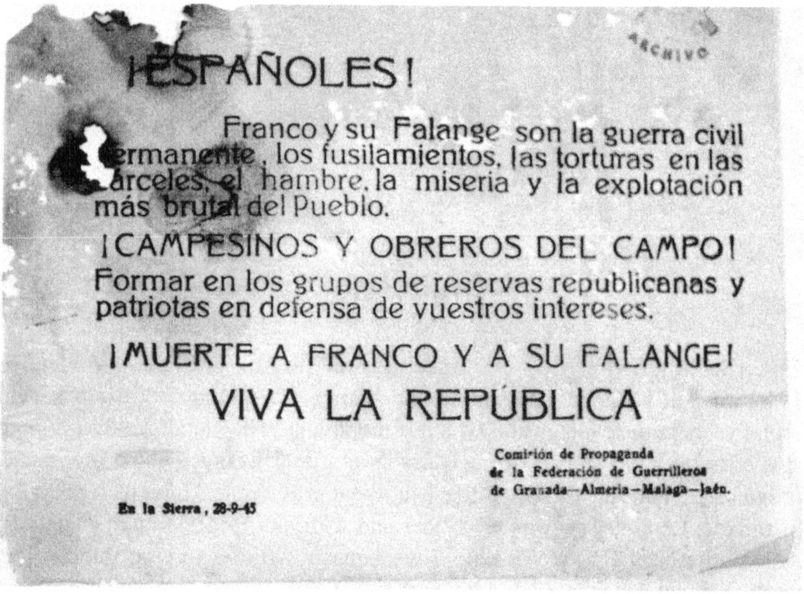
¡ESPAÑOLES!

Franco y su Falange son la guerra civil permanente, los fusilamientos, las torturas en las cárceles, el hambre, la miseria y la explotación más brutal del Pueblo.

¡CAMPESINOS Y OBREROS DEL CAMPO!

Formar en los grupos de reservas republicanas y patriotas en defensa de vuestros intereses.

¡MUERTE A FRANCO Y A SU FALANGE!

VIVA LA REPÚBLICA

Comisión de Propaganda de la Federación de Guerrilleros de Granada–Almeria–Malaga–Jaén.

En la Sierra, 28-9-45

A guerrilla pamphlet calling for a rising against the Franco regime

hole, Vías launched his campaign, making contact with fugitives, dissidents and country folk in the province of Málaga, organising meetings and committees, and editing a clandestine publication called *Por la Républica*. He sought to extend his activities throughout the province, from Coín and Alhaurín el Grande to Yunquera, Álora and Colmenar.

Claiming he had gained great support among the rural community, he reported: "They call us guerrillas and not bandits as before. We've contributed to the enemy having to declare this a war zone." Vías maintained that he was opposed to acts of banditry. He insisted later to the police that under his command the group had not taken part in any holdup or violent crime and he condemned another group which robbed a farmhouse. He was only awaiting the change of regime, he said.

Vías was arrested on November 15, 1945, given away by Eugenio Navarro, one of those who had come in the same boat from Algeria. Navarro, who had fought on the Teruel front, spent three years in the concentration camps of Oran, later working for the Americans in the Red Cross. When he was detained and interrogated, he revealed to the police that he was to meet Vías in the Plaza de la Merced in Málaga at 7pm. The first guerrilla chief was seized, although only after a fierce struggle.

In jail, Vías refused to talk and suffered weeks of torture. Blows rained down all over his body. He tried to commit suicide by cutting his veins and with his blood he wrote on his cell wall: "I am doing this not through fear but because I do not want to serve as a plaything for the taunts of my executioners. Long live the Republic!" A letter detailing his sufferings and his defiance reached the foreign press and the name of Ramón Vías acquired legendary status.

The month of May, 1946, was disastrous for the incipient guerrilla movement. Vías's reputation expanded when on May 1 he escaped from Málaga's provincial prison with 25 other inmates. They fled via a tunnel dug from the infirmary bathrooms to the exterior. For three weeks the authorities organised a large-scale hunt, without success. Meanwhile, the man who had taken the place of Vías, Alfredo Cabello Gómez-Acebo, cast about for some way to smuggle him out of the city. But on May 21, Cabello, a native of Zamora, of good family, with qualifications in law and journalism, was detained by the police in Málaga's main street, Calle Larios. His fall led to the arrest of 69 others and Cabello was executed two years later.

Vías was unable to escape from the city and on May 25 the police discovered where he was staying. He and three others were confronted in a city street and died in a fusillade of bullets. Some wondered whether the authorities had deliberately connived at his prison escape in order to eliminate a man who already had become a hero for his courage under torture and represented a nuisance for the Regime. The more cynical also speculated that perhaps certain members of the Communist Party, for their own particular reasons, were not over-interested in rescuing Vías.

At that critical moment the Party picked a veteran of the war and the French resistance as the new guerrilla chief, a man who became a legend, controlling a mini-army of about 150 men. He was the most elusive of the guerrilla leaders and one of the toughest, the most enigmatic and the most charismatic. Hs name was Roberto.

9. Roberto takes command

WAS ROBERTO A HERO? Or a bloody criminal? A symbol of valiant resistance to the dictatorship? Or a shameful informer? For some who fought in the mountains of Málaga and Granada he was an icon of the anti-Franco struggle, for others a contemptible traitor.

Considering later events, it could be regarded as grim irony that the man who would become one of the most notorious and controversial guerrilla leaders was born in Don Quixote country. In life and death Roberto, nom de guerre, was something of an enigma. His real name, José Muñoz Lozano, was unknown to those in his guerrilla group or to the authorities trying to hunt him down. For five years the Civil Guard were under the impression it was Juan José Romero Pérez. Ordered by the Communist Party to organise the anti-Franco resistance, Roberto set about unifying the groups of fugitives and rebels hiding out in the Tejeda and Almijara mountains, enforcing a rigid discipline and demanding total loyalty. Thanks to kidnappings, merciless vengeance against alleged informers, and violent clashes with the government forces, he was to create a serious problem for the Regime. Until the denouement — inexplicable for his followers and still a matter of debate.

By all accounts, Roberto had a taste for tobacco, strong coffee and pretty women. Although from a working-class background, he had a sophisticated veneer, the perfect disguise for an urban activist. A smooth talker with a contagious laugh, he was always ready to crack a joke and this sense of humour and his lively, black eyes contributed to his success with the other sex. According to a report in military archives, he liked to stroll through Málaga disguised as an army officer, whistling one of his favourite tunes, *"In a Persian market place"*. Although his knowledge of music was limited, he enjoyed Spanish operetta and classical numbers. However, once in the sierras of Málaga and Granada, where his word was law, he revealed the steel under that surface charm as he tried to mould a motley band of idealists and runaways into a fighting force.

Roberto's mother, Engracia, gave birth to him on September 3, 1914, in the dull provincial city of Ciudad Real, set amid the wide, bleak plains of La Mancha. Engracia and her husband Ramón soon moved to Madrid, where Roberto first worked as a bellboy in one of the big hotels before finding a job in a shop selling perfume. When the Civil War broke out, law and order crumbled in the besieged capital and death squads patrolled the streets. Anarchists seized the shop's owner, but Roberto reportedly saved him from execution. His interest in politics led him to join the Juventud Socialista Unificada, a leftwing youth group, and in August, 1936, one month after General Franco initiated the military rebellion, he became a member of the Spanish Communist Party.

José Muñoz Lozano (Roberto)

Roberto enlisted in the Republican army as it struggled to organise resistance to the Nationalist forces, which besieged Madrid and were advancing across the rest of Spain. His military career is wrapped in mystery as recollections of his comrades in the Maquis and the official records are in conflict. He apparently enlisted in the Batallón de Acero (the Steel Battalion) and, according to some accounts, reached the rank of commander in the 46th Division. However, there appears to be no proof of this. An official bulletin of the Ministry of Defence (number 239, page 1058) shows that on May 10, 1938, Corporal José Muñoz Lozano was promoted to infantry sergeant on the orders of the commander of the 53rd Brigada Mixta, but no further promotion is recorded.

Adding to the Roberto enigma, Spain's military archives in Ávila contain no details of his service. A likely explanation is that his records, like many others, were lost or destroyed in the war. However, sceptics see this as confirmation of their belief that he was a Francoist stooge with an invented background.

Among the half a million people who died in the three-year Civil War, was a brother of Roberto. He fell in combat. When in 1939 Franco's Nationalist forces, aided by Germany and Italy, finally crushed Republican resistance and thousands of men, women and children fled into France, Roberto was among them. He passed through various French concentration camps, including Saint Cyprien, Barcarés, and Argelès-sur-Mer. The Spaniards, betrayed by the democratic nations which had failed to come to their aid against Fascism, were treated harshly by the French. In Argelès, conditions were nightmarish. The camp was located on a beach and initially, in the chill of winter, the inmates slept on the sand. As many as 80,000 refugees struggled to survive and hunger, sickness and the lack of water and latrines took a heavy toll.

The Communist ex-combatants immediately started organising themselves and Roberto's conduct provoked some criticism. According to a report in the archives in Madrid of the Partido Comunista de España: "Muñoz joined one of the Communist-only groups and his behaviour was correct until he was promoted to lieutenant in his company, which caused him to distance himself from the other comrades, to mix more with the Spanish company chief, who was a real son of a bitch, and to create an unsympathetic atmosphere among the comrades."

The French authorities showed little sympathy for the refugees. They offered them several unattractive options: enlist in the French Foreign Legion, return to Spain (where jail or death would almost certainly follow), or join a workers' battalion. Roberto joined the Groupes de Travailleurs Étrangers, workers' groups organised by the Pétain collaborationist regime. No doubt he wanted to escape the bad conditions in the camp, but this did not meet with party approval. The Party did not forgive or forget those who failed to follow the official line. The report declared: "His attitude was weak since he should have refused to escape following the indications of the Party which at that time were being strongly insisted upon."

Sent north to work for the Nazis, Roberto later said he was employed in a German submarine base until May, 1944, when — coinciding with the Allies' Normandy landings — he joined the French Resistance. There he distinguished himself, chiefly in the Indre et Loire region. Former Republican soldiers who had fled from Fascism in their own country became the backbone of the Resistance in its heroic struggle against the German occupation. More than 4,000 Spaniards took part in the Maquis uprising in Paris in August, 1944, and Spanish fighters were among the first members of the liberating forces to enter the city. On August 24, 20 or so of the armoured half-tracks of the Ninth Company of the Leclerc Division which rumbled through Paris to the city hall bore the names of Civil War battles, Ebro, Guadalajara, Madrid, Teruel…

Roberto would later proudly remind his fellow guerrillas in Andalusia that he had fought in "the Ninth" and he gave the name "Novena Brigada" to his Málaga group. However, he himself was not among the liberators of Paris as on August 20 he was wounded in combat and spent three weeks in hospital. Later, he was credited with creating a division of 1,700 guerrillas and assuming command of a brigade of the Forces Françaises de l'Intérieur.

According to Roberto (under interrogation), he met the exiled Communist leader Santiago Carrillo who persuaded him to return to Spain to fight against the Regime. Leaving his wife, Consolación Rodríguez Herades, in France and travelling under a false identity, he crossed the frontier and entered the Basque Country. Years later Consolación, a native of Málaga, returned too and with her daughter Pepita lived in an apartment in a working-class area of central Madrid.

Guerrilla territory: Sierra Almijara on the Málaga-Granada provincial border

She died in the mid-1990s in an old folks' home. In Bilbao Roberto contacted other party militants through an activist named Ramiro Fuentes Ochoa, who soon had to escape to Madrid after the police arrested a number of Communists in the summer of 1945. Roberto participated in various holdups, including one at a bank in the Baracaldo suburb of Bilbao which yielded 60,000 pesetas for party funds. He carried a pistol concealed in a sling on his arm. After travelling over the north of Spain and to Madrid to make contact with guerrillas and party chiefs, he was sent to Andalusia where he renewed contact with Fuentes Ochoa who was organising the clandestine Communist resistance to the dictatorship.

At first Roberto lived in Málaga, gathering information and coordinating activities. Then the events of May, 1946, thrust him into the leadership of the local guerrilla movement. The first chief, Ramón Vías, fell to police bullets and his substitute, Alfredo Cabello Gómez-Acebo, was arrested. The order came from the Party: "Comrade Roberto, to the mountains!" It could be seen as a punishment for his failure to help Vías escape. In any case, the prospect of leaving the city for the sierra was not at all appealing to a man like José Muñoz, especially because of his physical disabilities — he was lame due to a war wound in the left knee. But, faithful to his ideological convictions, he began the last adventure of a life full of ups and downs, organising the guerrilla struggle in the mountains of Málaga and Granada provinces.

Very soon the name of Roberto became a byword for rebellion and defiance as the guerrilla campaign gathered momentum, posing a worrying challenge to the authorities.

10. Creating an army

INITIALLY, ROBERTO had no easy task in building a guerrilla group. The potential recruits were a mixture of Communists, Socialists, unionists, anarchists, fugitives from Francoist repression, young adventurers without any political belief and, without doubt, some unscrupulous thieves. A number of these dissidents held a meeting in a mountain shack to discuss Roberto's proposals. At times the debate became violent. Some were more interested in common crime than in Roberto's objectives, others did not want to be dominated by Communists and many simply did not trust this stranger with a Madrid accent. Roberto needed all his linguistic talent and force of conviction but decisive support came from Los Frailes, three determined, tenacious brothers from the village of Torrox.

With their help, around the month of September, 1946, the Agrupación del Roberto was formed. Making use of his war experience, Roberto introduced military discipline. His methods proved effective, at least in the early years. Indeed, Antonio Díaz Carmona, an officer who spent a number of his 37 years in the Civil Guard battling the guerrillas, commented: "We believe that the most perfect and disciplined organisation, from 1945 until its extinction, was that of Roberto in Andalusia." In the opinion of Lt Col Francisco Aguado Sánchez in his *History of the Civil Guard*, "Roberto was, by a large margin, the most fearsome of all the terrorist elements that the Communist Party licensed to alter public order."

Nine men, three of them from Frigiliana, formed Roberto's personal guard. Another *aguanoso*, Antonio García Martín (Gaspar), a charcoal maker and convinced Communist who enlisted in October, 1947, acted as liaison chief. In charge of propaganda and editing an underground bulletin entitled *Por la República* was Francisco Sánchez Girón (Paquillo). Born in Argentina, he came from Africa by night, was captured and sentenced to death but escaped from Almería prison. The group consisted of two "battalions", divided into parties of up to 12 men.

One of Los Frailes, Manuel Jurado Martín (Clemente), was Roberto's right-hand man and another, Antonio (Felipe), commanded the Sixth Battalion, with Sebastián Martín Vozmediano, of Frigiliana, as his aide. The Sixth Battalion set

Roberto's most trusted lieutenants: left to right, Felipe, Paquillo and Clemente

up camp in the mountains near Frigiliana and Cómpeta. It operated within the Axarquía, roaming over the Tejeda and Almijara sierras, but also in Granada province, including the area of Alhama de Granada and the sierra of Loja and into the south of Córdoba province.

The Seventh Battalion centred its activities in the mountains behind Almuñécar and Motril, in the Alpujarras (the southern flank of the Sierra Nevada) and into Almería province. The agrupación (group) included men from Torrox and Almuñécar, Nerja natives like the ex-mayor Manuel Martín Rico, a dozen or so from the Río de la Miel among them the brothers Francisco and José López Centurión, and about 20 youngsters from the Granada village of Agrón where one night all the military conscripts decided to enlist in Roberto's army instead of Franco's.

To supply the guerrillas and obtain recruits, Roberto organised a network of *enlaces*, or collaborators, and campaigned to gain the sympathy and support of the country folk. "One could estimate that he had four to five thousand men on his side, passive for the moment but ready to go into action at the first order from Roberto," the Málaga Civil Governor, Manuel García del Olmo, informed Madrid.

The aim was made clear in *Mundo Obrero*, the organ of the Communist Party (February 17, 1949): "The guerrillas are becoming the organisers and political directors of the rural inhabitants... The guerrilla voice is the voice of the people. The guerrilla chiefs are not people who have come in from afar and talk of general things. No. They talk of what happens in the village, of the exploitation suffered by the peasants, they explain what they ought to do in every concrete case, what type of organisation they should adopt."

In fact, the dreams of the Communist politburo and *Mundo Obrero*'s optimistic words, written in Toulouse or Paris, were far removed from the people of Frigiliana and their family members isolated in the mountains. From time to time up to 50 guerrillas would march into the villages and hamlets of Granada and Málaga, raise the Republican flag and pronounce political speeches. They seized any available arms and dealt out blows, or stronger punishment, to the Falangists they came across.

Thus, in October, 1947, two companies took Rescate, an isolated group of dwellings in the next valley to the Río de la Miel. The occupation lasted eight hours. In March, 1948, the guerrillas daringly invaded a farm in the hills behind Almuñécar and organised a fiesta there. The property belonged to the Marquesa de Cázulas "a lady of lofty lineage with whom the guerrillas have more than once had to settle accounts," declared *Mundo Obrero*, which made considerable propaganda out of the incident. After killing some of the Marquesa's lambs, the guerrillas and local inhabitants enjoyed a banquet. "It was a Republican day in the Almijara, in the fief of the Marquesa de Cázulas, who that day had to pay for the great fiesta of the people and their fighters, who had gone there to orientate and educate politically the peasants." Such operations were effective as propaganda. But many of the villagers were alarmed by them, fearing first the blows of the guerrillas and afterwards the reaction of the Civil Guard when they were informed.

Often the guerrilla had to march large distances by night, avoiding frequented paths and crossing rocky terrain gouged by steep-sided valleys. This was difficult going for a lame man like Roberto, but he had the help of a determined, wellbuilt bodyguard, José Martín Navas (Tomás). One of three brothers (los Panzones) of Frigiliana, Tomás accompanied the chief on all his journeys and acquired the nickname "Roberto's horse" because on tougher stretches he carried him on his back. Armed with rifle and pistol, he not only cared for the leader's safety but was always ready to bring him his coffee and, as Roberto trusted nobody, he alone had the responsibility for preparing his food.

Roberto never went anywhere unarmed. As his left leg was shorter than the other, he wore special boots, the left one fitted with a platform sole. A small pistol was concealed in a hollow in the heel. He was a commander who imposed respect and fear. José López Centurión (Rodolfo), a *guerrillero* from the Río de la Miel, tells how one day Roberto drew his pistol and threatened to kill him because he had left his shotgun hanging from a pine tree for a few seconds. What Roberto did know how to do was gain people's confidence by caring for their needs. He negotiated with the muleteers trading in blackmarket goods, buying from them sausages, cod, canned goods and, on at least one occasion, brandy to warm them in the depth of winter.

Sometimes too he demonstrated unexpected compassion. When Vicente, one of the Artabús brothers of Frigiliana, threatened to hang a village youngster if he did not bring food, Roberto intervened on the boy's behalf. Incidents like this

José Martín Navas, known as "Roberto's horse"

Ana "La Tangerina", Roberto's lover

provoked fierce arguments with one of his most violent lieutenants, Felipe (one of three brothers nicknamed "Los Frailes" – the monks).

Quite often Roberto disappeared from the mountains to make contact with supporters or party officials. He assumed disguise, carrying false identity documents and pretending to be a travelling salesman, an insurance agent, or any trade that would help him pass undetected. Who could guess that the nondescript individual, accompanied by a dowdy woman with a shopping bag, who boarded a rural bus or travelled on the railway that linked Ventas de Zafarraya with Málaga was a notorious outlaw hunted all over by the Civil Guard?

The "wife" was part of the disguise. On various occasions this role was played by Dolores, daughter of the owners of the Venta Panaderos, a remote inn in the mountains above Frigiliana, where guerrillas, Civil Guards and muleteers would drop in for refreshment and information. At other times it was his preferred lover, the beautiful Ana Gutiérrez Rodríguez, known as La Tangerina because she had been born in Tangier.

11. Attack in Calle Franco

IT WAS in the year 1946 that the anti-Franco guerrillas, *la gente de la sierra* as they were known to the villagers (the name Maquis was an import from France), really began to make an impact on life in Frigiliana. On April 9 an incident occurred right in the middle of the village. One of the better-off residents, Justo López Navas, received a letter demanding payment of 150,000 pesetas. Apparently he refused to pay and several armed men came looking for him. They made their way along Calle Francisco Franco, the main street, and entered the house where the López family was dining. According to the official report, there was a scuffle and Clemente (El Fraile) fired several bullets which hit a door. López managed to slip out on to his terrace and give the alarm, whereupon the intruders took flight, firing their weapons as they ran down the street to frighten off anybody tempted to block their escape.

The Civil Guard had been keeping watch on suspected dangerous subversives, i.e. Communists; they claimed the party's local committee held meetings in a carpenter's shop close to López Navas's house. Now the guards hauled in nine men for interrogation. Among them were the Artabús brothers, Sebastián and Vicente Martín Vozmediano, and Manuel Triviño Cerezo (Matutero), all of whom later fled to the sierra. Another detainee, Sebastián Platero Navas, later disappeared in very murky circumstances.

In September an incident which left an impression on the whole province occurred within Frigiliana's boundaries. The Maquis tried to kidnap the owner of the smallholding Los Almendros, Miguel Ángel Herrero, a wellknown figure, vice president of the Málaga Juvenile Court and treasurer of the Children's Protection Board. When Herrero tried to resist, he and his foreman Antonio Lomas Orihuela were killed.

Daily the authorities grew more concerned about the situation. A police report in November, 1946, complained at the lack of energy among many officers approaching retirement. It recommended "much more dynamic" efforts, asserting that "Málaga is the cradle of Spanish Communism and a breeding ground of common delinquents". There were frequent warnings of suspicious movements by craft in Algeria and Morocco, loaded with arms and "transporting elements of the Communist Party and exiled Reds who intend to make clandestine landings on the peninsula". The government reinforced its vigilance on the African and Andalusian coasts and shipped Regulares, the Moorish troops so loved by Franco, from Morocco to Málaga. The Communists knew about police movements because the Politburo in France employed a radio listening service to intercept coded Civil Guard reports.

According to some historians, the guerrilla problem had already been liquidated by the the Franco Regime by the year 1947. In other regions it was true that the battle was largely lost. But the situation was very different in Málaga and Granada. The years of maximum activity were only just arriving. A state of war existed in the mountainous area between Almuñécar, Nerja, Frigiliana, Torrox and Cómpeta. "Economic coups" (i.e. holdups and kidnappings) and *"ajusticiamentos"* (executions) by the guerrilla and thrashings, searches and shootings by the Regime's forces created an atmosphere of terror, although nothing of this appeared in the official press or radio.

To combat the Maquis the government took vigorous measures. The command of the Civil Guards in Granada and Málaga was unified and four companies of Spanish soldiers and a troop of Moroccans were posted to the zone. Two companies of the Policía Armada (known as "the greys" for the colour of their uniform) were ordered to give support. Already, in August, 1941, the then Director General of the Guards, General Álvarez-Arenas, had outlined official policy regarding "the fugitives dedicated to banditry": "We shouldn't hold back in the means employed...no matter how energetic or tough they are. We have to wage total war on the enemies in the countryside until they are totally exterminated, and as their actions are very much facilitated by their accomplices and comrades, identical tactics have to be followed with them with the modifications

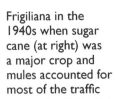

Frigiliana in the 1940s when sugar cane (at right) was a major crop and mules accounted for most of the traffic
Photo: Padial de Nerja

that circumstances may impose…" The man who succeeded Álvarez-Arenas as chief of the Benemérita (as the force is also called, ironically by its enemies) did not stand out for his tenderness either. General Camilo Alonso Vega, friend of Franco with whom he had studied at the Toledo military academy, gained the nickname "Don Camulo" for his stubbornness.

To make sure that enemies of the state could not encounter any loophole, a series of laws had been introduced: those of Represión de la Masonería y el Comunismo, de Seguridad del Estado, de Rebelión Militar and (in 1947) Delitos de Bandidaje y Terrorismo. At a meeting in January, 1947, the Civil Guard chiefs agreed "to shoot without previous warning at those who flee". This effectively opened the way to a dirty war. The so-called Ley de Fugas (literally "law of flight") allowed the forces of order to punish by death any suspicious action.

Everyday life in the villages of the Axarquía became ever more difficult. This was especially so in Frigiliana, from which an exceptionally large number of men fled to the sierras, 21 from a population of only 2,000. Automatically, their families and friends were suspects. The village found itself trapped between rival — equally ruthless — protagonists. It was occupied by government forces, the Civil Guards, soldiers and Moorish troops brought from Morocco. Every movement was tightly controlled. When a villager passed before the barracks with the national flag flying outside, it was advisable for him to doff his hat. To pass through the controls at the exits from the village the farmers needed a safe-conduct issued by the Civil Guard. A campesino could be fined 25 pesetas for not carrying a safe-conduct, but more probable was a beating if the guard at the control was one of *"los malos"* (the bad ones). If one intended to work in the mountains, a paper was also needed from the Company specifying where one was going and for what reason. When going to work in the fields, it was forbidden to take food for more than one person.

Even the sugar cane was subject to official control. To make it more difficult for outlaws to hide, the Civil Guard ordered farmers to tie the cane in clumps, forming open "streets". Farmers were obliged to deposit the keys to their *cortijos* (farmhouses) in the barracks every night. The Civil Guard also ordered anybody returning to the village after sunset to pass the night in the cemetery, until the parish priest fiercely protested. One old custom continued: every evening at sunset the church bells sounded the Toque de Ánimas, warning everybody that it was time to return home to eat.

The increasingly tough tactics adopted by the authorities drove more villagers to flee to the mountains. Early in 1947 Roberto's group consisted only of 16 men from Granada, seven from Málaga and five from Almería. But soon the recruits were coming in droves until, at the end of the year, there were 124 guerrillas. The brutality of some Civil Guards was particularly significant in Frigiliana. One was nicknamed "The Atomic Bomb" for his explosive charac-

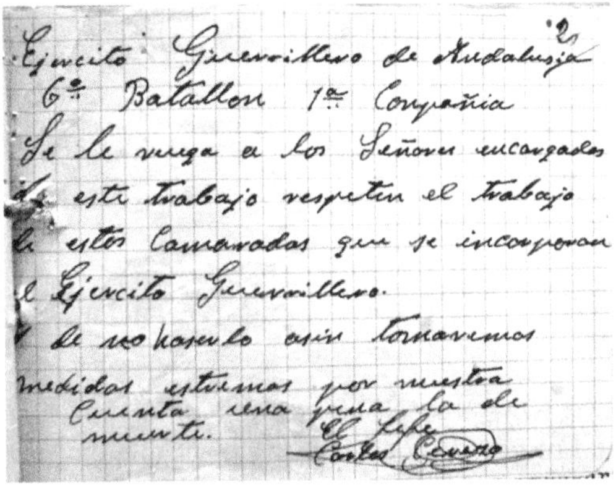

2

Ejercito Guerrillero de Andalucia
6º Batallon 1ª Compañia
Se le ruega a los Señores encargados
de este trabajo respeten el trabajo
de estos Camaradas que se incorporan
al Ejercito Guerrillero.
de no hacerlo asin tomaremos
medidas estremas por nuestra
Cuenta una pena la de
muerte.
El Jefe
Carlos [illegible]

Sebastián, one of the three Artabús brothers who fled to the sierra leaving this threatening note

ter. But the most notorious was Cabo Largo (big corporal). Hefty and arrogant, Antonio González Bueno became a figure of fear thanks to the beatings he administered. Nobody knows just how many men were driven to flee by his repeated threat: "If by tomorrow you're not in the sierra or Barcelona, I'll kill you." His efforts to boost the number of guerrillas inspired the suspicion that he was playing a double game. The more rebels there were the more food they required and some villagers claimed he himself was selling them supplies.

Some of those in the mountains were Communists and idealists, others credulous youngsters seeking a better life. José Martín Navas, a 45-year-old charcoal-maker who had spent years in prison for his political opinions and his Civil War activities, took the name "Tomás" in the sierra where he soon became Roberto's bodyguard. In the first months of 1947, another veteran Republican, José Pérez Moles (nickname Ranica), resident in El Acebuchal, and three youngsters, Miguel Cerezo González (Jaimito), Antonio Platero Ayllón (Ricardo) and José Sánchez Martín (Domingo) fled. In October they were joined by José Rojas Álvarez (Arturo). On June 1 three brothers, Blas, Sebastián y Vicente Martín Vozmediano (nickname "Artabús"), were making charcoal at the Cortijo El Daire when they heard the Civil Guard was about to detain them. They quickly abandoned their task and marched off. In his report to Málaga, Cabo Largo described them as "of very bad conduct, morally, publicly and privately" and stressed their Communist connection. As with all the village "suspects", the past actions of the Artabuses were documented by the guards, although the files piling up in the barracks abounded in errors, mixing facts, gossip and defamation. That of Miguel Cerezo, who spent less than a year in the sierra, was typical, reporting that he was an idler and leftwing sympathiser. Tomás harboured "dangerous leftwing ideas", and Ranica, born in Fornes (Granada), was "the author of innumerable crimes".

12. Life in the sierra

LEGEND AND MYTH can cast a romantic aura over the struggle of a valiant band of guerrillas against an implacable dictator. The reality is usually a little different. Obtaining money through ransoms paid for the numerous kidnap victims and at first Roberto's band were able to buy food and other necessities using a network of sympathisers. But towards the end, hungry and harried on all sides, it was a miserable existence up there in the mountains.

In their early days the *guerrilleros* had considerable success and at their peak they enjoyed some euphoric moments, as when they would march into a remote hamlet before the astonished gaze of the inhabitants, flying the Republican flag and singing the Guerrilla Anthem:

"Across plains and mountains
free guerrillas march,
the best fighters
of land and city...
Conquerors of fascism,
to the final battle, Spaniards!
Death to Franco! Death!
Long live liberty!"

Roberto tried to impose military-style discipline, appointing commanders, lieutenants and sergeants. His mini-army wore jackets, corduroy trousers and khaki shirts. Blue berets and sandals completed the uniform, plus armbands in the colours of the Republican flag and bearing the initials of the National Guerrilla Army (ENG). Each man was given a nom de guerre, a method of imbuing them with a new disciplined attitude while also confusing the enemy.

The task of identification was made even more difficult for the authorities as the guerrillas already had their village nicknames, whose use was forbidden by Roberto. Thus Espartero and Tomarroque were Julián and Máximo in the sierra. Sometimes the names were selected as a homage to fallen comrades, but others were simply picturesque, as with Espantanubes (cloud scarer), Mierda-

Guerrilla way station: the Imán farmhouse high in the sierra between Frigiliana and the Río de la Miel

frita (Fried Shit) and Caraquemada (Burnt Face). Roberto explained to his group that "the Communist fighter must give an example". He urged them to learn to read and write and to study the Guerrilla Manual, a political-military guide to guerrilla strategy.

General Manuel Prieto López, who as a young Civil Guard officer took part in the fight against Roberto's men, described him as an "authentic politician", although a comrade in the sierra believed "Roberto was more a soldier than a politician. In military meetings he would explain what was the mission of the Communist *guerrillero*." Lieutenant Colonel Eulogio Limia Pérez, chief of the anti-guerrilla campaign in Granada province, said the "repression and extermination" of the outlaws was difficult, partly because of the rural population's collaboration and partly because of "the perfect physical training, sobriety, resistance to fatigue and personal courage of almost all the members and their commanders".

According to one rebel, Enrique Urbano (Fermín), of the Río de la Miel, near Nerja, Roberto used to assert: "A good *guerrillero* has to eat heartily, shit hard and show he has balls to the point of death." He was not exaggerating. To survive in the sierra, a guerrilla needed to have feet and legs of steel, a cast-iron stomach, a lion's lungs, the instincts of a tiger and unquenchable determination.

There was no place for doubts or errors. Usually the guerrillas did not seek confrontations with the forces opposing them, particularly as they lacked weapons and ammunition. They preferred sabotage and kidnapping, while disseminating anti-Franco propaganda. When a conflict did occur, they tried to inflict damage on the attackers and then make a getaway as fast as possible. By means of night marches of up to 30 kilometres over the mountains, Roberto's men gave the impression that they were much more numerous than they in fact were.

The guerrillas moved through the darkness with the help of guides, men of the Axarquía who knew every inch of the sierras. When passing over mud or dust, the last in line would attach a branch to his waist to sweep away the footprints. On the whole they avoided caves, which became death traps if they were discovered inside; on a number of occasions the Civil Guards wiped out fugitives by tossing grenades or dynamite into caves where they had taken refuge. The guerrillas signalled to one another by imitating the hoot of an owl and at other times by clicking two stones together. They slept where they could on the ground, hidden among the pines and the scrub and sheltered by a jacket or a blanket. When torrential rain fell for several consecutive weeks in winter, a not infrequent occurrence in the Axarquía, they tried to protect themselves with pieces of canvas. Despite being so close to the Mediterranean and Africa, high up in the Sierra Almijara snow and frost are not uncommon and Roberto and his men were easy prey for throat and respiratory illnesses.

When a group split off from another, they arranged to leave a note explaining their movements in a tube hidden in a tree trunk or under a stone, or they placed a stone in a previously agreed position. Accomplices in the farmhouses had their own system of signals: to warn of enemy movements, they would hang out a sheet or leave a black cloth on a tree branch, or leave a window half open or the firewood in a certain spot.

Arming the numerous recruits was not easy. Shotguns, useful at close range, were the usual weapon of the foot soldiers. Group leaders had sub-machineguns (like the Sten, a British make), pistols (9mm Astra or Colt .45), and hand grenades. A coveted weapon, rare in the Sierra Almijara, was the Tommy Gun, the .45 mm Thompson sub-machinegun, a favourite of Chicago gangsters and American marines. Lack of ammunition was the big problem, although the guerrillas manufactured their own bullets. Apart from the supplies brought from Africa in the early years, they depended on arms stolen, bought, or seized in encounters with the Franco forces. The Civil Guard, which also suffered armament headaches, used the Schmeisser sub-machinegun, called *"el naranjero"* (the orange-seller) because the first delivery from the German factory was paid for with a shipment of oranges.

Communication with the outside world was necessarily limited in the sierra. *La Pirenaica*, the radio station directed by La Pasionaria in Moscow, pumped

POR LA REPÚBLICA

ORGANO DEL EJERCITO GUERRILLERO DE ANDALUCIA
(Fundado por el héroe Nacional, Ramón Vias.) Nº 30.

SUCEDA LO QUE SUCEDA EN EL MUNDO, sigan EL CAMINO QUE LLEVAN O MEJOREN LAS RELACIONES ENTRE LAS PRINCIPALES POTENCIAS DE LAS NACIONES UNIDAS, LOS ESPAÑOLES REPUBLICANOS TENEMOS UN MANDATO, ESCRITO CON SANGRE DE MAS DE UN MILLON DE COMPATRIOTAS; ESE MANDATO ES NO DESCANSAR Y LUCHAR UNIDOS HASTA QUE EL PUEBLO RECOBRE SU LIBERTAD Y ESPAÑA SEA SOBERANA E INDEPENDIENTE.

CAMPESINOS, OBREROS, PATRIOTAS EN GENERAL: AYUDAD INCONDICIONALMENTE AL EJERCITO GUERRILLERO A COMBATIR Y ANIQUILAR A LOS EXPLOTADORES QUE ... DE VUESTRO TRABAJO ROBANDOOS LOS PRODUCTOS Y VERDUGOS ... TORTURAN Y ASESINAN ... PUEBLO ESPAÑOL Y ... NUESTRA PATRIA.

SALUDO DE AÑO NUEVO AL PUEBLO ANTIFRANQUISTA ESPAÑOL.

Al finalizar el año 1.948 y comenzar el 49, el Ejército Guerrillero de Andalucía dirige un cariñoso saludo de combate a todos los españoles antifranquistas que en la medida de sus posibilidades, contribuyan, allí donde se encuentren, al desarrollo de la lucha por el derrocamiento del tiránico régimen franquista y el restablecimiento de la República.

Dirigimos nuestro saludo, a todos los que ansian y defienden la libertad y la independencia de la patria; a los obreros y obreras que en fábricas, talleres, oficinas, laboratorios etc, organizan plantes y huelgas para conseguir mejores condiciones de vida y protestan de las iniquidades del régimen; a los humildes agricultores que con interminables sudores trabajan día y noche para labrar las reducidas y esquilmadas parcelas de tierra que la codicia insaciable de los terratenientes

(Pasa a la 3ª página)

GRAN DESCALABRO DE LAS FUERZAS REPRESIVAS FRANQUISTAS.

VEINTICINCO MUERTOS Y QUINCE HERIDOS, MOROS Y GUARDIAS CIVILES, SIN NOVEDAD POR NUESTRA PARTE, ESTRATEGICO BALANCE DE ONCE HORAS DE COMBATE.

El día 6 de diciembre de 1.948, un nutrido contingente de fuerzas de la Guardia Civil, que constituyen la civilización asalvajada del siglo veinte en nuestra patria, en combinación con sus entrañables camaradas, los moros, salvajes sin civilización, mandadas por oficiales franquistas de opereta, que le superan en instinto vandalico, intentaron sorprender y cercar parte de las fuerzas del 6º Bon de la Agrupación Guerrillera de Granada que se encontraban en una posición del cerro del Lucero, término de Cómpeta (Málaga).

Al apuntar el día sonaron las primeras ráfagas, disparadas por los civiles dando comienzo un combate que duró hasta el anochecer y terminó con un balance catastrófico para el enemigo, que tuvo 25 muertos y 15 heridos, moros y guardias civiles, entre los que se encuentran un teniente de Regulares, un brigada de la Guardia Civil y cabo y sargentos de ambas fuerzas.

Las fuerzas enemigas que componian de dos Compañías de moros- los de Rebate; Frigiliana y Nerja- y civiles de todos los puestos costeros, los de Resinera, Juyena y de todos los pueblos que circundan la sierra; en total unos 600 hombres.

La moral de enemigo (si es que al principio tenia alguna) quedó anulada desde los primeros momentos cuando el fuego certero de las armas guerrilleras.....

(Pasa a la página siguiente).

FELICITACION

El Estado Mayor del Ejército Guerrillero de Andalucía felicita a las fuerzas del 6º Bón de la Agrupación de Granada que actuaron el 6 de diciembre de 1.948 en el cerro del Lucero frente a fuerzas enemigas inmensamente superiores en número. Elogia en términos generales el heroismo y disciplina de nuestros camaradas durante las once horas de combate en el que el enemigo sufrió un serio descalabro.

En la montaña, diciembre de 1.948. EL JEFE DEL EJERCITO.—Paulino.

PARTIDO COMUNISTA DE ESPAÑA — ARCHIVO — COMITE CENTRAL

ARCHIVO

Por la República, a guerrilla propaganda sheet, claimed 25 attackers were killed in the battle of Cerro Lucero

out anti-Franco propaganda. Radio contact was possible with the Communist Party, which ran a surprisingly sophisticated eavesdropping service. As Santiago Carrillo later explained: "We possessed a radio listening centre, staffed by operators and decoding experts who had worked in the Republic's war fleet. These maintained radio contact with guerrilla groups and Party organisations, besides picking up Civil Guard and police messages."

From time to time, the guerrillas bought from a herdsman, or stole, a goat or a pig and cooked it. Occasionally they could enjoy *migas* (fried breadcrumbs or semolina) or a stew of chick peas with some shreds of bacon. More usually they ate cold food, a diet of herrings or tinned tuna with a piece of bread. Often they were on the move or there was a patrol nearby and it was too dangerous to light a fire, so that days could pass without their consuming hot food or drink. Sometimes they went for days without eating at all.

Each man carried a knapsack with food, ammunition and his meagre possessions. In the mountains even transporting water from a spring to the encampment was a laborious task, usually reserved for the lower ranks. When they could, the men paid farmers' wives to wash their clothes, but it was difficult to maintain personal hygiene; it was not surprising that often they smelled bad and bugs gave them problems.

Roberto banned moustaches and long hair and insisted that his men should shave before going on patrol. In his book *Bandolerismo contemporáneo*, Colonel Díaz Carmona asserted: "El Roberto was a fanatic with extremist ideas, well-trained, an outstanding personality… His outlaws were truly afraid of him, as he had them controlled by an iron discipline. He did not allow the slightest weakness in their criminal act…he did not tolerate anybody having a moustache or beard on the grounds they were proof of little personality and the recourse of misfits etc."

Díaz Carmona, who played an active part in the anti-guerrilla campaign from his Civil Guard base in the small town of Alhama de Granada, recalled the control that Roberto exercised over his men. El Rubén, a *guerrillero* who surrendered to the Guardia Civil, was asked why he had not fled previously. He replied that once, when he was thinking of escaping, Roberto clapped him on the shoulder and said: "Ay Rubén, you're carrying the whole mountain on your shoulders!" According to Rubén, "Roberto guessed what everybody was thinking, so that one didn't dare think anything bad."

To *la gente de la sierra*, the Venta de los Panaderos must have seemed like a mirage, that solitary building lost amid precipitous terrain where a traveller could enjoy all the luxuries he dreamed about, food, warmth, drinks, soft beds. The inn has entered into the mythology of the sierras. Today it is abandoned and in ruins, but then its situation below the Puerto de Frigiliana pass made it a meeting point for all those who travelled between Málaga and Granada. There

Venta Panaderos, the inn used by both sides in the guerrilla war

the muleteers could gulp down a stiff drink or a plate of chick peas to give them strength for the climb up to the pass. And there one moment the Civil Guard would enter and the next the Maquis. The inn served both sides. It was easy to let slip information, true or false, in the Venta, knowing that it would be transmitted to the enemy. There are many anecdotes of how the Guards suddenly entered the inn, discovered meals which the Maquis had ordered and proceeded to scoff the food themselves.

To warn the guerrillas of any danger, the innkeepers, Paco Manuela (Francisco Rodríguez Ramírez) and his wife, Ana Herrero, would hang out a sheet on the rooftop. As tightrope-walkers they had few equals. It was a profitable game, but a risky one. When in 1947 a patrol halted Paco proceeding along a lonely track with a hefty cargo, he may have been able to justify why he was carrying so much merchandise, such as tobacco, lanterns, oil, sausage, bacon, sugar and beans, but the 12 pairs of socks were difficult to explain. Finally he confessed that men armed with machineguns had forced him to buy all those items.

The couple had two sons and four daughters, one of whom, the pretty Dolores, acted as companion to Roberto on his travels in order to aid his disguise as a respectable, married man. She may or may not have been his lover; everybody has a different opinion.

The fact that at the same time a Frigiliana man who was very friendly with a Civil Guard was courting another daughter created a tense situation. So much so that Roberto's men, convinced he was an informer (which he denied until his dying day), threatened him with a nasty accident. In fear of his life, he decided not to venture out of the village. In the end, the Venta Panaderos owners, Paco and Ana, and others in the family suffered interrogation and prison sentences.

Initially, the guerrillas were promised 500 pesetas a month by their leaders, but they didn't always receive it. Of the cash obtained from kidnappings (hundreds of thousands of pesetas in some cases), 50 per cent was sent (theoretically at least) to the Communist command in Madrid, 20 per cent was for the guerrillas, and 30 per cent for their families. The accounts were kept by the leaders, who at first scrupulously remunerated the collaborators who were supplying them with food.

According to one former guerrilla from Almuñécar, Roberto told him: "You will have a lot of money, but it's not yours. If you can't take the discipline, we'll give you cash and you can go wherever you want." Events would contradict that promise. If anybody disagreed with the commanders and thought of returning to his village, it was best to keep one's mouth shut. Roberto did not allow his followers to return home nor to give themselves up to the Civil Guard for fear they would give away their helpers and the guerrilla hideouts.

Despite the Communist propaganda, a number of the fugitives once they were in the sierra felt they had been tricked. They were sadly disenchanted by the conditions. Promises of a better life, of money and food, turned out to be far from the reality. Up there they found less freedom than there was in the village. They resented the discipline imposed by Roberto in his bid to create an efficient force. Some disliked wearing uniform because it made it difficult to move near the villages without being identified. And they were unhappy about being forbidden to visit their families. The lack of womenfolk must also have provoked a good deal of frustration among lusty young men. For disciplinary reasons sexual relations were prohibited and also the consumption of alcohol. "We were like monks," recalls one *guerrillero.*

Some attempt was made to educate the members of the group. Communists gave cultural talks and explained the general theories of Marxism. Some took advantage of the opportunity to learn to read and write, but it is doubtful if the Marxist dialectic provoked much interest among illiterate peasants, lacking any political education and more interested in where the next meal was coming from. According to two former guerrillas whose accounts appear in this book, there was a marked division between the rank and file and the most fervent Communists, especially those of the high command. This reached the point where one could not trust one's own comrades as in every group, in the purest Stalinist style, informers lurked, ready to report to their superiors. Falling asleep while on guard, showing a lack of morale or losing a weapon were serious crimes. And those who stepped out of line could not expect clemency.

Several guerrillas, when they realised their lives were in danger, decided to throw themselves on the mercy of the authorities. Miguel Cerezo, shocked by his experiences in the sierra, ran back to Frigiliana but could not risk staying in

Antonio Urbano (El Duende)

the village and had to join the Spanish Legion. José López Centurión, from the Río de la Miel valley, fled from the sierra with a sentence of death hanging over him and gave himself up. Another man from Río de la Miel, Antonio Urbano Muñoz (El Duende), after helping a prisoner of the Maquis to escape, felt threatened by both sides. Fearing his ex-comrades would kill him, he hid inside a farm oven,which was still warm from use.

Later he took refuge in a grotto under a pigsty, a few metres away from a Civil Guard post and a detachment of soldiers. Finally, he surrendered and spent time in prison, but survived to run a bar in Nerja for many years.

Roberto "gave special importance to his men's psychological attitudes, reserving the best for the Liaison Group (a type of personal guard), assigning the most fanatical to command groups and the craftiest to the role of spies and informers within the organisation. To retain the newer recruits, he applied a process of 'political responsibility'. It consisted initially in distributing them among the veterans and selecting them to commit killings, which they had to carry out, like it or not. These terror tactics, allied with an implacable persecution of deserters, hunting them down and murdering them, as happened in some cases, undoubtedly produced an internal strengthening of the group."

The words are those of Francisco Aguado Sánchez, who as a Civil Guard lieutenant colonel had access to all that force's files and wrote the "official" version of the conflict, not sparing his praise for the Benemérita while denigrating the "bandits". His text is dotted with the words "eliminated", "liquidated" and "exterminated".

The truth is, what with the official repression and the deeds of the Maquis, a climate of fear enveloped the *pueblos* and the *cortijos* (farmhouses) of the Axarquía, and also many of those in the sierra. For the countryfolk accused of betrayal there was no court martial or other chance to show their innocence. The guerrillas executed a number of alleged traitors, delivering what *Mundo Obrero* termed "the unappealable justice of the people". As always occurs in such cases, sometimes those who denounced the supposed traitors were merely seeking revenge or settling accounts.

13. Los desaparecidos

WITH SO MANY of their relatives in the sierra many village residents were suspected of being sympathisers or actively aiding the Maquis. Frigiliana lived under martial law and a curfew was imposed. Besides various Civil Guard detachments, a troop of Regulares was posted to the village. Soldiers and Guards stationed themselves at strategic points, in La Molineta (controlling the road to Nerja), in El Ingenio (the old palace of the Counts of Frigiliana), in Santo Cristo (a route to the cultivated land) and in the Molino de Lízar (above the village on the edge of the sierra). Within the boundaries of Nerja lay the Cortijo de las Moras, the mere mention of the name being enough to make many tremble because of its reputation as a torture centre.

Interrogations, shootouts, murders and kidnappings were regular occurrences. In February, 1947, two youngsters, Ángel Sánchez García and Sebastián Navas Iranzo, were loading a mule with fodder at the Cortijo La Morea when a group of armed men arrived. They sent Navas to Frigiliana with two letters (one for the Civil Guard to throw them off the scent and the other for the family) demanding a ransom of 75,000 pesetas and then they took Sánchez off to a hiding place in the sierra. Sixty years later he remembers every detail of his ordeal. His ransom was paid and he was promptly freed.

Antonio Ortiz Torres was not so fortunate. He was kidnapped on June 3, 1947, in Acebuchal, a small community deeper in the mountains than Frigiliana. El Maquis, among them the three Artabús brothers, demanded 30,000 pesetas for him. The Civil Guard archives hold a short radio report: "Málaga headquarters chief to Director General Seville — Yesterday evening bandit group showed up at Acebuchal kidnapping a civilian who later was found dead no further details known. Forces mobilised, interprovincial sector and I am going to direct operations." Those of the sierra killed Ortiz in the Barranco de las Majaillas.

The situation of the inhabitants of El Acebuchal grew more difficult by the day as one moment the Maquis would pass by there and the next the Civil Guard. The hamlet's mayor, Baldomero Torres López, thought his last moment had come when armed men seized him and demanded 40,000 pesetas. They were about to take him off up the mountain, but in the end, for one reason or

Three who disappeared: left to right, Manuel Santisteban Gutiérrez, Manuel García Herrero and Sebastián Platero Navas

another, they let him go free. In August, 1947, there was another kidnapping at a Frigiliana farm near the Río Seco. This time five armed men grabbed Paulino Fernández Ortega, aged 50, a Cómpeta native. Apparently they believed, mistakenly, he had a large amount of money stashed away and asked his wife for 150,000 pesetas. The ransom was not paid and the victim was shot. His decomposed body was found three weeks later. Three Frigiliana men were allegedly involved in the killing, Vicente Martín Vozmediano, Antonio Platero Ayllón and Antonio Rojas Álvarez.

At about that time, possibly provoked by the lack of success in controlling the guerrilla, a death squadron went into action. Four villagers "disappeared".

Night had fallen when three armed men suddenly emerged from the darkness at a spot where three members of the same family were making lime. Manuel Rodríguez Santisteban, then a youngster of some 15 years, vividly recalls the moment: "We were preparing a limekiln near El Acebuchal. As it was night I and my father were resting. My uncle, Manuel Santisteban Gutiérrez, went on working, throwing wood on the fire. He was a bachelor, about 20 years old. Suddenly these three men in civilian dress carrying guns arrived. They said they were from the Maquis. It seems they were looking for my uncle because they asked our names. Then they told my uncle he had to accompany them and they took him away down the valley. Everything happened in a few minutes. He was never seen again. They say he was taken over to Granada province and probably tortured and murdered. We don't know for certain who those three men were, of the Maquis or of the Civil Guard. All I know is that my father and I were very scared. The next morning we abandoned the kiln and returned to the village."

Indications are that Santisteban, with his hands bound, was taken up to the Puerto de Frigiliana where the Ley de Fugas was applied. Manuel Rodríguez had another disagreeable experience. In January, 1952, he was obliged to help bury an uncle by marriage, Lomas, the last *guerrillero* of Frigiliana, after he had been gunned down by the Civil Guard. Enough was enough and in 1958 he moved to Madrid, where he made a prosperous new life for himself.

On August 14, 1947, Sebastián Platero Navas, a 37-year-old farm worker with a wife and four children, went to the sierra to work and did not return. He had previously been detained on suspicion of being a Maquis sympathiser. His family believes that he was accused of helping the guerrillas with firewood and food and for this was shot in the Barranco de la Rambla, near the Frigiliana pass, and his body taken to Fornes (Granada). However, no death on or about that date is to be found in the Fornes registry, although there is an entry reporting the death of "an unknown" who was "killed in the sierra from gunshots on November 5 as a consequence of a meeting with the police force".

Two others disappeared that August 14, while they were collecting esparto on the mountain: Manuel García Herrero (nickname Leva), aged 43, already under suspicion of collaborating with the guerrilla, and one of his three sons, Manulillo, a dumb boy of 15. Civil Guard sources indicated that they had been shot and their bodies delivered to the Vélez-Málaga cemetery, with the allegation that they were "bandits killed in a skirmish". Nevertheless, their names do not figure in the Civil Registry nor in the archives of the San Juan de Vélez parish church. Another version, impossible to confirm, suggests that the Civil Guard was not involved and that for reasons unknown one of the Maquis, an in-law, killed the father and, when his son continued to cry and make a fuss, killed him too.

It was dangerous to ask questions about the fate of a relative who had vanished, particularly if a suspicion existed that the Civil Guard was responsible. Any contact with the authorities could only create problems. Thus, when a brother, a father, or a husband failed to return home, the safest was to keep quiet. The only indications of what happened to those who disappeared are to be found in the Civil Guard files, which reported that 12 "unknown" men were killed in the vicinity of Frigiliana, Torrox and Cómpeta between September and December, 1947. Official reports show that on September 28 two "*bandoleros*" who could not be identified were liquidated in an encounter in the Puerto Blanquillo and on November 5 two outlaws fell in La Rambla near the Puerto de Frigiliana. And on December 19 three "unidentified bandits" were shot in the area of Canillas de Albaida. The only certainty is that the bones of many victims of that pitiless war remain in the crevices and ravines of the mountains.

The Maquis also killed many people, and sometimes for very murky reasons. But, in contrast to groups like the Basque separatists, they did not plant bombs aimed at killing indiscriminately nor did they shoot police and Civil Guards in the back, nor target their families. Even Manuel Prieto López, a retired Civil Guard general, who was particularly active in the battle against Roberto and his men, says: "There were many deaths caused by the *bandoleros*, but all were in confrontations. They never employed the ETA terrorist system of shooting in the back. Because of this, I have a certain respect and appreciation for the Maquis."

Whatever the case, the year 1948 was one of the bloodiest in the Frigiliana zone. On February 21 the guerrilla achieved a spectacular economic coup under the noses of the Civil Guard when they stole 950 kilos of flour from a mill belonging to the de la Torre company at La Molineta, a huddle of dwellings and mills on a curve in the track to Nerja. According to *Mundo Obrero*, the booty consisted not of 950 kilos but of 1,800 and the guerrillas distributed free bread to the villagers, a popular gesture which, unfortunately, nobody can recall.

Normally, Roberto's men avoided direct confrontation with the Regime's forces, especially the military draftees. However, in March they staged an ambush in the Sierra de Cázulas, a few kilometres to the east of Frigiliana in the province of Granada, where some soldiers were guarding workers cutting pine trees. The guerrillas killed seven infantrymen, wounded five others and seized a quantity of arms and munitions. It was a blow which could only infuriate the military and toughen the repression, but for Clemente (El Fraile) it was a triumph. In a communiqué, he said: "The whole Seventh Group returned to their positions singing the guerrilla hymn and with the flag of the Republic flying."

During the guerrillas' most successful era, kidnappings produced considerable amounts of cash and, according to Frigiliana residents, some families grew rich from the sale of food to Roberto and his men. Even so, it was a dangerous game. There was always the risk of trickery and betrayal. One of the points where the people of the sierra picked up food was at the Cortijo de Los Caños. The villager who carried the food there did so under the threat of death. The Maquis had not forgiven him for murdering a Republican (apparently in cold blood) at the end of the Civil War. To save his life, he agreed to work for the guerrillas. When the Civil Guard found out what was going on at Los Caños, they set up an ambush. On July 1, 1948, they surprised a group of guerrillas and killed Francisco Cecilia Cecilia (Porrete), of Almuñécar. In the confusion of the skirmish, Joaquín Centurión, a Niño de la Noche and one of the most experienced guerrillas, was isolated from his companions. Some days later the Guard trapped and killed him at Los Peñoncillos, near El Acebuchal.

Two months later, Roberto's men, apparently convinced that somebody had betrayed them, wiped out three members of the Orihuela family of Frigiliana when they were working at Los Caños. A bulletin signed by Clemente declared: "As they paid so will all those who harm our units and patriots. It is what our people demand and it is what we fulfil."

14. Fiasco on Cerro Lucero

DETERMINED to crush the Maquis once and for all, in the summer of 1948 the authorities ordered the residents of Acebuchal to abandon their houses. The hamlet, five kilometres from Frigiliana on the traditional muleteers' route between Málaga and Granada, offered easy access to the guerrillas and the inhabitants were suspected of aiding them with food and information. Some 200 residents had to leave their homes and seek shelter in Frigiliana, Cómpeta and Torrox.

In December word reached the authorities that Roberto was organising a big meeting of his men in a camp located below the summit of Cerro Lucero. It was a golden opportunity to wipe out the group and a large-scale operation involving both Civil Guards and soldiers was mounted. They launched a dawn attack, but the guerrillas, though taken by surprise, were well-positioned on the heights and held off the attackers all day. By night they slipped away, suffering only a few wounded. The Communist propaganda claimed that they had killed 25 Guards and Moorish soldiers, an obviously exaggerated figure, but the attack was certainly a dismal failure.

As they fought for their lives on the slopes of El Lucero, the guerrillas knew nothing of distant events which would result in their being abandoned to their fate. Hurling themselves over precipitous terrain, sleeping on the ground, gambling their lives at every moment, they could not imagine that the Communist Party's executive committee was considering terminating their movement. They knew nothing of a meeting in the Kremlin in September, 1948, when Stalin advised the Spanish leaders to put more emphasis on infiltrating Franco's vertical syndicates. Already it was clear that the armed struggle was getting nowhere, but the party chiefs showed a strange inertia in the face of the facts. News of the change in tactics was going to take years to reach the Sierra Almijara.

Meanwhile, *Mundo Obrero* continued its forecasts of imminent victory, and with its denunciations. In its February 10, 1949, issue, it declared: "One of the most frequent locations for Francoist crimes is in Andalusia with the continuing assassination of countryfolk. 'Shooting while trying to escape' is the criminal law of the Civil Guard. Frigiliana, a tiny village in Málaga province, has seen its humble streets soaked with blood. The terror of the Civil Guard has fallen like

Ruins of the Civil Guard post on the Cerro Lucero summit

a black shadow over its houses." The report referred to the death of José Cerezo Rodríguez, who was surprised with others taking food to the sierra. The Guards attacked, throwing grenades, and Cerezo fell mortally wounded.

But, if the village inhabitants could not expect much mercy from the Civil Guard, neither could they trust in the benevolence of the people of the sierra. The Maquis never forgave those who betrayed their comrades, as they demonstrated on more than one occasion. Miguel Moreno González, a Nerja Falangist, helped the Guards to identify collaborators with the Niños de la Noche, directed by Julio Ramos Corral. That occurred in 1937. In his statement to the authorities, he said: "I beg that these patrols are carried out with great precaution so that nobody can suspect that I was the accuser because if I am in the countryside they could kill myself and my family." His fear was justified. Twelve years later, on April 16, 1949, guerrillas led by Vicente Martín Vozmediano seized Moreno and demanded a ransom of 75,000 pesetas. The Civil Guard reported: "As it was already night they took shelter from the rain within the walls of a Frigiliana farmhouse and it appears that the victim tried to free himself using his own knife, which the outlaw snatched away from him and dealt him a deep cut in the throat cutting his jugular."

Another settling of accounts, a particularly horrifying crime, occurred in August, 1949. One of the villagers informed the Civil Guard that he had seen a group of 10 to 12 *"bandoleros"* taking off to the sierra Francisco Iranzo Herrero. The Maquis had warned this witness they would string him up from a pine tree if he gave away their presence. Among the kidnappers, who were armed

Francisco Iranzo Herrero

with sub-machine-guns, rifles, shotguns and grenades, were three Frigiliana men, Vicente Martín Vozmediano, Antonio Rojas Álvarez and Antonio García Martín.

On August 16 a badly scrawled note appeared on the door of the school in the village main street. It read: "El Bendita and El Terrible are at the Cruz de Napoleón, you can be sure they are there." Somebody had found the bodies, it appears, but preferred not to report the discovery directly to the barracks. The security forces began searching the Higuerón river valley. A few metres up the hillside from the Cross of Napoleon (a spot where in the 19th century some thieves had killed a youngster named Napoleon), they found Paco Bendita, Francisco Iranzo Herrero, a 25-year-old bachelor, and El Terrible, José López Jurado, a 35-year-old goatherd, married with two children. The two had been hung from pine trees with esparto cord (cause of death according to the Civil Registry: "in consequence of suspension"). The bodies were terribly mutilated, suggesting they had been tortured. According to the people of the sierra, they were guilty of betrayal.

Confrontations continued. And the deaths. But these were not reflected in the news reports of the time. The few inhabitants of Frigiliana who saw a newspaper learned that, in contrast with the rest of the world, Spain was a picture of tranquillity. As Franco was to explain later, it was not convenient to publish details of the conflict "for political and security reasons". The guerrillas did not exist, except in foreign news as when *Sur de Málaga* reported that the Italians were employing "guerrilla tactics against the bandit Giuliano in Sicily".

A frequent headline in the Falangist press was "Tremendous welcome for the Caudillo". According to the Generalísimo's speeches, Spain was enjoying an unprecedented era of peace and prosperity despite the intrigues and infiltrations of the Bolsheviks. Thus he informed parliament in May, 1949, that "almost all those who committed offences during the Red revolution had been reintegrated into national life". The number of those in prison for crimes of all types was only 38,000 because "the redemption of sentences through work and the penal system is today the most humane and advanced among all civilised nations".

15. Shake-up in the Civil Guard

A VERY RARE allusion to the continuing violent struggle appeared in the local press on September 20, 1949. Málaga's Civil and Military Governors were reported to have attended the burial in the provincial capital of Corporal Antonio Toribio Tejada and the guard Antonio García Reyes, "killed near Cómpeta in the course of duty". In fact, three days earlier the Benemérita had suffered a reverse in a furious battle on Cerro Verde, a steep hillside near Acebuchal. Learning of the presence of the guerrillas, at least 100 guards and soldiers had besieged them. All day long the noise of submachineguns, shotguns and grenades echoed about the jagged mountain ridges. Two guerrillas were killed, Rafael Jurado Martín (Nico) from Torrox, one of Los Frailes, and Miguel Ángel García Platero (Espartero) from Frigiliana. The official report said Espartero was found dead after the battle. But witnesses say that after Espartero surrendered a lieutenant questioned him, did not like his answers and shot him. The Ley de Fugas. Besides losing two men, the Civil Guard suffered several wounded.

Life for members of the Benemérita was hardly a bed of roses. Most had little education and enlisted to escape the lack of work and poverty of their villages. Badly paid (around 12 pesetas a day), they lived far from home in dilapidated barracks in places where many of the locals preferred to avoid contact with them. Patrolling for days at a time through the sierras in search of the guerrillas, they slept where they could, knowing that often they were being tracked by the enemy. On a number of occasions the guerrillas had opportunities to kill guards but resisted the temptation, preferring to remain hidden. When the Civil Guard set up ambushes, they often had to make night marches, using local guides to negotiate paths that they did not know. They built an observation post on the summit of the Lucero peak, a bleak,

Killed in action: Civil Guard
Antonio García Reyes

windswept spot reached by a precipitous path. From there they could dominate the heights and valleys of the Sierra Almijara. A squad of five or six men kept watch, using binoculars (when available) and sending messages via reflecting mirrors. It was a strategic spot but very exposed and the observers, who were relieved every two weeks, were no doubt both bored and nervous, knowing that they themselves were under surveillance.

Discipline was strict and errors were not pardoned. Mesas de Ibor, a tiny village in the north of Cáceres province, was a witness to the severity of some officers. Informed in April, 1945, that a Maquis band had attacked the barracks there and carried off arms and uniforms, in the presence of all the inhabitants a lieutenant colonel shot a corporal and three guards. Punishment did not normally go to such lengths, but the pressure to obtain results was extremely strong. To look good in the eyes of their superiors, commanders had to exaggerate their successes and conceal their faults. On various occasions the bodies deposited at cemeteries and labelled *"bandoleros"* were those of guiltless country people. The explanation offered for so many deaths and so few prisoners taken in confrontations was that the outlaws fell victim in shootouts provoked by their fierce resistance. There were no public inquests. And nobody had the nerve to ask why there were so few wounded.

Civil Guards died too. Manuel Prieto López, a retired general, recalls: "The *bandoleros* killed many Civil Guards. There's a plaque to the fallen in the Granada military headquarters with the names of three of my colleagues, three lieutenants, and of various non-commissioned officers and guards, to a total of 60." To encourage the forces of order, the Regime rewarded them with decorations, promotions and cash prizes. The Cross of Military Merit was the medal most frequently awarded and many guards pocketed monetary compensation for distinguished action. A guard who succeeded in detaining or killing a guerrilla leader received 3,000 pesetas, so that chiefs like Roberto really did have a price on their heads.

Expulsions and penalties for lack of zeal were common. The failure of the attack on Cerro Verde in September, 1949, and the lack of progress in the campaign against Roberto's group provoked a

Civil Guards aid an injured comrade after a clash with guerrillas

Eulogio Limia Pérez

number of sackings and the naming of new commanders. Captain Ismael Quilis Alfonso, who had commanded detachments in Frigiliana, Nerja and Cómpeta, was sentenced to two years in a military prison "for lack of initiative and activity". A sergeant accused of negligence and disobedience received a sentence of four years and three corporals sentences of six months. In October Lieutenant Colonel Ángel Fernández Montes de Oca, who had acquired a fearsome reputation after his performance in Córdoba province, took charge of the 137 Comandancia, the Civil Guard area command in Málaga, and Lieutenant Colonel Eulogio Limia Pérez was appointed to head the 136 Comandancia in Granada. With Montes de Oca arrived two other hardliners, Captain Joaquín Fernández Muñoz and Lieutenant Francisco Giménez Reyna, posted to Nerja and Frigiliana. Under the new officers there came an important change in tactics.

Limia Pérez noted that in Granada "the province's state in general was one of genuine panic among the forces of order, proprietors, authorities and functionaries". This officer had gained experience in crushing the guerrillas in Toledo and Ciudad Real and now, given special powers, he set out to undermine the rebels by taking aim at their collaborators and their families. One night about 300 guards surrounded the communities of Salar and Loja in Granada province. In the first there were 93 arrests and in the second 61.

The operations of the Regime's forces were equally vigorous in Málaga. Civil Guards emptied the farms in the Barranco de Huit, near Torrox, and detained many residents in the Río de la Miel area. All former guerrillas who were at liberty in their villages were rounded up. In some places families suspected of giving shelter to the guerrillas were ejected from their houses which were then burned. The jails were filled with families accused of having helped the people of the sierra. Prieto López, then a captain heading the Civil Guard post at Torrox, distributed hundreds of leaflets all over the Axarquía offering a passport to escape abroad to anybody who delivered the guerrilla leader. "The life is guaranteed of whoever kills Roberto," he promised. Prieto already had experience with informers in Granada where an extraordinary case of treachery had occurred. Tarbes (José Luis Merediz Víctores), first chief of staff of the Agrupación de Granada, who had infiltrated from the French resistance, became an invaluable police informer. When his comrades learned of his betrayal, he was executed and his body tossed into a lime kiln at Órgiva in the Alpujarras.

An important factor in the Frigiliana area was the work of the *contrapartidas*, a tactic as crafty as it was effective. These groups of Civil Guards acted as *agents provocateurs*. Wearing civilian clothes and posing as members of the Maquis, they would suddenly arrive at a farmhouse and ask for help. It was a way to uncover the collaborators, but the false Maquis also threatened the country-dwellers and committed outrages in order to discredit the guerrillas. Very soon the peasants did not know whom they could trust. Life was particularly difficult for the goatherds and shepherds in the sierra; on the one hand the Maquis counted on their support, on the other the government forces insisted their duty was to report on the movements of the "outlaws". A number paid with the supreme penalty. As the repression grew ever more severe and the guerrillas were liquidated, ever more frequent in Frigiliana parish church's registry of deaths were such notes as "He delivered his soul to the Lord in the sierra" and "He did not receive the last rites".

Manuel Prieto López

SE GARANTIZA la VIDA al que MATE al "ROBERTO" SEA QUIEN SEA

Todos los que se PRESENTAN nos dicen que si no se vienen MAS es porque el "ROBERTO" os dice que os matamo, pero que si SUPIERAIS la VERDAD del trato que damos, dejariais sólo al "Roberto" y al Estado Mayor, y os presentariais.

No dudarlo y VENIRSE que no os arrepentireis.

ROBERTO: ¿Por que tienes tanto MIEDO que siempre estás en el toldo RODEADO de los enlaces.? ¿es que no te FIAS de los demas? Acuérdate que el "FELIPILLO" y el "LORENZO" eran de tu confianza.....

ROBERTO: ¿Te acuerdas de "TARVES", tu compañero de la escuela francesa de de Pou.? Se que dices que le ODIAS cordialmente. Por él, que como sabes, TRABAJO conmigo, detuve a tu Jefe "RAMIRO" y a "MARIANO" y tú te escapaste de milagro. ¿TE ACUERDAS?

Espero conseguir que alguno de tus compañeros de hoy, me ayuden a acabar contigo.

¿Tú que opinas de eso?

Incluso al "Clemente" o al "Felipe" o a otro cualquiera que traiga tu cabeza, LE FACILITARIA un pasaporte para el extranjero. Si alguno se atreve por MUCHOS crímenes que tenga, que se pongan en contacto conmigo bien por carta, o por alguna persona de confianza y discreta, y que ponga incluso las condiciones que quiera de garantía.

"¿Que te parece Roberto?"

Torrox Febrero-Marzo 1951
El Capitán de la Guardia Civil

In this leaflet Captain Prieto López guarantees the life of any guerrilla who kills Roberto

16. The crime at La Loma de las Vacas

IN 1950 THERE occurred one of the most terrible incidents in Frigiliana's recent history. Two days after three young men had been arrested by the Civil Guard their mutilated bodies were dumped at the village cemetery. Their deaths were directly linked to an attack on a Moorish soldier which occurred on the morning of April 20, 1950. Mohamed Ben Abdela, one of the detachment of Regulares stationed in Frigiliana, decided to go to an irrigation channel on the edge of the village to wash himself. He had stripped off his clothes when suddenly he received three axe blows on the head and clavicle and fell to the ground spurting blood. The culprit, according to the Civil Guard, was Antonio Platero Martín, a 20-year-old unmarried labourer, known as El Moreno. Immediately, he and two companions, José Castillo Moreno (Pepe Mocha) and Antonio Sánchez Martín (Lomas), fled to the sierra.

The Civil Guard had good reason to believe that El Moreno was helping the rebels and six weeks before the incident they had confronted him and pressured him to collaborate with the authorities in tracking down the "outlaws". El Moreno found himself in a terrible dilemma. He wanted to flee to the mountains but two leading guerrillas, the Frailes brothers, did not trust him. They insisted that first he must commit some act to demonstrate his commitment (and also to minimise the possibility that later he would change his mind and betray them). Thus, finding himself between the devil and the deep blue sea, El Moreno opted to put himself definitively on the other side of the law.

Although Ben Abdela eventually recovered from his wounds, his comrades in the Regulares were enraged and discharged their fury by destroying El Moreno's house and all his possessions. Large numbers of guards and Regulares combed the area around the village but failed to catch the runaways. Doubtless the Civil Guards felt frustrated by their lack of success and wanted vengeance.

The officer responsible for suppressing banditry in the zone was Captain Joaquín Fernández Muñoz, a 42-year-old native of Bailén (Jaén) based in the neighbouring village of Torrox. This officer had already established a fearsome reputation for harshness in Córdoba province and, according to the villagers, had declared that for each of his men who died three or more of the guerrillas would fall. Whether this was true or not, the Civil Guard went looking for "the usual suspects", those who had relatives in the sierra. On April 21 they arrested three young men. A patrol picked up Manuel Martín Ruiz, aged 18, as he was returning from the spot where he had been preparing a charcoal kiln. His father, Sebastián, was in the sierra. Another youngster, Antonio García Martín, aged 22, had just returned home from work when his wife told him he had to report to the barracks. His brother, Ángel, was in the sierra. Also called to the barracks was Antonio Triviño Cerezo, aged 26, whose wife was about to give birth. His brother, Manuel, was in the sierra. None of the three — their families and neighbours insist to this day — had committed any offence.

The three never returned home. Manuel Martín and the two Antonios spent the night in the barracks. The next morning various witnesses saw the guards ordering them into a vehicle which left the village. For 36 hours their families, without news and desperate, searched for them. They had been taken to an olive oil factory known as La Maquinilla in the Molineta, a group of buildings in an area known as La Loma de las Vacas (the Hill of the Cows) on the road to Nerja. During the day a woman saw them looking out of a window. They asked her for water, which she gave them.

That night the three were taken from La Maquinilla and apparently handed over to the Regulares. For some hours they were beaten and dragged about in the area of La Loma de las Vacas before being finished off by gunshots. On the morning of April 23 their bodies were loaded on a donkey and dumped at the cemetery.

The village was profoundly shocked and indignant. The priest, Don Domingo Campillo Gascón, parish priest between 1949 and 1959, a man big in both stature and courage, decided to hold a full-scale mass. He ordered the church bell to be rung, put on his most impressive vestments and with the choirboys strode through the village to the cemetery, passing in front of the barracks. Inspired by his example, amid a tension that was almost tangible the inhabitants walked in silence to attend the funeral under the hostile gaze of a host of Civil Guards. It was an unprecedented act of solidarity and defiance.

In this highly charged atmosphere, a furious Captain Fernández Muñoz called to the barracks the most influential residents who had attended the funeral, including the mayor, the doctor and the teachers. There he scolded them, accusing them of being hypocrites, and the guards gave them a beating. According to several villagers and also some guards, the Francoists in the village, alarmed by the guerrilla threat, had previously encouraged the Civil Guard to get tough and because of this the guards felt betrayed.

Don Domingo was also called to the barracks, but he refused to go. Instead, the captain had no choice but to go to the priest's office where a ferocious confrontation took place. The Civil Guard launched an investigation in which Lieutenant Francisco Giménez Reyna went as far as accusing the priest of

Their bodies were delivered to Frigiliana cemetery: left to right, Antonio Triviño Cerezo, Antonio García Martín and Manuel Martín Ruiz,

organising an "anti-patriotic" demonstration. The accusation reached the ears of the bishop, who called Don Domingo to Málaga where he was advised to adopt a more diplomatic attitude.

The same day that the trio's remains were deposited in the cemetery the Civil Guard questioned three women related to the men who had fled to the sierra. It is not difficult to imagine the physical and mental pressure employed to extract confessions from them, especially when Captain Fernández Muñoz was in charge of the interrogation. In the end, El Moreno's mother, Florencia Martín Navas, a 51-year-old widow, admitted that she had recently bought 12 pieces of tobacco and 35 shotgun cartridges with money her son had received from the guerrillas. So that the seller in Málaga would recognise her, she had carried a basket with two hens in it, half-covered by a red cloth. Later she took the purchases in a sack to the mountains with the pretext that she was going to see her son who was making charcoal in the area of Alcóncar, up the river from Frigiliana. Two months earlier she had taken to the same area seven pairs of esparto sandals, seven loaves of bread and two kilos of sausage. There she met some guerrillas from Frigiliana, the Panzón brothers, Zumbo and Matutero. Altogether her son had received 5,000 pesetas from the outlaws to make a number of purchases and she had been paid a thousand or so pesetas.

Josefa Moreno Moreno, aged 51, widow and mother of Pepe Mocha, confessed that for about two years she had been buying food and clothing in Nerja and Vélez-Málaga, which her son delivered to the people of the sierra. Altogether she had received 1,500 pesetas. Ana Santisteban Gutiérrez, aged 26, said that on three occasions — more "out of fear and necessity" than anything else — her husband, Lomas, had taken sausages to the sierra. He had received 700 pesetas. When Lomas fled, he took with him a small pistol which he had found near the river and which she had hidden beneath a mattress. In the yellowing

Don Domingo, Frigiliana's parish priest, clashed with the Civil Guard over the deaths of the three young men, Lieutenant Francisco Giménez Reyna (right) accusing him of organising an "anti-patriotic" demonstration

documents in the military archives, the women's thumbprints at the bottom of their statements contrast sharply with the firm, confident signature of Fernández Muñoz. The captain reported: "The three detained women have a bad reputation, and have leftwing ideas." The three were sent to Málaga's provincial prison for women and later were sentenced to two years behind bars.

Meanwhile, it was necessary to keep up appearances, even if it were only for internal consumption, and the Civil Guard quickly organised an investigation into the deaths of the three young men. The official version of the incident bore little resemblance to what actually happened, as reported by witnesses in the village.

Málaga's Civil Governor informed the authorities in Madrid: "Around 1.30am on April 23, a group covering the zone known as the Loma de Vacas, in the Frigiliana district, observed the presence of three unknown persons proceeding with caution and when they were near enough they were ordered to halt in the name of the Civil Guard. The unknown persons then took flight in an attempt to escape, a manoeuvre prevented by the forces who, when they realised their orders were being disobeyed, opened fire, causing the death of the abovementioned individuals."

The inquest (never made public) was hardly an impartial affair. Fernández Muñoz named a junior officer, Lieutenant Juan Domínguez Rojo, as examining magistrate. The lieutenant called two witnesses. First, the captain himself gave evidence. Fernández Muñoz declared under oath that he had posted patrols at various points around Frigiliana following the attack on the Moorish soldier. He himself was on guard on the Loma de las Vacas with a sergeant, a corporal and a guard.

The inquest report noted: "...at one thirty today (in the early morning) they sighted several unknown persons and, as they approached, the guards could see there were three of them. At a convenient distance the officer ordered them to halt in the name of the Civil Guard but, far from obeying, they took flight. The order to halt was given several times but failed to detain them, the witness then ordering shots to be fired in the air. As this too was not effective, in fact far from stopping they redoubled their speed, the members of the patrol were obliged to open fire with the result that within a few moments all the fugitives fell to the ground, apparently dead."

The second witness was Sergeant Manuel Sevilla Ortega whose evidence reflected almost word for word that of his captain. The only other witnesses were the doctors of Torrox and Frigiliana. Their report indicated that the three died "owing to gunshot wounds". They did not mention if they had found other injuries on the bodies.

Lieutenant Juan Domínguez took little time to reach his verdict. On April 24 he signed his report which said: "...the action was carried out without the intervening force bearing any responsibility. It has complied and interpreted well and faithfully its regulations, leaving the Honour of the Corps in good standing, on putting to death three individuals who were indisputably collaborating with the bandits and who, if this had not occurred, would have been among those sowing alarm and anxiety in this zone among peaceful, honourable citizens."

The inquest report was sent to military headquarters in Málaga and in July reached the Auditoría de Granada (the judicial authorities). The judicial verdict was clear: the facts "do not constitute an offence" and "the Benemérita acted in compliance with its orders". On July 24 the Captain General of Granada declared the affair closed. There was no blame to apportion.

Down the years all the efforts on the part of the victims' families to establish the facts have proved unsuccessful. They have encountered only a wall of silence. In 1996 a Nerja lawyer, representing Antonia Triviño Martín, Virtudes Martín Ruiz, Antonio Martín Ruiz, Antonio García Triviño and Ana Agudo Navas, approached the Historic Studies Service at Civil Guard headquarters in Madrid and the Capitanía General (military headquarters) in Seville seeking access to any document that could throw light on the affair. He drew a blank.

No information was forthcoming about any inquest proceedings. The details reported here only came to light when the author was checking Andalusia's military archives. The official version of the incident — radically different from that presented by people of the village — turned up in a document of the Capitanía

General de Granada (Case 355/50, lodged in File 779-37 of the Togado Militar (military judiciary) of Almería).

In Frigiliana the families continue to hope that one day the memory of those who died on the Loma de las Vacas will be rehabilitated.

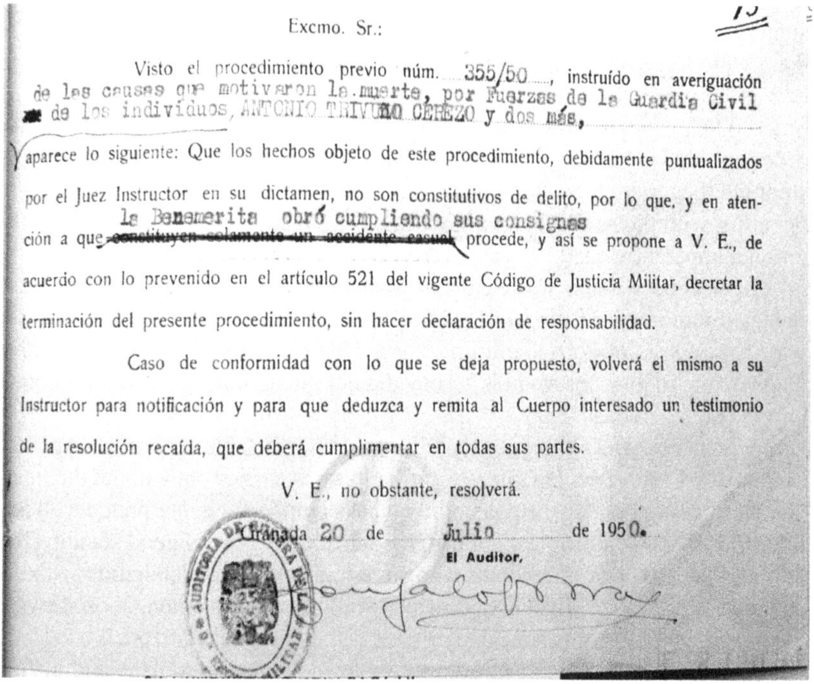

Excmo. Sr.:

Visto el procedimiento previo núm. 355/50, instruído en averiguación
de las causas que motivaron la muerte, por Fuerzas de la Guardia Civil
de los individuos, ANTONIO TRIVIÑO CEREZO y dos más,
aparece lo siguiente: Que los hechos objeto de este procedimiento, debidamente puntualizados por el Juez Instructor en su dictamen, no son constitutivos de delito, por lo que, y en atención a que la Benemerita obró cumpliendo sus consignas ~~constituyen solamente un accidente casual~~ procede, y así se propone a V. E., de acuerdo con lo prevenido en el artículo 521 del vigente Código de Justicia Militar, decretar la terminación del presente procedimiento, sin hacer declaración de responsabilidad.

Caso de conformidad con lo que se deja propuesto, volverá el mismo a su Instructor para notificación y para que deduzca y remita al Cuerpo interesado un testimonio de la resolución recaída, que deberá cumplimentar en todas sus partes.

V. E., no obstante, resolverá.

Granada 20 de Julio de 1950.

El Auditor,

The military command in Granada formally shelves the investigation into the Frigiliana deaths, noting the Civil Guard "acted in compliance with orders"

17. All exits barred

THOUGH INCREASINGLY harassed and with their supply lines cut, the guerrillas still had the ability to stir up trouble for the forces of order. They moved by night with amazing rapidity from one spot to another, from the Alhama de Granada area to Las Alpujarras. On May 17, 1950, they killed three guards in a shootout in the Barranco del Lobo in the Sierra de Loja, but six guerrillas fell too. And six more died, including Mocha of Frigiliana, on July 17 in an ambush at a farmhouse near Alhama. On October 28 a skirmish lasting several hours occurred on the Loma del Cuerno, a hillside in the Loja mountains. Sixteen Civil Guards battled, according to their estimates, against 80 guerrillas, among them four or five from Frigiliana. A corporal and a guard were killed and the Maquis group escaped in the darkness.

But these were the death throes. The arrest of supporters, the betrayals and the desertions were destroying the information and supply network, isolating the guerrillas and contributing to their demoralisation. As the Civil Guard tightened the screws, the guerrillas were reduced to boiling animal bones to make soup and eating leaves, berries and raw potatoes. Each day was a purgatory. To try to halt the desertions, the court martials in the sierra and the death sentences were becoming more frequent. Towards the end, paranoia surged among Roberto and his men. No deviations from the party line, nor arguments about tactics, nor complaints about the rigid discipline were permitted. In his attempt to retain control, Roberto became more ruthless. Courts martial were held and at least 16 guerrillas accused of lack of revolutionary spirit or of treason were *"ajusticiado"* (executed). The phrase "he must be sent for flour" was a euphemism for the sentence of death. Just as, when it was learned that a comrade had been "sent to the Sierra Nevada", everybody could guess his fate.

Sebastián Martín Navas, of Frigiliana, was tossed over a cliff when he apparently lost his mind on learning of the death of his son at the hands of the Civil Guard. Another from the village, Antonio Platero Ayllón, fell into disfavour due to his indiscretions and was thrown down a well. In Platero's case, it's possible he was put to death beforehand by means of a technique frequently employed. They called it "putting on the tie" and three or four guerrillas shared the responsibility. Taking the victim away from the encampment, they placed a greased, sliding cord of esparto around his neck, then without warning two heaved at the ends while a third pushed him in the back with his knee. Death usually came swiftly and the method had the advantage that it did not waste bullets. The body was thrown into a gully or crevice.

In such a way two of the Centurión family from Nerja died. Francisco Centurión Centurión (Florentino in the Maquis), brother of the leading *guerrillero* Joaquín Centurión (Juanito), was accused of having slept on guard duty and of intending to desert. He was executed in the Sierra de Loja. In the case of Francisco López Centurión (Lucas), the suspicion, apparently mistaken, that he was about to give himself up was enough to condemn him. His execution occurred in the Sierra de Cázulas and his remains were almost certainly buried in the Otívar (Granada) cemetery.

Half a century later his brother José (guerrilla name Rodolfo), an indomitable type who fled in fear of suffering the same fate, was still struggling to obtain official confirmation of Francisco's final resting place (see his testimony, page 132).

The Sixth Battalion, cornered in the mountains between Frigiliana and the Zafarraya pass, lost contact with the Seventh Battalion in the Alpujarras and the Sierra Nevada. Suffering stronger and stronger repression, Roberto must have understood that he and his band had been abandoned. The Party was not going to offer any help. There were no arms and no food, and — so distant from France — there was little chance of escaping via the northern frontier. At the end of 1950 or the beginning of 1951 members of the high command apparently engaged in a fierce argument about future tactics. It was suggested that they should dissolve the guerrilla force and reorganise it with only those who could be most trusted. Roberto was thinking of abandoning the sierra, but the Frailes, Paquillo and others refused to accept that the years of struggle had been in vain. Even so, the situation was reaching crisis point.

On January 20, 1951, the Frigiliana town council held an extraordinary meeting to congratulate the Civil Guard under the command of Lieutenant Rafael Domínguez for "the capture and extermination of various bandits in the sierra of this district". A few days later, in February, Limia Pérez issued an ultimatum to the "deceived outlaws". Pamphlets distributed across the region warned: "Your days are numbered. We shall totally crush you within a few months and I offer you this sole chance to save your lives. Do not be so stupid as to believe that a ridiculous and ignorant little chieftain like the tyrant who commands you can have any influence on behalf of Communism in Spain, a cause definitively lost since the end of the war."

The guerrillas continued to fall victim to the bullets of the Civil Guard. Among those from Frigiliana were Blas Martín Vozmediano, who died in January, 1951, Blas Martín Navas (Gonzalo) and José Sánchez Martín (Domingo),

Servicios
Fuerzas de la 137 Comandancia (Málaga), consiguen dar muerte a dos peligrosos bandoleros

A Civil Guard bulletin reports two *bandoleros* have been killed

gunned down in February, and José Rojas Álvarez (Arturo), killed in April. Antonio García Martín (Gaspar) was trapped by the guards in July and, rather than surrender, killed himself. In August Antonio Rojas Álvarez (Carlillos) y Bautista Acosta Urdiales (Máximo) were killed. Directly involved in some of these deaths and various others was Vicente el Artabús, who in March surrendered in Frigiliana and, arrayed in a Civil Guard uniform, led the guards to a number of guerrilla hideouts.

Limia Pérez's tactics were working. Ninety men died in shootouts between October, 1949, and September, 1951. Another 13 were captured, 21 gave themselves up, six fled and 16 were "ajusticiado" (executed) by their own comrades. In that period the estimated strength of the group fell from 109 to 28, according to the (suspect) calculations of Limia Pérez.

By June, 1951, the guerrillas' situation was unsustainable and Roberto slipped away from the sierra in order to prepare the evacuation of the few followers he had left. He said he would obtain the documentation necessary for them to leave Spain and he carried more than sufficient funds, 500,000 pesetas according to one guerrilla. First he went to Málaga, staying for one week in a house in Churriana. He obtained an identity card bearing the name Jaime Costa Arévalo and travelled to Madrid, where he lodged in Hilarión Eslava street. With him were his lover La Tangerina (introduced as his wife) and Paquillo, Francisco Sánchez Girón.

18. Roberto arrested

EXACTLY HOW the authorities discovered Roberto's whereabouts has never been revealed, although among those suspected of betrayal was La Cascaja, María Martín Godoy, owner of a Torrox farm. The most wanted man in Spain and his companions were relaxing in a bar in the Plaza de España in the centre of Madrid when they were confronted by a squad of Civil Guards led by Sergeant Alonso Ansó (for his "zeal, coolness and resolution" Ansó was rewarded with promotion and 3,000 pesetas). The man who identified Roberto, it appears, was none other than Vicente of Frigiliana, the turncoat guerrilla. Taken to Madrid for this task, he concealed his face with a moustache and hat when he entered the bar.

For the Civil Guard it was a moment of triumph and celebration. After all these years at last they had in their hands the most notorious guerrilla leader, even if they were not sure of his correct name. Roberto's arrest is recorded thus in the Civil Guard archives: "On September 26, 1951, special forces of Málaga headquarters with the collaboration of those of national headquarters, directed by Lt Col Ángel Fernández Montes de Oca, Málaga commander, detained in Madrid the chief leader of the so-called Agrupación de Guerrilleros de Andalucía which had committed so many crimes, holdups and acts of vandalism in this province, particularly in the Málaga-Granada border area, its principal field of operations. Called José Lozano Muñoz (sic), El Roberto, an individual who stood out in the Red zone during the War of Liberation with the rank of Commander and who, trained in the Terrorism Academy of Tolosus (sic) (Francia), was sent to Spain by the Communist Party in order to organise in our country and commit acts of terrorism."

The three detainees were transferred to Málaga. A lengthy interrogation of Roberto was carried out in a barracks in the Malagueta area of the provincial capital. Or in a chalet in El Limonar residential area. Or in a house in Huétor-Vega near Granada. Or perhaps in all these places...reports are contradictory because all the questioning was done in the greatest secrecy so as not to alert the guerrillas still at liberty. What is certain is that Roberto began to talk — under what sort of physical or mental pressure, heaven knows — and he did not stop.

He betrayed all his faithful comrades and helped the Civil Guard to prepare an ingenious trap to detain them.

Before leaving the sierra, Roberto had cut in two a banknote of five *duros* (25 pesetas), one half for himself, one half for his colleagues. He said the trustworthy person who would come with the half note he retained would fix up the necessary paperwork. Indeed, an individual with the piece of bank note did make contact with those still in the sierra. Messages supposedly sent by Roberto — still in Madrid, the guerrillas believed — informed them of the plan to flee Spain: Roberto and Paquillo had organised the details of their flight to Africa and they must go to Málaga in pairs.

The Civil Guard had planned their ambush to the last detail and the survivors in the sierra walked straight into it. Following instructions, the guerrillas spent some days hidden in a primitive farmhouse near the village of Cajiz, within the district of Vélez-Málaga, where they were photographed to prepare false identification. They buried their weapons there and then proceeded to the coast. In Málaga a lorry covered at the rear with an awning awaited them. When they climbed aboard, they found some "bricklayers" already there, apparently employed in loading and unloading the vehicle. But the bricklayers were Civil Guards in disguise and, once the lorry was in motion, they jumped on the unsuspecting, unarmed guerrillas. Instead of heading for Algeciras, where a ship was supposed to be awaiting them, the lorry drove directly to a barracks. Thus all the leading members of Roberto's group ended in detention.

AMNISTIA

Se garantiza la vida a todos los que se presenten, menos a los siguientes criminales: "Roberto" "Clemente" "Felipe" "Mario" "Andrés" "Gaspar" "Jorge" y "Galindo".

De estos **TAMBIEN** se les **GARANTIZA** la vida, al que mate al "Roberto." o entregue algún Grupo completo.

Cuando salgais de "patrulla" a suministrar, el "responsable" diciendo que vá a ver al "patriota" de la "base", puede **AVISARNOS** y si **CAE** la patrulla completa, le **GARANTIZAMOS** la vida al "responsable"

Como el "responsable" sabe donde está la "posición" o por lo menos el "punto nota", tenemos mucho **INTERES**, en que se **PRESENTEN** «responsables», por que nos harán buenos **SERVICIOS** Tener mucho cuidado al leer la propaganda, porque Roberto os amenazará.=Si «Roberto» pregunta, que quién quiere irse no decirlo, que es para matarlo como ha hecho otras veces.

VENIRSE QUE NOS HACEIS FALTA

Torrox Febrero-Marzo, 1951

El Capitán de la Guardia Civil,

This Civil Guard leaflet guaranteed amnesty for guerrillas who surrendered

19. Death in Granada

IT WAS ONE of those winter days the citizens of Granada take for granted, cold but bathed in dazzling light. A day to bring to mind the sentiments of the 20th-century's most famous *granadino*, the poet García Lorca, who once noted: "The hours are longer and sweeter there than in any other Spanish town." Lorca met his death in the madness of the Spanish Civil War and on this brilliant morning members of another firing squad were preparing their weapons. The first rays of the sun were gilding the snows of the Sierra Nevada that towers above the city when, at 7am, with the temperature close to freezing point, they escorted a prisoner to the municipal cemetery.

The ritual was brief and brutal. The shots rang out and the condemned man, blindfolded and erect but almost certainly destroyed by months of interrogation, slumped to the ground, where an officer applied the coup de grace. Of the victim's last moments we know nothing, not even whether he uttered any words of farewell, of repentance or defiance. The inhabitants of Granada went about their business, unaware of the death in their city of a legendary figure. Only a few could perceive, perhaps, a hint of irony in the reflections of the journalist who on that Thursday morning in January, 1953, started his column on the front page of *Ideal*, a local newspaper, with the comment: "Days without history have their charm too. They have, among other things, the ineffable charm of peace..." Indeed, peace had descended, the peace of death. The years of struggle were over. The execution of José Muñoz Lozano, El Roberto, removed one of the most troublesome thorns nagging the flesh of the Regime.

EVERYBODY has a theory about what happened after Roberto's detention in Madrid. There are still those who refuse to believe that he betrayed all his men. Others insist that he was a Fifth Columnist infiltrated by the Regime, that his execution was a charade, and that another person died before the firing squad while he escaped to South America. But the facts appear incontrovertible. So why did Roberto turn informer?

Franco's police were notorious for their brutality and their lack of scruples about torturing prisoners so there can be little doubt that Roberto endured horrendous interrogation, which was carried out over months. As one would expect, ill-treatment was not something the authorities would admit to, and — according to a letter from the Civil Guard headquarters to the military judge in Granada — Roberto "offered himself freely and spontaneously to collaborate with this body". The former guerrilla López Centurión subscribes to that version: "He gave himself up to the National Police and said he would deliver up all the people of the sierra if they would give him a passport for South America."

However, Tomás, his faithful bodyguard and "horse", loyal to the end, believed that Roberto was trying to spare his mistress La Tangerina (see the words of Antonia Triviño Martín, page 185). "They began to mistreat her and through her they made him talk," he believed. Another ex-guerrilla, Victoriano Sánchez Ramos (Isidro), told local historian Romero Navas that Roberto turned against his men because he believed his former colleagues who had surrendered to the authorities had betrayed him.

In a bid to shift responsibility and escape execution, Roberto sent to his death Ricardo Beneyto Sapena (nom de guerre, Argüelles), one of the Communists who had collaborated with American agents in North Africa training Spaniards for guerrilla warfare. Roberto told his interrogators that Beneyto was the chief of the whole guerrilla movement in Andalusia. Beneyto was already serving 30 years for military rebellion, but Roberto's evidence was enough to have him retried and executed in 1956.

After the detention of Roberto and his men, there followed exhaustive interrogations, face-to-face confrontations, pursuit of suspected collaborators and trials before military tribunals. La Tangerina was sentenced to two years in prison, but for Roberto and his faithful lieutenants, Paquillo and the two Fraile brothers, there was no possibility of clemency. All four were tried and shot in Granada.

Of the 21 Frigiliana men who were in the sierra, three suffered the same fate; on May 6,1953, Sebastián Martín Vozmediano went before a firing squad in Granada and on April 3, 1954, Antonio Platero Martín (Silverio) and Manuel Triviño Cerezo (Valeriano) were executed in Málaga. Jailed for 30 years, Ángel García Martín (Marcelo), José Martín Navas (Tomás) and Vicente Martín Vozmediano did not serve all their sentences thanks to various pardons. Antonio Ruíz Cerezo (Yelo) also spent some years behind bars. Miguel Cerezo González (Jaimito) escaped the vengeance of his former comrades by enlisting in the Spanish Legion, before settling in Barcelona. The others from Frigiliana had already perished in the sierra, in shootouts, through suicide, or executed by their comrades.

For the loyal forces of the Regime there were eulogies, medals, cash rewards and promotions. The daily paper *Sur* carried news on January 31, 1952, of a "Brilliant homage to the Civil Guard in Alfarnate for cleaning up banditry". Two of the most feared Civil Guard officers in the Axarquía, Fernández Montes de Oca, and his deputy, Joaquín Fernández Muñoz, were present as the Civil Governor, García del Olmo, decorated Captain Francisco Jiménez Sánchez with the Cross of Military Merit, declaring: "It was necessary to achieve peace in our Fatherland and that order and tranquillity in the countryside has been obtained with heroism, intelligence and moral victory..." In a report to the ministry in Madrid, the Governor urged that Montes de Oca should be awarded the Commendation of Civil Merit and did not stint praise for his "patient, delicate and extraordinary work". The inhabitants, he said, had been "terrorised, with the fields almost abandoned" and had feared to make journeys by road. Now, the problem had been resolved. The province was left "without a single bandit and completely normal".

The leading figure in crushing Roberto's guerrillas in Granada province, Limia Pérez, declared in a report dated September, 1951: "This individual, with the powers given him by the Party and his qualities of character, intelligence and ability to command, which he has demonstrated since arriving in the sierra, rapidly made himself respected by all..." In victory Limia Pérez could afford to be magnanimous and he had personal reasons for emphasising the toughness of the rebels: it was a way of inflating his success in annihilating the Red menace. In 1957, in his *General outline of the problem of banditry*, he described Roberto as a "person of a certain erudition, of cool and reflexive temperament, of great energy", adding: "His has been the most disciplined group, with Roberto exercising a total and energetic command, on both the military and political side, 23 outlaws having been executed in the sierra on his orders for disobeying instructions and showing doubtful loyalty."

At his court martial Roberto was confronted with a large list of crimes committed by men under his command, including responsibility for the death of 31 soldiers, the murder of 59 other persons and the killing of 20 of his own group. It was difficult for him to evade the consequences, although right at the last moment he tried to save himself, according to a former comrade, fellow guerrilla Sánchez Ramos. By order of the Military Governor he had to remain for at least 12 hours in the prison chapel "in order that the priest's attention to the condemned may be as efficient as possible and that the prisoner receives the desired spiritual aid in his final moments". At the 11th hour Roberto asked for a delay in his execution, claiming he had something more to tell. But the judge denied this plea and thus, on January 22, 1953, Roberto faced an execution squad.

The next day, squeezed between reports on "mysterious balloons in Japan" and "a North American Super Fortress shot down in Manchuria", the Granada daily newspaper *Patria* informed its readers of the end of one of the country's most hunted men in exactly six lines. *Ideal* gave the news more importance, eight lines: "Yesterday morning the sentence dictated by a court martial, which imposed two death penalties, was carried out against José Muñoz Lozano, alias

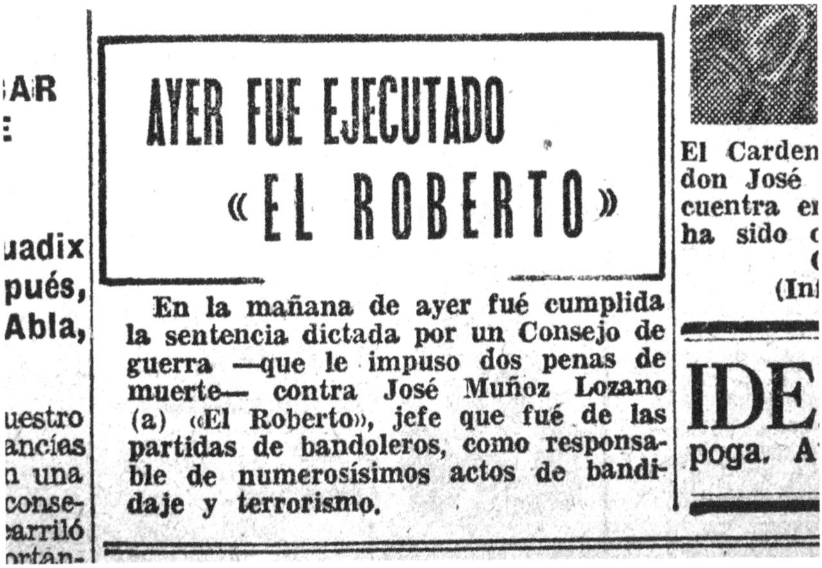

AYER FUE EJECUTADO «EL ROBERTO»

En la mañana de ayer fué cumplida la sentencia dictada por un Consejo de guerra —que le impuso dos penas de muerte— contra José Muñoz Lozano (a) «El Roberto», jefe que fué de las partidas de bandoleros, como responsable de numerosísimos actos de bandidaje y terrorismo.

Roberto's execution was dismissed in a few lines in the Granada press

'Roberto', the ex-leader of bandit gangs, responsible for numerous acts of brigandry and terrorism."

The newpapers dedicated more space to revealing that matador Antonio Ordóñez had cut two ears in Mexico and that singer Juanito Valderrama with his Gran Compañía Lírica was coming to the Gran Teatro Isabel la Católica. They also reflected the change in the international climate as the Cold War intensified: an economic-military agreement was imminent between Madrid and Washington, where Eisenhower had just assumed the presidency. Meanwhile, the citizens of Granada were forming queues outside the Aliator cinema to see William Holden and Barbara Swanson in *The Twilight of the Gods*.

Among the few of Roberto's group who did survive were six members of the Seventh Battalion, among them Enrique Urbano Sánchez (Fermín), of the Río de la Miel, a nephew of El Duende. In 1952 they made a hazardous, clandestine journey on foot from Motril on the Granada coast to the Pyrenees with Franco's police on their heels all the way. Against all odds, they managed to cross the snow-covered mountain barrier to seek sanctuary in France as political refugees.

After a 100-day trek guided only by the North Star and a school map, they were free. Behind they left their comrades, their families, their villages, the sierras of Andalusia, the years of struggle…

Epilogue

The impossible war

EVERY YEAR, on the first Sunday of October, a convoy of buses winds it way along tortuous roads through the mountains of Cuenca province to reach the remote village of Santa Cruz de Moya. They come from all over the country, from the north and south, and also from France. This day the streets of humble, half-abandoned Santa Cruz are filled with people. Several hundred trek up a hill overlooking the village to a monument to the anti-Franco guerrilla movement. They wave the flags of the Republic, there are impassioned speeches, emotions overflow. The crowd gives precedence to some special pilgrims, old and fragile, who move with care over the rocky ground. They are the last *guerrilleros*, the few who remain. After a short ceremony, the veterans place wreaths in homage to the comrades and relatives who fell. Then the crowd, fists raised, restraining their tears with difficulty, sing the hymns of the Republic and of the resistance, songs which defy the years and the destruction of their dreams.

Santa Cruz was chosen for this homage because there on November 7, 1949, one of the strongest guerrilla groups — the Agrupación Guerrillera de Levante y Aragón (AGLA) — suffered a crushing blow. The Civil Guard attacked an encampment on the nearby Cerro Moreno and killed 12 leading rebels. The Santa Cruz monument is apparently the only one in the whole of Spain which commemorates those who fought in the sierras against the Franco Regime. You won't find any similar memorial in the villages of the Sierra Almijara, nor in other parts of Andalusia. In Frigiliana about 30 inhabitants lost their lives at the hands of one side or the other and many men and women spent years in prison. But the history of those years of the guerrilla only lives on in the memories of the pensioners.

From any point of view it is difficult to justify such sacrifice and so much suffering. Because — and it is easy to talk with hindsight — everything indicates it was a war condemned to failure from the start. In the whole of Spain it is estimated (the figures are the subject of debate) 100,000 men and women collaborated with the movement and of, perhaps, 10,000 guerrillas more than 5,000 died or were imprisoned. Did these sacrifices and the years of struggle against a firmly entrenched dictatorship serve any useful purpose? With even more basis one could ask: how is it possible that the PCE (the Spanish Communist Party) persisted with armed struggle when already by the year 1947 it clearly appeared to be a lost cause? Even more difficult to understand: why did Roberto's men continue in the sierra until 1952 when the guerrillas had disappeared virtually everywhere else in the country?

The anti-Francoists' dream that the end of World War Two would signal the fall of the Caudillo's regime is understandable. But the Communist leaders seem to have demonstrated an astonishing shortsightedness in view of the Allies' public declarations. At the very moment when men and arms were arriving on the Málaga and Granada beaches and the anti-Francoists had begun looking forward to an invasion by the Allies, the warning of the betrayal to come (a repetition of the betrayal during the Civil War) was resounding through the British parliament. On May 24, 1944, Prime Minister Winston Churchill expressed his gratitude to Spain for not having entered the war and he added: "I hope that (Spain) will be a strong influence for the peace of the Mediterranean after the war. Internal political problems in Spain are a matter for the Spaniards themselves. It is not for us — that is, the government — to meddle in them."

The fact that a leftwing government soon took power in Britain did not change official policy, as Ernest Bevin, the new Foreign Secretary, showed on August 20, 1945, when he asserted: "The question of the Regime in Spain is something that the Spanish people must decide." And, indeed, instead of expelling the Generalísimo, the Allied troops halted at the Pyrenees.

After the world war, because of its friendship with Hitler and Mussolini, the Franco regime found itself treated as a pariah by the international community and excluded from the United Nations. But Franco was already moving with his usual agility to convert himself into an essential ally against the menace of the Soviet Union. To demonstrate that he supported democratic values, he concocted the Fuero de los Españoles, a charter of rights theoretically guaranteeing civil liberties, and suppressed the Fascist salute at official ceremonies. In fact, nothing had changed. Franco (memorably described by a monarchist ex-member of his government, Pedro Sáinz Rodríguez, as "a sphinx without a secret") spoke of "wearing a democratic suit as an insurance policy". But, when a minister suggested an amnesty for political prisoners, he replied: "We don't wipe the slate clean."

The Allies' intentions were spelled out on March 4, 1946, a few days after the execution in Spain of 10 anti-Franco activists, including Cristino García, a hero of the French resistance. France, Britain and the United States made a tripartite declaration: "There is no intention of interfering in the internal affairs of Spain. The Spanish people themselves must in the long run work out their own

The Republican flag flies at Santa Cruz de Moya next to a monument which honours those who fell in the guerrilla movement

destiny." If anything was needed to underline the change in the international climate, it came the following day when Churchill made his famous speech about the "Iron Curtain". The Cold War had truly begun.

In those circumstances, who was going to come to the aid of a movement organised by the Communists? Without support from outside, it was evident that the guerrilla struggle had very little chance of success. Nonetheless, it appears that the Communist strategists turned a blind eye to these details. And to others. From the start the movement's tactics appeared badly thought-out. The Communists launched a guerrilla invasion from France into the Arán valley in the Pyrenees in October, 1944, a very inopportune moment. Some generals and monarchists were questioning the continuity of Franco as chief and conspiring with the exiled Don Juan de Borbón to establish a constitutional, democratic monarchy. When the guerrillas, altogether about 7,000, crossed the frontier, the military closed ranks. Once more Franco could appeal to their patriotism to defend the country against the Red menace. Waiting for the invaders was an army of 40,000 men and only an urgent call to the guerrillas to retreat avoided a massacre.

Sir Samuel Hoare, the British ambassador in Madrid, reported to London: "The reckless movement of a few hundred Spanish adventurers on the frontier has given him the chance of posing as the champion of Spain against a Red invasion. It has also provided him with a pretext for arresting and executing a formidable number of his political opponents."

The exiles did not properly take into account another factor: the true situation within the country. It was easy to talk in Communist propaganda of political education and defending the peasants, but theory and reality don't always agree. After the violence of the Civil War, Spain had been crushed by years of hunger and harsh repression. Nobody could blame the inhabitants of a small village like Frigiliana — pressured and terrorised on one side by the Regime's forces and on the other by the guerrillas — if they only thought about living in peace. Roberto's men and those of other groups found themselves in a similar situation to that of Che Guevara when he tried to organise a revolution among the indiff-erent peasants of Bolivia.

In his book *Maquis*, Secundino Serrano notes that, while Republican leaders in exile were embroiled in sterile personal quarrels, "Inside the country organisations of the masses scarcely existed and the militants of parties and Republican unions were dead, in jail or in exile. Survival was the main objective of the silent majority with Republican and democratic ideas." José Aurelio Romero Navas, a Málaga historian who has studied in depth events in the Axarquía, declares in his book *The guerrilla in 1945*: "One of the things which turned out to be a tremendous error on the part of the organisers of the guerrilla was the belief that everybody was awaiting their arrival so that the people would rise up against the dictator. We don't understand why they did not check beforehand the situation in the countryside and whether there was any intention to support the movement or, due to the harsh regime, not do so."

Doubtless the Politburo believed that the armed struggle would serve the purpose of ensuring it could not be ignored in any agreement on the future of the country. But at what price? The Party either did not know or did not want to recognise the reality, to judge by the grandiloquent statements in its monthly magazine *Nuestra Bandera*. In January, 1948, ignoring the losses already suffered, it spoke of "the people's hardened attacking vanguard, expanding by their struggle the mortal wounding of Francoism and laying the ground for future liberty". "All across the country," it went on, "the guerrillas grow in number and their actions extend and multiply...the people support and protect them." What the strategists in exile took time to understand was that the movement was losing its collaborators in the villages who, owing to the increasing repression, were fleeing to the sierra.

True enough, in some regions for a time the Maquis created a serious problem for the authorities. The security forces had to recruit more men, establish special anti-guerrilla schools, and station thousands of men — including Moorish soldiers, legionnaires, the Policía Armada and the much-feared Brigada Político-Social (plainclothes political police) — in the more troubled areas. There it was dangerous to pass along roads and through the countryside by night, and in some places by day too. In Granada alone Roberto's group collected 8.2 million pesetas from 193 kidnapppings and 429 holdups, according to Lieutenant Colonel Eulogio Limia Pérez, the ruthless Civil Guard chief in that province; the figures of Málaga province were lower but not by much. During the years of fiercest conflict the Regime tried to minimise the seriousness of the problem because the existence of the Maquis damaged Spain's international image. The Regime needed to send a message that within the country all was peaceful and that the government was supported by the people. Thus, the Maquis, the only opposition of importance, was an irritating thorn in the foot for the dictatorship.

Nevertheless, the Maquis made little impression on the cities where, thanks to the censorship, most inhabitants did not know what was going on in places like Galicia, Asturias, Cuenca and the mountains of Andalusia. The failure to transfer the struggle to the cities indicated that it was a lost cause, theorises Serrano, pointing out: "Except in isolated cases, only the rural environment favoured the guerrilla campaign and it was conservative, usually preferring those in command whether they were Francoists or the Maquis, and hardly susceptible to revolutionary adventures."

There were many who refused to help a guerrilla movement controlled by the PCE. The PSOE (the Socialist party) and the CNT (the anarchists) were suspicious of Communist intentions and preferred a peaceful transition. In fact, the anarchists found the guerrilla struggle counter-productive as it provoked harsher repression, making it even more difficult to organise clandestine activities. The Socialists tried to create an alliance with the monarchists, but the Caudillo, as astute as ever, made a pre-emptive move to consolidate his regime. While the exiled politicians fought among themselves, in August, 1948, Franco met Don Juan de Borbón (son and heir of Spain's exiled king) and agreed to the restoration of the monarchy and that Don Juan's son, Juan Carlos, should study in Spain.

It was time for a change of tactics by the PCE, but the stimulus came not from the Central Committee in Madrid nor the Politburo in France but, as though to confirm all the Francoist accusations about the source of Red conspiracy, from the Kremlin. In February, 1948, Santiago Carrillo, who was directing the Maquis, and Enrique Lister visited Belgrade to seek technical advice on the guerrilla struggle and also help in sending in parachutists to reinforce the Agrupación del Levante. The only aid obtained was a sum of money. The Spaniards were unaware that a rupture was imminent in relations between Tito and Moscow. No doubt concerned about their visit to the rebellious Yugoslavia, the Kremlin then invited the Spanish Communists to a meeting, an extremely rare honour.

In September, three leading members, Santiago Carrillo, Dolores Ibárruri (La Pasionaria) and Francisco Antón (for some years Ibárruri's lover) entered a large room in the Kremlin where they were received by Stalin, Molotov, Voroshilov and Suslov. "Their greetings were very friendly," La Pasionaria relates in her memoirs (where she mentions receiving the gift of an Alsatian dog called "Maquis" from a Spanish guerrilla chief). The Soviet leaders invited the Spanish trio to tea and cakes. Stalin, in boots and military uniform unadorned by any decoration, smoked a pipe and made sketches on a pad during the conversation. A cosy scene. In his memoirs, Carrillo admitted his astonishment at finding himself in the presence of Big Brother. "We returned to our *dacha* in an elevated state of euphoria after our interview with the man we considered chief of the world revolutionary movement."

It's not easy to understand his respect for one of the monsters of the 20th century when it was already known that he had liquidated thousands of persons, including many of the Russians who had fought in Spain alongside the Republicans. Despite this, according to *Nuestra Bandera*'s September-October edition in 1948, Stalin continued to be the "shining guide for Spanish Communists". But then Carrillo himself did not hesitate when it was necessary to eliminate somebody deemed to be a danger. He made that clear in a speech in Toulouse in 1945 when he said: "Let us resolutely liquidate agents of provocation. Every informer must pay with his life for his betrayal." It was advice which Roberto later put into practice in the Sierra Almijara. What Carrillo called "the laws of the underground" ruled during the Franco era. He confessed (in an interview with the Spanish publication *El País Semanal*, January 9, 2005): "...sometimes, to protect the Party, you had to commit injustices, such as sidelining or separating persons who were perhaps collaborating with the police. And that I have accepted, with all its consequences. Even, in some cases, I have had to eliminate a person, that's true..."

During the Kremlin meeting, Stalin advised the Spaniards to infiltrate the organisations of the masses, chiefly the government-controlled unions known as the "vertical syndicates". He also told them they should employ the guerrillas to protect the Party hierarchy inside Spain rather than in armed struggle. He arranged for the PCE to be given half a million dollars, "the only gold we received from Moscow", according to Carrillo. On returning to France, the leaders called a meeting in a chateau on the outskirts of Paris of the Politburo, the executive committee of the Catalan Socialist party (PSUC) and various other delegates. There were some who opposed the change in tactics, but who could say "No" to Stalin? It was decided to dissolve the guerrilla movement. Unfortunately, it appears that nobody thought of communicating this message to the guerrillas in the mountains of Málaga and Granada. Youngsters from Andalusian villages went on fleeing to the sierra to join Roberto's group and the battle continued.

Enrique Líster, veteran warrior and Carrillo's bitter rival, made the accusation in his book *How Carrillo destroyed the PCE* that "for him the guerrillas

La Pasionaria and Santiago Carrillo at a Communist Party rally on their return to Spain after Franco's death

were no more than a means to manoeuvre his way to be head of the Party". Lister claimed that the Maquis did not receive the necessary support and in the end "instead of giving some political content to the dissolution, it was preferred to disband them by stealth, introducing in the groups intrigue, rivalries and provocation in order to justify their liquidation. Once the decision to end the guerrilla war was taken, there should have been a public statement explaining why it was being done, and the pertinent means should have been taken to save the *guerrilleros* and those who could be persecuted for collaborating with them."

Carrillo believed that the Maquis would attract support from Andalusia's people with their "very strong leftwing traditions, with a very radical agricultural proletariat, along with a team of very reliable comrades of proven fighting spirit". Later, however, he admitted that he had under-estimated the moral and material damage suffered by the people due to war and repression. He confessed to the Party (or at least to La Pasionaria) the errors involving the war in the sierras in a self-criticism made in June, 1952, an astonishing piece of self-flagellation quoted by Gregorio Morán in his devastating book *The greatness and the misery of the PCE*. It is understandable that his confession was kept a secret: the contents of its 75 pages would have rendered speechless a good many of the men who followed the orders of the guerrilla chiefs.

"We never succeeded in making the guerrilla struggle a mass struggle, in which the peasants took an active part, working the land by day and taking up arms by night…" admitted Carrillo. While in 1947 the Party was shrinking in the cities due to the greater repression, collaborators in the countryside were joining the guerrillas. "We did not appreciate that the numerical increase was a symptom of weakness rather than strength…the groups were starting a dangerous process of isolation from the masses which inevitably accelerated their breakdown."

Enumerating his own and the Party's errors, Carrillo declared that militants sent from France revealed "weak political and ideological training and a lack of ability to understand the vital problems of the working class". The Party had not realised in time the change in the imperialist camp and its support for the Franco dictatorship. In addition, admitted Carrillo: "We over-estimated the importance of the guerrilla struggle…and we did not manage to withdraw in time at least a part of our forces…" He said he could have avoided some of his mistakes if he had taken note of the works of Stalin, "our great teacher and leader", adding "It is clear that, with greater ideological preparation, greater knowledge of the work of the Bolsheviks, and studying more seriously and completely comrade Stalin, I would have worked better."

The delay in ending the guerrilla war and organising a proper withdrawal is difficult to explain. Inertia? Political blindness? Gregorio Morán offers an explanation of why Carrillo waited until the spring of 1951 to order the withdrawal: only the secretary-general, La Pasionaria, could approve the order and she was in Moscow suffering from a serious illness (she was six months in bed, attended by several doctors and helped by an antibiotic only obtainable from the United States through high-level contacts).

By 1950 many of the guerrilla groups had been annihilated. Some Socialists were lucky as they were helped to escape by their party leader, Indalecio Prieto. He personally organised the embarkation on October 23, 1948, of the last group of 31 men on the Asturias coast and they were shipped to San Juan de Luz. The Communist Party made an effort to rescue the guerrillas of the AGLA, the agrupación in eastern Spain which had up to 210 members in the provinces of Cuenca, Teruel, Castellón and Valencia. After the slaughter near Santa Cruz de Moya, the AGLA's days were numbered and Carrillo sent his representatives to the area, boasting that they organised marches of the guerrillas across the Pyrenees with the help of "dozens of guides".

But little was done to save the other survivors fleeing from the bullets of Franco's forces. There was some justification for the Party's lack of energy: in September, 1950, the PCE was declared illegal in France where its militants were detained or banished, creating obvious difficulties. Roberto and his men were distant, very distant from these events. Neither arms, nor food, nor any type of aid reached their hideaways in the Sierra Almijara. The volunteers from

Frigiliana, Nerja, Almuñécar, Agrón, Salar, Alhama, from all the communities of the south were abandoned to their fate. Carrillo has tried to explain this lack of support, pointing out that — despite its efforts — the Party in exile lost all contact with the Andalusian militants for some years.

Whatever the case, it appears the Politburo in France had forgotten their very existence to judge by Carrillo's astounding statement, in his conversations with Regis Debray and Max Gallo, that in 1950 there no longer remained any organised guerrillas in Spain. In fact, Roberto's group still continued active, although day by day it was more isolated and harassed. It operated in a wide area, kidnapping, liquidating alleged traitors, engaging in shootouts, from the mountains of Loja to those near Motril, from the sierras of Almijara and Tejeda to the provinces of Jaén and Almería.

When did Roberto learn of the change in tactics? What passed through his head, a man of some intelligence and much better informed through his contacts with the Central Committee in Madrid than the men under his command? By 1950 Roberto and his lieutenants must have realised that the battle was lost, but they refused to accept the reality. So many years in the sierra for nothing? And how could they withdraw? There were no ships to transport them to Africa and France was out of reach. In addition, it was very likely that the French police, in the current atmosphere of hostility towards the Communists, would hand over any fugitives to the Francoist authorities. There was no possibility of help from any source. Roberto and his men had fallen into a trap with no exit.

The cost of that impossible war is difficult to calculate. Historians do not agree about the figures. The great irony is that, once it had won the battle, the Regime inflated the figures so as to give more importance to its triumph while the Communist Party preferred to forget all about its failure.

Even so, it seems that over the whole country as many as 100,000 persons collaborated with the Maquis, of whom more than 19,000 were arrested. Of some 10,000 guerrillas, more than half were killed or ended behind bars; 2,173 died in skirmishes, 467 were captured and 546 surrendered, and another 2,374 were arrested. The Civil Guard lost 257 men and 370 were injured. Twenty-three policemen and 27 soldiers died. More than 1,800 skirmishes occurred and the guerrillas were responsible for 953 deaths, 538 acts of sabotage, 5,963 hold-ups and 845 kidnappings. These are the statistics quoted by Francisco Aguado Sánchez, officer of the Civil Guard, who had privileged access to the force's archives.

Analysing these official figures for the years 1943-1952, Valentina Fernández Vargas, in *La resistencia interior en la España de Franco*, arrived at the following calculations: In Málaga the Maquis suffered 186 dead, 23 wounded and captured, 150 detained and 87 surrendered. The guerrillas committed 82 executions, 141 kidnappings, 28 acts of sabotage and 352 holdups. There were

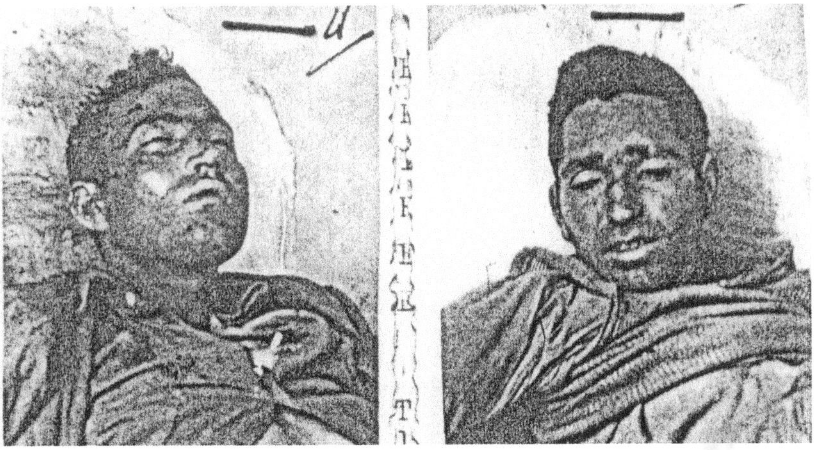

Civil Guard photos of two unidentified guerrillas killed in an action in Granada province in which José Pérez Moles also met his death

149 clashes with the forces of order. Collaborators arrested totalled 2,103. The Civil Guard suffered 22 deaths and 14 injured and the army lost eight men and had nine wounded. One policeman was killed.

In Granada, 155 guerrillas were killed, 34 captured, 140 arrested and 72 gave themselves up. They carried out 73 killings, 188 kidnappings, 34 sabotages and 426 holdups. There were 151 skirmishes. Altogether 1,883 collaborators were detained. The Civil Guard lost 31 men and 47 were wounded. Seven soldiers were killed and 10 wounded. Also, five policement died.

Limia Pérez, who experienced the situation at first hand, estimated that a total of 340 men passed through Roberto's group. He put the total number of guerrillas in Spain at 2,824, of which 2,235 were killed or captured. He blamed the conflicting figures on errors of calculation and information. During the 1939-1945 period there were many fugitives who did not form part of the guerrilla movement and later many collaborators, or sympathisers, were branded *"bandoleros"* when they were not. The historian Hartmut Heine reached similar conclusions with regard to the figures (although he calculated that overall up to 1,000 Civil Guards lost their lives). Certainly many of those who were killed by the government forces were not guerrillas. The case of the three Frigiliana youngsters killed at La Loma de las Vacas is a clear example.

What the figures do not reveal is the human effect of the years of war. They do not cover those who were exiled, the broken families, the ruined lives. One cannot measure suffering nor fear, nor the courage of those who did not abandon their principles and values in the face of the overwhelming pressures that invaded their villages and shaped the lives of a whole generation.

PART TWO

The way it was: personal testimony

"There were moments when I believed my moment had come. I was keen to get out of there because they were sending people to their death."

Francisco Martín Triviño (Paco el Gordo — Paco the Big One), esparto weaver, born in Frigiliana on October 26, 1906, the oldest inhabitant when he died on April 1, 2005.

When Azaña took over as president of the Republic, they released all those who were in prison. That was when they tossed all the religious images into the street. The leftwingers took the saints and burned them. People from other places came and wanted to set fire to the church too but it was agreed not to burn it, only the saints. They took them to the end of the village, to the threshing ground, and burned them.

It was in Franco's time when they brought half Morocco here. The Moors were Franco's favourites and he brought them. Here there were nothing but Moors. They picked me up during the Movement in 1937 because I was in a leftwing party, the Communists. I was a town councillor. No more than three or four of the village were detained because many people had fled when Franco's troops came. I was a member of the supplies committee. It hadn't harmed anybody, it just searched for food, but they picked me up. After holding me in Frigiliana for three months, they organised an excursion and took us to Torrox and to Vélez, then to Málaga and from there to Seville. They killed eight persons from Frigiliana in Torrox because they were on the war committee. They got rid of them and of others because they knocked down the saints, nothing more.

Fear, that's what one felt when Franco came in, when you realised that you couldn't speak. He imposed the law by which all those who had been in the wrong place were picked up. Not many people got out of jail. When they took us there, there were 4,000 and more in the Málaga prison. Every night, at the time when you got the little food they gave, you heard: "They've taken away 60 or 70 in the bus." To get rid of them, to kill them. The next day the same. Every night. You knew because, when this happened, some of them only got hit by a bullet in the hand and they came back to the jail. Then they would finish them off, you heard it: bang, bang, bang. By that we knew that those they took away were nearby. The cemetery was close and we would count: one, two, three…*

There were moments when I believed my moment had come. I was keen to get out of there because they were sending people to their death. When the place was almost empty, they ordered those with minor sentences to go to one side, so-and-so, so-and-so, until there were 50. We told ourselves: "Now it's our turn." But they said: "Don't be alarmed. Bring your belongings. You're going to work." That was a relief. They took us to the exit and then put us on a train. We were off to Seville.

In Seville province I was working for a contractor on the Guadalquivir canal**. They brought 100 from Málaga, first one group of 50, then another. I received pay, one *peseta* for each child and two for my wife. As I already had a family in the village, a wife and three children, I received five *pesetas* a day for digging the canal. There was nothing else, just pick and shovel, pick and shovel.

The strictness came from Franco. Here in the village Paco (Franco) didn't have any Spaniards. He only had Moors. He didn't trust the Spanish, not one of them. When I was working on the dyke in Seville, they brought a lieutenant colonel to Franco and he promoted him to general on the spot. They brought him to where all of us were at the bottom of the canal. It was the first time I'd seen Franco. He was on a hillock and he had very short sideburns. The fuss they made on both sides of the canal so he could pass! But he was only there a matter of seconds. And we went on working.

Some prisoners did more and some did less. But the job was done. There were a hell of a lot of us in the camp, 100 from Málaga but altogether a thousand or so from all parts, from the North, from all over. There were prisoners who had not been tried and were serving under six years. When they brought in a new law, they were allowed to leave.

Fifty-two months went by in that way. I was there from 1937 to 1941 and in 41 they kicked me out. When they detained me, I had a little girl eight days old and when I returned she was four years old. The year after I returned my wife died.

To tell the truth, I didn't want to come back because I liked it there. After coming from jail, it was wonderful. We were fixing up a drain which passed beneath the canal. They fed me. And I and another, Plácido Triviño, el Botero, who always went around with me, were put in charge of the vehicle with the food. They greeted me and made a fuss when I came. I'd come from the camp with two melons and sell them at five *reales* (one *real* was a quarter of a *peseta*). I was making money.

So, believe me, I'd no wish to come back. Because I asked: "Why am I going? To see my enemies? So that my enemies can kill me?" And the enemies were still here. Maybe they could do nothing, but... I got two months' pay from the contractor and, when I came back to the village, I lived from working on the land and in the sierra. I preferred the sierra. Instead of being on the land, where you had to work from morning to night, I went to the mountains and by 10 or 11 in the morning I was already back home. For a long time I worked with esparto, making big baskets and panniers as there were a lot of mules.

There were mules and donkeys, mules and donkeys, nothing more except two vehicles of the Company. Just as every house now has one or two cars, then every house had one or two mules or donkeys, to work in the sierra. Every day you'd go out to the mountains, always early, at four, five or six, according to the work you were doing. Some went for esparto, others for the tree trunks, another for firewood. I used to sell wood along the street. Later they fenced it off and now you can't go to the sierra. It's finished.

The toughest time under Franco came when everything was rationed. The "*traspelo*" (*estraperlo* or black market) started. There was no lack of bread because every day I would go for a sack of bread. I used to bring a sackful from Játar in Granada province. One day I'd go up, the next come back down, one day up, the next down. That's how it was for two years.

In the 1940s there were still muleteers who took fish from here to Granada. Later that came to an end and the mules weren't used any more because there were vans and they could carry more. It was a very bad time, very miserable.

It's not that long ago that they got rid of the people of the sierra. During their time I stopped going up and down the mountains, because I was in the police files and I said to myself: "The Civil Guards are going to grab me somewhere up the river and I won't come back." So I quit. The people of the sierra and the guards were everywhere. There were more *civiles* than you could shake a stick at. We were at war. That's how it was in Frigiliana. In other places they'd say: "You're from Frigiliana? Oh, that's the worst place of all!"

As we were always at war, it was just Moors and guards here. The sierra was close at hand so, after the Civil War, all those who were afraid they'd be picked up and killed stayed in the sierra.

There was a farm where the people of the sierra used to stop. The owner was one of those who took them food. He had mules and land and he'd fill a big basket with food and then throw a bit of manure over the top. Who was going to look in there? They said they'd taken away his son to cause him harm and he was taken away to give the impression that he'd been kidnapped. They took him up the mountain and demanded a lot of money from the father. He said he didn't have it but somebody gave him a bit, another gave him a little until he'd collected the cash to take to the people of the sierra. Then they released the son. That's what they made out, but then, two or three days after the son came back, they bought a farm. Where did the money come from? From the people of the sierra, where else? Those were treacherous times.

I feared the *civiles*, but I wasn't afraid of those of the sierra. I even went in search of them. But they didn't show up. They were hiding and they didn't reveal themselves unless they wanted to.

My second wife, Rosario la Caída, lost her husband*** when they (the Civil Guard) took him off and killed him up by the Frigiliana Pass. She was left with four children, the oldest 14 or younger. They killed a brother of Rosario too. He was one of three they killed at the Loma de las Vacas because they had relatives in the sierra. Rosario, who came to live with me in 1955, also had a brother, Zumbo, in the sierra, but he was saved. He gave himself up here, they took him to Barcelona and he died up there. A whole bunch of people from the village are in Barcelona. I've never wanted to go. I've been there but only because of the family.

The Civil Guard threw out all the folk from Acebuchal and left it empty, except for the goatherds. It was on a mule track and there was a small village but they didn't want anybody there. Everybody had to come back to the village every night, in daylight not in the darkness. And here in the village they didn't want anybody in the street at midnight. You had to be in bed. What a nasty bunch the *civiles* were! For my part I don't like any of them.

There was one here called El Puebla who gave me a beating without knowing what for. "Come on — confess! Confess!" I told him: "Tell me what you want and I'll say yes or no. Tell me what you want me to say." I didn't tell him anything but finally the son of a bitch stopped beating me. "You know who I am?" he asked. "Why do they say I'm bad? Ask in the village." Do you know how he ended up? Blowing out his brains. He never did any good and also he went chasing women. He went to Málaga, managed to draw out the Civil Guards' pay and spent it on a woman. Then he killed himself in Nerja. Good riddance, I say. A bad type. He did nothing except beat up folk.

One of the villagers who gave himself up was Vicente. He was a leader in the sierra, in charge of organising them. But then he came down and went with the Civil Guards, dressed as one so nobody would recognise him. He caused the death of two brothers who were in the sierra. The Civil Guard killed them, but he pointed them out. That was what finished off the people of the sierra. The guards found them wherever they were, because he led them to the spot.

Vicente was in touch with his wife who lived in the Chorruelo (a Frigiliana street). He came in through the garden to their house and his wife went and talked to the guards, to arrange that if he surrendered nothing would happen to him. That was when all this was fixed up. They gave him free passage, to win him over, and Vicente was with the people of the sierra one moment, then with the Civil Guards. As he knew where the guerrillas were, he would go with the guards in search of them. They seized a few high up at the Pedregal. It worked well. He did more damage than anybody. Vicente killed one young fellow, who was knocked around and hanged. A bad business that. But Vicente was safe in the barracks. Nobody could touch him there.

After Franco's death they paid me an indemnity, one million *pesetas* (6,000 euros). They adjusted the amount according to the time I was a prisoner. It came out at one *duro* a day, almost the same as a day's pay (a *duro* was the equivalent of five *pesetas*).

**Estimates of the number of prisoners executed by firing squad and the garrote in Málaga in the period February-December, 1937, vary from 1,884, quoted by historian Antonio Nadal, to more than 2,400. Altogether more than 4,000 persons executed during the Civil War were buried in mass graves at the San Rafael cemetery. Dozens of other mass graves exist in the villages of the province. Various organisations are working to have the remains exhumed. In the Prisión Provincial, according to the researcher Encarnación Barranquero, "The most anxious moments came when they called those they were going to execute. There were individuals who committed suicide or tried to do so because they could not endure, day after day, the fear that they would be called."*

***The Canal of the Lower Guadalquivir — known as "The Prisoners' Canal" — was one of many projects constructed by forced labour. Following the Civil War thousands of men accused of opposing the Franco regime had to work in military penal colonies. The 158-kilometre waterway, four metres deep, transformed an area of 80,000 hectares into irrigated ricefields.*

**** Sebastián Platero Navas, who disappeared in August, 1947, when he went to work in the sierra.*

"Democracy should have authority and respect for decent persons. The criminals are enjoying the doctrine of human rights and we decent folk are suffering."

Federico de la Torre Núñez, born July 10, 1935, ex-mayor of Frigiliana, retired schoolteacher, former manager of the de la Torre company.

The first of the de la Torre family to appear in the church records goes 11 generations back. Sometime after 1640 the death of Pedro de la Torre is recorded by the church. Pedro appears as first mayor of Frigiliana in the year 1640, when the municipality was founded. It is possible that there were two generations here before him, which would make me the 13th generation. So the first de la Torres came here when the area was repopulated after the expulsion of the Moriscos.

The lord of Frigiliana was given the title of "count", for contributing financially to the defeat and expulsion of the Moriscos. He brought settlers from elsewhere and the first de la Torre came among the founders, 44 of them I believe. The Count of Frigiliana's surname was Manrique de Lara and there still lives a count in Morón de la Frontera. Frigiliana's lands later passed through inheritance between the noble familes to the Dukes of Fernán Núñez. Then in 1929 the de la Torre family bought the sierra and the Ingenio from the Fernán Núñez.

The title of Count of Frigiliana was created by Doña Juana la Loca, but it was Felipe II, her grandson, who in 1580 gave it to the lord of this village. And that's when they began to build this building, the Ingenio, as the palace of the counts. Before that, the counts had a family seat, a very big house, where the main street makes a 90-degree turn. We still call it "the palace bend".

In 1929 the de la Torre family paid 138,000 pesetas to purchase the sierra, the Ingenio, the Civil Guard barracks and land below the cemetery. The barracks is still ours. They formed the de la Torre Company, which is devoted mostly to producing molasses and some building projects. Now I'm the one who manages all this.

The Arabs brought sugar cane to Spain and the Spaniards took it to America, and then when the colonies were being lost, it came back here from America. My great-grandfather began to manufacture molasses about 1840. There were small factories before. The Conde's employees made molasses and apparently the Moors too.

This idea of rich and poor is a relative concept. Here, those who had nothing or very little thought themselves poor. And those who had something they called them "the rich ones". But "a rich man" of Frigiliana was nothing in Vélez-Málaga. These are relative concepts and very local.

It's true that, compared to the others, we had a lot: a farm of 2,500 hectares and this very big building. We had saw-mills, we had lorries, we had the molasses factory. But it's also true that there were a lot of us. The thing is that we were together. A father might die or be getting on and he would share out what he had, but we were always united. Today we make up the 37 members of the company, almost all in Málaga.

The sierra was the property of de la Torre and so here one could buy esparto and thyme. People used a cauldron to make oil of thyme, for medicinal purposes, and face creams used as a cosmetic by the ladies. Then there was the timber. As the sierra produced a great deal, every year we made about 300,000 boxes for the raisins. In summer they were sold here, in Torrox, in Cómpeta, in Sayalonga, in all those places thousands of boxes were sold.

Also people went to the mountains for firewood because in those days you cooked with wood as there was no butane gas. The village has had electricity since the end of the 19th century. It was produced by water power at six small stations, three in the Torrox river and three in the Chíllar. Now they're abandoned.

Sugar cane was the main crop here. We couldn't use all the cane produced in Frigiliana because we were only selling part of it as molasses. So, after milling what we needed for the year, we took the rest, especially that from the Molineta and below, to the Larios mill in Nerja. Larios took everything. We haven't milled any for the past 20 years or so. We now prepare the molasses with imported juice.

In past years there was big consumption of products like potatoes and sweet potatoes. They were the principal crops, especially the sweet potato which mostly went to Madrid, Barcelona and Valencia and other big centres. Because in the 1950s things began to take off a bit economically. Very few countries would do business with us until the treaty was signed with the Americans and Spain was admitted to the United Nations. Although we didn't have as many problems as before, there was still a lot of scarcity. It's the only period, say the old-timers, when farming had a certain splendour. There was big demand for the crops.

My first memories go back to the year 1941 or 1942. At that time there were only three or four radios in Frigiliana. There was one in the Casino, another in my uncle Federico's house and another in Don Victor's. A lot of people went to the Casino, particularly, at the time of the news bulletins, because it was during the world war.

When I first went to school in 1941, there was a lack of everything. The children wore very patched clothing and there were fleas at school. When I came home from school, my mother "deloused" me as they said. She checked my head and clothing to see if I had brought back fleas.

Many people came begging. Here the land was much more equally divided than in Nerja where there were many folk who lived only from the sea. As there was so little money, people hardly bought fish or they bought it very cheap. They went more for the basics, above all flour to make *migas* and bread. In Frigiliana virtually everybody had a bit of farmland and they sowed things that allowed them to eat all year around. They grew maize, for example, which they stored for making *migas* or maize bread, which was really bad.

Figs were another handy resource. They were dried and pressed between esparto mats so that worms couldn't get in. All winter one ate figs to help down the *migas*. Then, when autumn arrived and the grapes had been dried, the raisin beds were dug up to sow chick peas. This is how I saw it as a kid, that period of shortages.

Even so, Frigiliana didn't have as many people asking for help as those that came from Nerja. Some inhabitants begged but mostly in a more discreet way. The more humble families went by night to the houses of those who had something. Instead of asking for money, they were more likely to ask for something material, promising they would pay later, as though ashamed of what they had to do. They were people with big families and so they lacked oil, flour, potatoes.

Then, to complicate matters, in 1947 the French began to send across the frontier certain men of the Republican Army who formed here what they called the Anti-Franco Guerrilla or the Maquis, imitating the French Resistance from which that word came. But in reality the behaviour of the guerrillas in our sierra was more that of bandits than of guerrillas, by the way they operated and the acts of vengeance. There were families here who threatened the people: "If you don't do this or the other, I'll tell my relation who's a guerrilla in the sierra." In other words, it was a revenge system, demanding payment for previous events.

The truth is that on various occasions the Civil Guard, as well, did not act very brilliantly. There were very ugly cases, like that of the three youngsters whom they killed at the Loma de las Vacas. Or that of a corporal who killed a father and his dumb son of 14 or 15. In the Civil Guard there were people who were not worthy to be members of the force, and they took advantage. All unworthy types take advantage of such moments to behave in uncivilised and inhuman ways. You can see what their game is when there's a chaotic situation. They show their savagery when they believe they have impunity.

Why did so many men from here go to the mountains? I think that was a general phenomenon all over Spain. One could better defend oneself in the rugged sierras. And, as is natural, it was where they had most clients and most activity.

Some indeed went off for fear of the Civil Guard, but others did so because they enjoyed it. The younger ones felt a certain admiration for the barbaric acts those people committed, regarding them as heroic acts. Youngsters mistakenly seek glory in these situations. In the epoch of the Spanish empire people sought glory in America and at that time they looked for it in the sierra.

I believe that most of them weren't very clear about where they were going. But then, up there, they indoctrinated them. On various occasions the Civil Guard picked up encyclopaedias and books in their camps and saw that somebody was indoctrinating them. I know there was a Frenchman who was a specialist in guerrilla war, who possibly came from the French Resistance, and it was he who organised the encampments. That man operated as deputy to Roberto and was better prepared than Roberto. Roberto was the chief because he was the Communist Party delegate, but the Frenchman was the organising brain of everything here.

The village had a very bad time. I was 11 when that began and 18 when it finished, and at that age one already sees things clearly. The people were very afraid, more than in the war. Because in the war there were two zones, on one side the Republicans and on the other the Nationalists, and as battles were fought the zones extended or shrank, and the people fled to one side or the other. But here the people lived between two fires. The guerrillas would appear before the folk who went out every day to the country and tell them: "Bring me food. Or bring me footwear, or whatever."If they didn't bring it, they killed them. And, if the Civil Guard found out that they had brought it, they did the same, beat them up or if it happened two or three times got rid of them. It was horrible.

One of the worst moments during the time of the guerrilla was when the people of the sierra killed two goatherds at the Cruz de Napoleón in the Higuerón river. They said it was for being informers, possibly because those men reported something to the Civil Guard. I'm not clear about that, but if you have to kill a person, then do it. But you don't have to be brutal with a dead man, right? Well, with them they cut off their testicles and hung them from a branch, or at least that's what I heard. I didn't see it. But it was brutal. The same when the Civil Guard killed three young fellows at the Loma de las Vacas, that too was brutal. Although there was a difference: they didn't mistreat them. They shot each in the head and that was the end of the story. It was still a brutality but to mistreat a corpse, that's going too far.

In the case of Acebuchal (a hamlet in the sierra near Frigiliana), the inhabitants had no choice but to become friends of the people of the sierra because they had no protection against them. The Civil Guard knew that they were involved and so, it was a little over the top, they obliged them to leave. To 60 families in Acebuchal they said: "Come on. Within two months there must be nobody here." Those who had money bought houses, in Frigiliana, Torrox or Cómpeta. But those without money had to leave too and some had no place to live. Half those people suffered a big trauma adapting to a new life.

The Civil Guard had some right on their side because they knew that the people of the sierra had a supply centre there. But those who issued the order should have realised that those people lived between two fires. They had to perform a balancing act on a tightrope.

A great many people, including men who had been in the war on Franco's side, took food to the people of the sierra. The Maquis who gave themselves up talked and gave away those who had helped them. To some the Civil Guard showed consideration and let them go away. Many went to America, to Argentina and to Brazil in the 50s, when the guerrilla was already almost defeated and beginning to surrender. Others were jailed and others...

Many people emigrated, some out of fear of the people of the sierra because they were compromised and the Civil Guard got to know. When they told what they knew, the guerrilla persecuted them, so they went away. As far as I remember, 25 to 30 familes went to America. And a couple of hundred families went from here to Barcelona, Madrid and Bilbao but that could not be blamed on the trouble with the people of the sierra. It was when Spain began to take off economically and those areas had a little industrial infrastructure. Most of the people went there in search of a better life because in industry you earned a bit more than on the land.

From 1954 or 1955 life here began to change and by 1962 the improvement accelerated. It was when the European countries and the United States decided to help Spain. I was the mayor here from 1969 to 1978, during the Transition. At that time the mayors were appointed by the Minister of the Interior, but on the recommendation of a province's civil governor. Two or three persons would be suggested as alcalde of a village and then the governor would ask for reports, chiefly from the Civil Guard and the priest.

The clergy had a great importance in Spain. Later things changed. Most of what they called the "progressive priests" went against Francoism. This was from 1973 when the priests began to preach and make public their views. But before then, up to 1973, they were Franco's principal allies.

Previously I had been a good Catholic, but after the priests started to lash out

I ceased to be one. I believe in God. I'm a profound believer. But I don't believe in the priestly declarations of any religion. The Catholic clerics are as harmful as the Moslems and the Buddhists. They're accommodating and hypocritical, lovers of power and all that…

Democracy should have authority and respect for decent persons. The criminals are enjoying the doctrine of human rights and we decent folk are suffering.

During Franco's last years, when the Civil Guard was not beating up and the police didn't trouble decent citizens, for me those were the best. In the early years there was a lot of violence. You have to recognise how things were. You're not doing yourself or anybody else a favour if you tell lies. The Civil Guard beat up whoever they liked and a no-account little corporal would make himself the boss of the village. Where there was a corporal who was a decent type, the village was different, but if he was a bad person, it was disastrous. However, during the last years of Franco, from 1965 or so, the Civil Guard only caused problems for the delinquents and those it had to deal with.

"We were the university. The higher education course of six years was very hard and the pupils all did it here. There were very few who could pay to go to school in Málaga."

Amparo Guerrero Rivas, schoolteacher in Frigiliana for 45 years, born in 1906 in Algarrobo (Málaga), died July 21, 2003. A square in the village bears her name.

I studied at a religious college in Málaga and then they appointed me as an interim teacher in Arenas, in Granada. I was too young to have a school of my own. I did another course in Fuensanta de Martos, a village in Jaén province. Then, as I had very high marks, they sent me to Málaga province and this village. My husband, Enrique Ginés Matas, exercised his right as my spouse to come here too and we arrived, with my daughter Carmen aged three months, in 1931. I spent 45 years teaching in Frigiliana.

At that time the village was very removed from worldly bustle. Communications were very bad, so bad that you had to walk to Nerja or, if a person was sick, on horseback. The women used to go to Nerja to buy things to sell here. There were no shops in Frigiliana, nor any bus, just a van owned by the Ingenio, the molasses factory.

The land produced nothing except sugar cane. People lived from the cane and the firewood and the thyme from the sierra. They made a lot of oil of thyme, boiling it in cauldrons with water from the river. It was a very simple life then, very traditional, family-oriented, isolated — there was only one access to the village.

One could come up the track from Nerja to the Ingenio to buy thyme, sugar cane and everything. The workers were paid in molasses. Those that produced the cane took it to the factory in the Ingenio where they milled it and then they took the molasses to deliver it to other little villages.

There were no cars, just the van used by the Ingenio employees to go to Málaga. If you wanted to go to Málaga, you had to go to Nerja and catch a bus in the morning. In the 1930s buses were still horse-drawn and they took five or six hours to get there.

If somebody fell sick, they brought the doctor from Nerja and if somebody had to be taken away they carried them by mule or donkey to Nerja. The hospital was in Málaga. Here in the Axarquía there was nothing, not even a clinic in Nerja. One person, my daughter's father-in-law who was one of the owners of the sugar mill, had a Ford, a small car. He was very caring. We'd call him and he'd make the car available for a sick person who needed to go to Málaga. Only later was there a van.

Mariano began running his small bus in 1937. If you wanted to go to Málaga, you had to book ahead so as to get enough people together to take advantage of the trip. Thus, if there was room for 10, 20 would go, doubled over, seated one on top of the other, and others outside on the mudguards, those that could cling on that is, as the road to Nerja was of stones. Once on the main road it was asphalt and they could hold on. The vehicle burned wood and smoke would be belching out and everybody on top of one another.

There were only two schools, one for each sex. The village had just over 2,000 inhabitants and I had 130 girls registered, just me, one mistress. I used to arrange them in groups. The classroom was a fine, big one with windows to the street and the countryside. It was built by the Dukes of Fernán Núñez, who owned all these mountains and the Ingenio. When the schools collapsed in the earthquakes of 1884, they constructed two schools. I was in one and my husband in the other. There was room for everybody, all seated on long benches attached to tables, and the floor full with the smallest girls.

Sometimes the bigger pupils helped me with the reading and writing lessons. One would write on the big blackboard for them to read and copy. The state sent books from Málaga, but very few. In 1936 two more schools were created and the classes were split in two, those who knew least for one teacher and those who knew more for the other. They continued until they were 14.

There were many registered but attendance was poor. The girls attended more. Fewer boys came because their fathers used them to help out tending a goat or a pig or looking for fodder for the cows or obtaining manure. The teacher had to fight to get them to attend, but the parents paid no attention.

If a pupil had to retake an exam, he had to go walking to Nerja in the early morning in September, because it wasn't worth putting on a bus just for one person and you had to ask for the service beforehand like a doctor's appointment. My husband would go walking with the children to Nerja so as not to leave them alone and to protect them and encourage them. Many owed their careers to my husband. Their parents couldn't support them in any college in the capital (Málaga), but he had sufficient education to coach them.

We were the university. The higher education course of six years was very hard and they all did it here. There were very few who could pay to go to school in Málaga. You can't imagine how many clever girls I had whose studies I facilitated until they matriculated. And we ourselves paid so they could do it. Those were the facilities we gave them, teaching and all. As teachers we started with a salary of 1,000 pesetas a year. Then it went up a little, to 4,000 pesetas.

Before the Civil War and the start of the Movimiento (the National Movement which ousted the Republican government), the situation was already tense. Already bombs were going off in religious centres. They insulted priests in the street, and that was before the war erupted. Here we had a very good priest. He wasn't here when the Movimiento happened as he was in the seminary doing some courses. At the start of the war they obliged the school to take down the crucifixes and they burned the church's holy images. They converted the church into a shop and a market. They killed the animals and displayed the meat there.

It was a lot later that the Maquis groups came. Life was difficult. Already the forces of order were in control. Many Moors and Nationalists came. Of course, the Maquis needed food and money and many from here were known. They went to the mountains because they had been the most active during the war years.

Things went on the same at school. I didn't suffer any sort of reprisal. I'd made it plain that I had no sympathy for Communism or anything like that. In fact, I was religious. After the 1940s, cars began to come and life got better. There was a big levelling of classes. In Franco's time one lived very well.

In recognition of his work over more than 35 years, my husband Enrique was named an honorary citizen of Frigiliana and a street was named after him. I went on teaching until 1976, when I retired at the age of 70. Later they awarded me the Cross of Alfonso X The Wise and the pupils and everybody bought me an emblem on which they inscribed details about me. I've got the big cross with its ribbon at the bottom of the wardrobe.

"We were on the way to the sierra when I threw myself on the ground and said: 'Kill me right here because my father has no money.'"

Ángel Sánchez García (Ángel Bernardo), peasant farmer, born in Frigiliana on March 3, 1928, kidnapped and held for ransom, died April, 2008.

Long ago a neighbour of mine in the countryside told me: 'Ángel, I'm going to die, but you're very young and you're going to see it all. There's going to come a big war, with everybody killing one another, a civil war. And after that there'll be a *guerrilla* (literally "small war"), where one brother kills another. You just see if this doesn't happen.' And that's how it was. I experienced the *guerrilla*. He told me about it and it happened. He was a very old man and I was a little kid of 10 or 11 at the time. He knew it. Maybe he read a lot, I don't know. I've always remembered what he told me.

Back in 1947, on February 27, Sebastián Navas and I were working at La Loma de las Vacas (the hill of the cows), near the village. I was 18 then. We were loading a mule with fodder when the people of the sierra suddenly arrived. It was around 4.30 or five in the afternoon. 'Come on, get in the farmhouse,' they ordered us. Then, inside, they told me: 'We're going to hit your father with a fine.'

I recognized Vicente, one of the Artabús brothers — that's the nickname they had — and one called Lomas, who came from the hamlet Acebuchal. The others were strangers. There was one from Torrox who was carrying a Russian machinegun, and the others had pistols. We talked and I tried to tell them that we had no money, that we were poor. They discussed things among themselves and then, about seven or eight in the evening, we left the farmhouse. It was dark already. We took the route toward the River Chíllar, me in the middle of them. There must have been eight or nine of them.

Before leaving the farm, they gave Navas a note to give to my father. Or rather two notes, one for the Civil Guard and one for my father demanding 75,000 pesetas from him. That was a lot of money then, a lot of money. They unloaded the mule and with a knife I gave them they cut the girth, so Navas went to the *pueblo* with the mule stripped, without harness or load. That's how they sent it to my father.

I went off with them to the mountains. We went via the Tablazos, to the Chíllar river, to the farm of Doña Aurora which they called Las Pepurras because it belonged to Pepe Herrero. We were going past Las Pepurras when I threw myself on the ground and said: 'Kill me right here because my father has no money.' I was afraid they were going to kill me because we had no money to pay. Naturally I was frightened because they had killed two or three men. They'd killed Paulino and they´d killed Miguel Moreno. So I said: "If you're going to kill me further on, just do it right here."

The fellow from Torrox took his machine-gun and hit me on the side and said: "Come on, come on! Get going!" And we kept going into the sierra, up above the waterfall for the electricity station. Up, up into the sierra until we reached the Barranco de las Higueras, above the Mina de Luz. There was a big cliff, very steep, and I couldn't get down it. They could get down fine, but not me so they lowered me down. In the last mine at the top of the ravine there was a cave and there I was two days and three nights.

By day they made me stand guard with them and we talked together. They told me that there were good people in the sierra, but one young fellow who was on guard with me said there were both good and bad folk up there. Another told me that they were going to win and, when they won, they would return the money to me and I would be a Don. At night they put me in the cave and I slept on the ground on some esparto grass.

The next day Antonio Platero, he of la Quiñona — they called him Chispa (Spark) in the *pueblo* — arrived with food. Then came the Frailes, brothers from Torrox. One was a commander. Sebastián, Vicente´s brother, came too. He was a lieutenant. We talked and they told me that they weren´t going to harm me and that, if they sent the money, soon I could go home. In the evening we went to a cave higher up and came down again in the morning. They kept a lookout on top of the Lomas Llanas cliff. I was always down below, in the ravine.

They wanted to explain why they were in the mountains. They said they were going to kick out Franco and were going to be the bosses. And they were going to restore the Republic. A youth who later gave himself up in Nerja — he was from Río de la Miel — said he went to the sierra because he was taking food to those people. The Civil Guard came looking for him and he jumped out of the window of his house and fled to the sierra.

In the morning, when they brought flour from the mill, we ate pancakes.

They called them *'tangarines'*. And at midday they brought fried meat. But I didn't eat much. I wasn't hungry. The people of the sierra were pretty gross — they grabbed the bread in their hands. They were very dirty. Some were clean, like the Frailes, but the older men were really dirty.

The Fraile who was in charge wore his star on a baton. He had a rifle, the one from Acebuchal had a shotgun and another one had a pistol. Vicente, of the Vozmediano family, was a captain and his brother Sebastián had a lieutenant's star on a baton too.

While I was in the sierra, my brother Antonio went off to take the money to the Barranco del Puerto. It's way down in the Río Seco. He left the village with a white cloth on his shoulder and went down the river singing "Long live Granada which is my home", as the kidnappers had instructed. Five or six appeared before him in the Barranco del Puerto and there he delivered the money, 75.000 pesetas. People of the village lent the cash to my father. At that time he was working with Don Justo López and he gave him a little. And the Company, de la Torre of the sugar factory, gave him another bit. Because we hadn't much money. We'd bought a farm a short time before and we had little.

We were up there three nights and two days and the third night they told us to come down. We descended from the sierra towards the *pueblo*. They were going to take me as far as the Chíllar river, but there were Civil Guards at the Fuente del Esparto so they turned back and left me alone above the Fuente. They told me: 'If the painter dies, what he has painted will die too.' It was their way of saying that, if the guards killed them, I too would die.

From that point I had to make my way alone to Frigiliana. It was eight in the evening and I didn't reach the village until seven in the morning. All night walking, all the damned night crossing the mountains until I got to the *pueblo*. As I could see nothing, I found myself in a hollow with no way out and had to go back. I had a tough time, I can tell you. Sometimes I was feeling good about things but other times really bad.

After I'd left those of the sierra, I rolled a cigarette and smoked it, so that if there were guards around they would see I was approaching. And I smoked all the way from there until I reached home, just in case there were Civil Guards who weren't aware of the situation, so they didn´t shoot before they knew who I was. When I got to the track to Frigiliana, then I was in better mood, more light-hearted.

The people of the sierra told me to go via the Portón entrance to the village, by the round terrace there, and to walk up below my home, as my mother was waiting for me. I entered through the terrace and arrived just below the house. When I called out, everybody waiting in the house came running out. The whole village was there in our house, a lot of people.

Afterwards, I saw no more of the people of the sierra. My father saw them in the countryside, in the vineyards, but I never saw them again. I had to report to the Civil Guard. I told them what I knew, nothing more. Among the guards was "the Atomic Bomb", who was a bad type. But they didn't meddle with me. I used to come from the countryside at night and I didn't notice them. They didn't interfere with me in any way.

I didn't get to school much. As my father had a lot of land and many olive trees, we would be picking olives until we finished them off. Only then would we come to the *pueblo* and that's when we went to school.

Life wasn't too bad. We worked hard, but, thank the Lord, we had enough to eat. My father bought a good farm and had a load of very good olives. My father was a livestock dealer, buying and selling mules. Don Justo López put up the cash and my father invested his labour and the profit was split between them. We bought a lot of farms, one in La Morea which was very good, and then another good one among the olive groves. It was nonstop work, in the countryside and in the mountains. I and my four brothers spent our lives working in the *campo* (on the land).

"At least 40 or 50 of the people of the sierra arrived, all with shotguns and machineguns. They treated me very well."

Sebastián Navas Iranzo (Vinagre), bachelor, farmworker, born on December 21, 1931, in Frigiliana, died February 16, 2007.

I was 15 or 16 in 1947 when I went to work with Ángel Bernardo, a son of the owner, on the farm La Morea. One day at about six in the evening at least 40 or 50 of the people of the sierra arrived, all with shotguns and machineguns. Some of them I knew. They treated me very well and didn't threaten me either when I was there or when I was in the village.

They gave me scraps of tobacco. "Take it," they said. "Smoke." I told them: "I don't smoke, I don't smoke." They held me there in La Morea until 11 o'clock at night. Then they took Ángel Bernardo away and held him in the sierra for two or three days. They sent me off to the village with a mule I used to carry fodder for the cows I had here. I can't say that I was afraid. I had to pull myself together when they sent me to the village.

They demanded a ransom of 75,000 pesetas and gave me two letters for Ángel's parents, written on a typewriter — they had a machine and all that sort of stuff. Up there were people who knew more than you can imagine. The letters said where they had to take the cash. The people of the sierra knew that people would give money to save Ángel's life. And, if they didn't give it, they would kill him — as they killed many who didn't pay.

The village had to raise the money. The rich folk gave it, the *señoritos*. They were very friendly because the father traded in mules and donkeys and also had a lot of land. But he wasn't rich. He'd pay them back the 75,000 pesetas when he could, but he had to find that amount for the people of the sierra.

The Civil Guard had found out about the kidnapping, but they didn't make any move until they saw Ángel, otherwise he'd have been killed. I was in the barracks I don't know how many times to give evidence and answer questions.

There was a Corporal González who was a bad one. They called him Cabo Largo (Big Corporal) because he was so big. But he treated me well. When I went to the barracks, he looked me over and said: "Nothing is going to happen to you. Tell me everything and you'll be all right." He even took me to his house and told his wife to give me food. I refused, so he said: "All right, go home and eat, then come back." Then he asked me questions and wrote it all on a typewriter.

Often the guards called people to the barracks and they suffered, but they never hit me, never touched me. Of course, I didn't have any relations in the sierra. There were no *señoritos* here. Those who had more land called themselves *"señoritos"*, but they weren't really rich. They were Franco supporters. There's nobody stranger than those folk. Those who were dying were Communists and now their families have become rich and the sons of the rich have turned Communist.

I always had money because even as a kid I earned a little. But it's not like today when people go to work on the land and by one or two pm they're back in the village. Before, you worked all day, right until dark, and there were no Sundays or Saturdays off. And no holidays. You stopped for a fiesta, but only for one day and not the whole day. You came back from the farm in the evening.

For entertainment there were no discos or anything like that. There was no money. You could have a glass of wine in the bar or at home. We used to make a lot of wine, more than 160 litres every year. And we drank it all between ourselves and friends who turned up or we invited. There were loads of bars and the Casino was the most important. There are more places to eat now but those who eat there are the foreigners and Spanish from other parts.

One fellow I knew who was in the sierra was El Duende (Antonio Urbano Muñoz). He was a smuggler from Río de la Miel. After he was in the sierra, he was in prison for quite a while. He was a very good type and I got on well with him. Later he had a bar in the Molineta and I passed by there a lot with my mule loaded with manure and fruit and tomatoes. I stopped to drink a glass of wine, or two, or three or four.

Some say El Duende cut off the ears of his victims when he was in the sierra but that's just an old wives' tale. There's another tale about how he once paid a visit to a neighbour in the Río de la Miel valley — he was from the Levante (east), which is what we call that part of Granada. "What's your name? Come here. We're going to kill you," he told the neighbour. They were doing away with many at that time. He told him: "Take off your underpants." He pulled the chap's underpants below his private parts and then he said: "You can go now — we've castrated you. We've cut off your privates." The fellow fled and back home he told his wife: "Look what they've done to me. They've cut off my privates." And she said: "Nonsense! You've just shit yourself." He'd shit himself from fear. And these are the stories that folk tell.

"It was a very miserable life. But I tell you something. There was more friendship. Now people are more detached from one another, even in the same family. They put on the television and they don't speak."

Antonio Acosta Martín, farmer and bricklayer, born in Frigiliana on February 5, 1940.

I remember when a loaf of bread cost 15 pesetas and a worker earned 15 pesetas a day. A litre of oil went for 24 or 25 pesetas, and that was bad, cloudy oil. The good stuff always went elsewhere because of what they owed from the war and had to pay to other countries. In Frigiliana everybody has olives because everybody has a bit of land. At that time, when you made oil, you had to do it at night so they didn't see you, because it was like contraband. Everything was very restricted but, if you brought in olives, the owner of the mill had to give you the oil. But it was finished in a flash. There were ration cards, but flour, wheat, lentils, chick peas came from Granada and all that was on the black market. Anybody who didn't get into that had a bad time of it.

Nerja was worse off than Frigiliana as almost all the land belonged to the Marquis of Larios and, as his company had a sugar mill, everywhere was sown with sugar cane and that was as far as the work went. They depended on the sea. They fished from rowboats and, when the sea was a little rough, there were no fish and nothing else.

A lot of people from Nerja came to the village begging from door to door. They would give them maybe a sweet potato or two or three potatoes or a bunch of grapes or a glass of wine — there was always something as every family had its own land. With figs, you dried them and put 70 or 80 kilos of them in a big esparto basket and then pressed it well under stones, otherwise the worms would eat them. Then all winter you ate figs.

The way in which the land was cultivated hadn't changed in centuries. Everybody trod the grapes for wine in the cortijos. First, you used a big beam with one end in a cavity in the wall. You put the baskets of grapes under the beam and on its free end you hung all the rocks you could so as to crush them. Afterwards you added water to the crushed residue and trod that to make another sort of wine, more like water, which they called *"aguapié"* (plonk).

From one Friday to the next you didn't drink. You waited until Friday to drink plonk. It was a very miserable life. But I tell you something. There was more friendship. Now people are more detached from one another, even in the same family. They put on the television and they don't speak. If you try to say something, they say: "Quiet, quiet." My mother was one of the few who knew how to read and knew it well. She read novels and in the evening the whole quarter would come to listen as she read one. Today you see nothing of that. There's less contact between families. Where's it going to end?

There was a good deal of solidarity among the villagers, although those in the lower part who had a bit of money were not friends with those who didn't. In the upper part of the village everybody would be out in the open air, talking and swapping tales. A very different relationship to that of today. People live more apart these days. Perhaps they live better, but…

My sister Pura couldn't stand *frigüelos* (beans). At Lízar (the cultivated area above the village), we harvested a great pile of beans so that every night we'd eat bean soup. There was nothing else. Those with a patch of land could look after themselves. One man used to say: "Hunger came by my house. But it didn't enter. It went past the door."

During the olive harvest the village would empty. Only the old folk and the little kids remained. Everybody went to the countryside as formerly olives were one of Frigiliana's main crops, along with grapes.

In those days men arrived in the village with loaded mules and donkeys. Like the tinsmiths who patched up the coffee pots or whatever. They'd come with their tools and fix things up. From Nerja people came with basketfuls of fish — and not only to the village. They would make a trip around the farms when it was the season to work the land. The same with the bakers who went from farm to farm, each with his own customers. Those who had a donkey went with that. If not, with a basket on the back.

There used to be at least 200 mules in Frigiliana. They weren't only needed on the land but were for use in the sierra, all of which belongs to the Company. You'd take your mule to the mountains and return by one or two in the afternoon, depending on the time it took to collect firewood, and you'd earned a day's pay. Then, after lunch, you went to your farm. Every day first the work in the sierra then in the afternoon to the land, cutting cane or collecting grapes, olives, potatoes and sowing lettuce, onions, cabbage. You didn't go shopping for food.

You used to put a load of oranges in a big box and throw sawdust on top, until you had 500 oranges. That was how you conserved them, like a fridge, and you took them out one by one, over time. Grapes...I've had bunches at Easter. If you cut them and hung them from the ceiling, they would last until Holy Week. Pomegranates too. You ate what you grew. There was nothing else. If you bought a kilo of sugar, you kept it in case anybody fell sick. We also had molasses. You could go to the Ingenio and bring back a jarful of molasses to eat with bread.

You were free to plant what you wanted, but sugar cane was worth money. If you needed cash, you could go to the Company, to the Ingenio, and ask for a thousand pesetas and they would give it you, on account. It helped lots of folk when they were in need. You always had the cane to take to the Company. You didn't take it to Nerja or anywhere else. The village lived more or less from its own resources, maybe few but enough.

When you brought oil from the mill, you poured it into a big earthenware vat. As they they used to give you the worst oil, the oil at the bottom of the pot was cloudy and worthless. Also you had the oil left over from frying fish. Instead of throwing that oil away, you kept it and when you had enough, you made soap to wash clothes. It was made by mixing it with caustic soda, boiling it and pouring it into a wooden tray. When it was set, you cut it with a knife.

My mother would put a bucket of water in the sun on the terrace and, when I came home in the evening, I'd go to the stable and use a rubber tube and a can with holes in it to have a shower. The stable was the bathroom and toilet. Water had to be brought from the fountain, but we did have electricity. In my home there was just one light bulb, of 20 or 30 watts, and a long cord. When we were upstairs, the light was there. If somebody visited us, we took it downstairs.

Everybody in my family went to school and learned to read thanks to my parents. Many of my friends would wrap a strap around a primer or some other book as though to carry it to school, but they didn't attend. My parents made us show them what they'd taught us and many times they went and asked the teacher.

As a kid, an incident that really made an impression on me was when they killed Don Ángel, a Málaga magistrate at his farm, the Cortijo del Almendro. I recall six or seven cars arriving from Málaga. You were used to seeing only the buses of Vicente and Mariano and the Company vehicle, but that day six or seven cars brought people from Málaga and all the kids went to the barracks to see them.

Many folk took food to the people of the sierra. One fellow gave them food at Los Caños farm in exchange for not being killed. It was because of what he had done previously, when he killed a Republican at the Frigiliana Pass. It happened that there was another man from Frigiliana with the same surname and a dapple-grey mule, exactly like that fellow's. One day, when he was bringing in a load of bread, the people of the sierra grabbed him. They were on the point of killing him when a man he knew turned up and asked: "Pepe, what are you doing here?" "Darned if I know. They've grabbed me to kill me and I haven't done a thing." And he was set free. But, if that fellow had not turned up, they would have killed him.

It was then that Ana Herrero, the landlady of the Venta Panaderos, fixed things. She had contacts with the Maquis and the Civil Guard. She arranged that the killer of the Republican should be spared if he took food to the people of the sierra. But three of the workers at Los Caños are said to have talked about this to the Civil Guard (who mounted an ambush). As a result the people of the sierra killed those three and their bodies were brought back to the village on the backs of mules.

People went to the sierra partly because of the pressure from the Civil Guard. An uncle of mine, Bautista Acosta, or Máximo, was one and he died in a shoot-out with the guards. Miguel Moreno, a Nerja man, was killed by the people of the sierra at a farm near the village. They kidnapped him to demand a ransom but there was a struggle, he tried to escape and was killed. They brought him to the village too across a mule's back.

Most of those of the sierra came from the Barrio Alto, the poorest quarter, always the worst. At night, if you saw the guards, you went inside to bed. If the guards arrived when you were sitting outside, they obliged you to go inside.

As a kid, I was friends with some of the Civil Guards. But one guard, a neighbour's son-in-law, beat a lot of folk in Frigiliana, for pleasure. One time he was in the sierra with another guard when they met two villagers each with a donkey. They took the harness off them and burned it, then gave the two a beating and sent them packing to the village, for no reason at all. That was very bad. That fellow doesn't get on with anybody. If he comes to the village, nobody will do anything to him, just the looks he gets are enough. He knows who I am but he passes me with his head bowed. He doesn't want to be friends with anybody because nobody wants friendship with him.

There were five brothers and sisters in my family. After doing three years' military service my brother went to Argentina in 1951 with three others. All Frigiliana didn't go because you couldn't just emigrate there. An employer had to confirm that he had work for you there, and the passage to Argentina was very expensive. Later my sister went to Argentina too, when my brother's brother-in-law arranged to marry her. A good many went from here and almost all to San Juan de Mendoza, partly because of the pressure and partly because there was no work. At that time you could live well in Argentina.

We didn't see anything of our family in America for 30 years or so. There was no money to travel. But around 1980 my brother visited and later my mother, by then 80 years old, went by herself to visit the family in Argentina. We took her to Málaga, she changed flights in Madrid and off she went to America...

"I went to the mountains because I was earning hardly anything. The guerrillas said you'd have money to enjoy yourself. But once you were mixed up in it you couldn't come back because you knew too much."

Miguel Cerezo González (El Canijo), factory worker, born in Frigiliana on June 2, 1927, joined Roberto's guerrilla group. Resident in Barcelona.

I was just a kid during the war, but I remember the militia and refugees who passed this way going towards Almería after Málaga had been taken. I couldn't go to school. There was a night school but you had to pay for it and my family didn't have the money. You worked all day on the land for a *duro* (five pesetas). My father was no longer alive so I was busy even as a kid. You had to work at anything, collecting wood or esparto or whatever was available. Nowadays the village folk know a bit more but then they were very ignorant. Many were illiterate and half of the parents didn't know how to read.

Working the land was very bad. People lived from the sierra. We made charcoal. First you have to collect the wood. You arrange the logs to make an oven, using up all the wood. There are always a few holes left on the top so you put some foliage there and throw soil on it. Then you set the oven on fire and it burns all night long, until the following morning or evening. At the bottom you would put some stones to act like vents. The smoke came out of there. When flames started coming out of the four vents, then it was cooked. You'd throw on some water to put out the fire and then you would fill sacks with the charcoal and carry them on your head. Kilometres and kilometres walking down the river bed with your face like shit, all black. That was no life.

In the esparto season you had to carry it to Nerja, down where the cemetery is, and they would weigh it with a scales. You would carry maybe three or four *arrobas* (34 or 46 kilos). Imagine how that weighed on your head. And you were going barefoot. They used to make lime too. My nephew, Antoñillo, has made it many times with his father in a pit with a pile of stones and timber. He made some when they were fixing up the church. He told me the priest supplied him with all the firewood and in return he gave him the lime to whitewash the new work. That was how deals were made.

I went to the mountains because I was earning hardly anything. Two or three of us were working up in the sierra when the guerrillas turned up. They fooled us. They said we'd be better paid and have money to enjoy ourselves. But once you were mixed up with them they'd got you — you couldn't come back because they said you knew too much.

It's true that the Civil Guard beat folk up so they would run away. There were guards who I think were conspiring with those of the sierra. I don't know… the blows they gave you for nothing. One day the one called Cabo Largo (Big Corporal) threw me in the armoury. Just as well that along came the lieutenant. It didn't matter if you were just a kid. He would grab anybody and kill them for any reason.

To leave the village and work in the land you had to go first to the Civil Guard to ask for a pass. Cabo Largo did what he pleased and gave the paper to whoever he wanted. Those who didn't get it couldn't go to the sierra or to work or do anything, except die of hunger. He would say: "Why are you coming here to ask for papers." He would give fellows a good beating and to many he'd say: "Off to the sierra with you."

He beat a lot of people who'd done nothing and didn't deserve it so that they would run away to the sierra. An old fellow told me: "I saw Cabo Largo go out at night many times. He went up the river alone, without any other Civil Guard." It would be to meet up and talk with them (the people of the sierra). He had something going with them, with the leaders.

Me and another chap called Antoñillo, or Chispa (the Spark), went off up there. They tricked us into joining them. We were kids and knew nothing. They fooled the young lads. They could pick them up because there was so much ignorance in those days. Antoñillo's elder brother, who was married and had two small children, told us: "I give you my word I'll come too tomorrow. Wait for me in this spot." That fellow had been in prison and in the war. We waited for him, but we learned later that he had gone off to Barcelona. He sold a small house he had and went to live in Santa Coloma in Barcelona. God's ways are known only to Him.

They paid us every month in the sierra. But what were you going to do with the money? From time to time we had a meeting and they had to pay you so you could buy food and many made money out of that. When they gave me money, I thought I was in heaven. I'm not sure if it was 5,000 or 6,000 pesetas. I didn't earn that much in three or four months. But there was no way I could send it to

View of the Sierra Almijara from the summit of El Lucero

anybody because within two days we had to move on.

Almost all those who joined were duped. Many of those who said they wanted to leave the sierra, well, they got rid of them. If you did quit, you were put in prison and had a bad time. And if you didn't go to prison, you had to leave the village because they (the people of the sierra) would come down to look for you and kill you. That's the way it was.

I didn't know what Communism was. I knew nothing at all about politics. Living in a village without being able to read and write, what could you know? Now, at the age I am, one thinks about things. But up there half of them, the lads from Nerja and other villages, were fooled. I only knew about the money they showed us. They showed off the money a lot.

Groups used to go out to try and raise cash. But not us. We did nothing more than look for water, spending perhaps four or five hours going for water in big containers. Up the mountains we had no alcohol of any sort, just water. They would order me: "You have to bring water, you have to bring this or that." And me barefoot, all day up there in the middle of the scrub. Two or three of you stayed there while those who had weapons went off. They gave you a one-barrel shotgun and two or three cartridges. I didn't even know how to fire it.

We lived on *migas* (fried bread crumbs) and boiled potatoes. When those in the black market passed coming from Granada, they would buy bread from them. If they had no money, they had to make a gift of it. In the sierra I only had old clothes, the same as in the village. No uniform, maybe that came later. The leaders slept with blankets and stuff, but all I had was a strip of blanket. There I was with my jacket over my face, on the ground amid the pines. You put down four branches and lay down there. You couldn't go in caves because it was dangerous — they caught many in caves.

Those who enjoyed themselves were the chiefs. Many of them made a lot of money. And there were the top brass who got new papers and changed their clothes and their names and went away from the sierra. They said they had to do business and that sort of thing.

Many a time I went to the Venta Panaderos for food. There were some troubles there, but they (the Maquis) were always watching with binoculars and when they saw there were no Civil Guards they would go down. But the big guys, those giving the orders, didn't go down. They sent the gullible ones. "You have to bring up so many sacks. We'll be watching," they said.

I saw Roberto a couple of times. He was lame from a war wound. He was very tough and he it was who commanded. El Fraile from Torrox was always with him, Clemente, who had a brother Felipe there too. Clemente was one of the political types who had been in the war. But those people didn't speak to you. They were always apart. They had their tarpaulins and tents and they had bodyguards. We were the foot soldiers, the slaves, the slaves.

Roberto was in command but he didn't get involved in skirmishes. He couldn't run and José el Panzón always carried him on his back. José was a very tough fellow. He was in prison a short time and then he came to Barcelona to live as his daughters and wife were here. And here he died of cancer.

The Frailes were scary. Felipe, the small one, who was a couple of years older than me, was a commander. They threatened to kill you. When you had to go some place and you didn't arrive in time, you were in their bad books. They were always watching you, they didn't trust you for the silliest things. Because of that there were many who disappeared. They said they had changed to another group, but you never saw them again. If they were going to kill somebody, they would say: "Come on. We have to go to that place and get there fast." They would take somebody off and you wouldn't see them again. "They've got rid of him," others would say. "They've liquidated him."

There were many young kids and, as the saying goes: "If you sleep with babes, you wake up covered in piss." But it didn't matter to the leaders. What they wanted was to swell the ranks to show they had a large force. They didn't try to teach Communism or politics. They didn't talk to us. They had us there as donkeys, to work. Sure, they tried to brainwash us. But what sort of politics was that? "When the war is over, we'll all be officers, we'll all be leaders." Illiterate leaders! You see what this was for, to suck you in. They were young lads and look, not one is left.

They told me in Frigiliana later that Roberto betrayed all his comrades and that all the leaders were in a plot to escape. They went to a beach waiting for a boat but they were picked up. They grabbed all the leaders, Roberto, the Frailes, the lot. I don't know what happened to them, whether they went to prison or they killed them. I've no idea.

Roberto wasn't a politician. When the war ended, all those who escaped took refuge in France and later they came back over the frontier and formed groups. They brought a few weapons and they were organising people to liberate Spain. "We'll kick out Franco or he'll disappear and we'll be in command." They were always saying the same.

I didn't even know who Franco was. I heard them talking about him and asked: "Who is he?" Because at that time there were no newspapers and nobody could read. All the youngsters who were in the sierra were illiterate. Those who could read among the chiefs looked after the books, taking note of this and that and how much money they'd collected. They carried wallets with bundles of banknotes. But if you looked at them, they would say: "What are you looking at? Get out of here!" Dogsbodies under the pines, that was us.

I thought a lot about my family. I didn't like it up there nor did any of the others. There were young kids among us and the chiefs would keep watch on them or swap them between groups putting them in groups of seven or eight, all older types. They would give you a bit of paper to take, you wouldn't know what was in it, and tell you: "You'll be all right. We're going to a new place, but you'll be fine."

Often there were shootouts with the Civil Guard but I was never in one. They would be waiting for the guards. When they said they had to go hunting, I didn't know what they were talking about. I thought: "It'll be to hunt rabbits." They would all go off, with guns, a Sten or a Thompson. And you stayed there with the cooks.

I was almost a year in the sierras of Granada and Málaga. I tramped all over the Málaga mountains and then I was over near Loja on the Granada side. When I asked one fellow why they were taking me to that side, he told me: "Because you tried to run off. So they are moving you to somewhere you don't know."

I had problems with the bosses over the loss of a shotgun. That was when I told myself: "I have to get out." I tried two times to get away and then they changed my group. They put me in the sierras of Granada which I knew nothing about. Then it was that one fellow from Almuñécar, called Olaya, told me: "You look bad." He was an older man who had been in prison. He said: "Tomorrow I'm heading out of here. I'm going to surrender." They had taken a command off him and given it to a younger fellow. If you had a command, you received more money. It was the leaders who controlled the money.

I went off with that fellow towards Almuñécar and then I came walking,

walking, walking until I reached Nerja. From Nerja I came up the river-bed and back to Frigiliana. I reached my house and my mother handed me over to the Civil Guard.

There was a company of Moorish troops in Frigiliana and their lieutenant was from the village. When my mother told him that Cabo Largo had me in the barracks, he went to the corporal and told him: "I'm taking him." I didn't go to prison. The rich types of the village didn't have a go at me because I was just a kid. I was too young to join the Legion, but the lieutenant arranged it. He said he would go to the church to fix the documents and he had the papers changed to show I was born in March instead of June.

I was three years in the Legion in Africa. The lieutenant sent me there so I would be away from the village, because if the people of the sierra caught you they'd finish you off. There were only legionnaires where I was, somewhere beyond Ceuta and Tetuán. Millán Astray, who founded the Legion, was there. Franco came many times when the Legion paraded. As there were so many illiterates, they created a school and that's where I learned to read and write. I went to class every day.

I was discharged in 1950, I think it was the eighth of November. I didn't come back to the village. There were Catalan lads there and my friends were discharged at the same time so I came with them to Badalona (on the outskirts of Barcelona). They told me: "There's loads of work in Barcelona. Are you going back to the sierra? Or are you going to work?"

I learned that there were no more people in the sierra. They had picked up almost all of them. Many gave themselves up and many that they hadn't caught were trying to escape. That was a lost cause.

So I came here and here I stayed. I found a Catalan country girl and we married. Her parents were from Almería. I had plenty of work. I was in factories and construction — there was a lot of construction. I worked at a factory until I retired. I've never thought of returning to the *pueblo* to live because my family is here. I have three children, one died, and four grandchildren. I've been back to the village many times on holiday but not even those Civil Guards were still there. José, a nephew of mine, was a Civil Guard but now he's in Nerja, also retired.

Almost all those who were in the sierra died. Antoñillo (Chispa), who was the same age as me, wanted to leave the guerrilla too, but they killed him. He left his girl pregnant. The baby's a grown man now. Then there were the three Artabús brothers, Vicente, Blas y Sebastián. They were making charcoal and left the oven burning to go and join up. The two younger ones died. Vicente was in another group but I saw him pass by many times.

Vicente was bad for the village and everything else. My elder brother had a charcoal oven. It takes months and months to build one of those before you take out the charcoal to sell. Vicente turned up and asked him: "Where is your brother Miguel?" He replied: "He's in the Legion. They took him away." Vicente denied it and said he had been killed by the Civil Guard. When my brother insisted I was in the Legion, he said: "I don't want to see you in the sierra again. Now watch what I'm going to do." He broke up the oven so that everything burned, and that was when my brother left Frigiliana. "I'm ruined," he said. And Vicente and he were friends, they were neighbours.

It was true that I was in the Legion. Vicente told my brother they were going to look for me there and kill me. Later Vicente came to live in Barcelona. I thought of going to see him one day, but for what? Why should I go and fight him? A cousin of mine told me: "Forget it. Let him go to hell." He was a fellow without scruples.

One of those in the sierra was the brother of my cousin Dolores, Yelo (Antonio Ruíz Cerezo). He'd been in the leftwing youth movement. He escaped from prison and fled to the sierra. One night he was on sentry duty and, when everybody was asleep, he took the leader's wallet with all the money and slipped away. He didn't give himself up. He married a woman in Nerja and with all that cash he bought a house. He never went out in the street. But after a couple of years, when everybody thought he was dead, a brother of his wife talked and they caught him.

They sent him to prison and he was taken up north. One of the other prisoners had a daughter who came to visit him. Yelo married her. He was already married in Nerja and had children but he married the other one and had three or four more. He came to Barcelona and went to work in an electricity station. I saw him there and told him: "They're looking for you." He said: "They can go to hell."

Another one who came to Barcelona was Zumbo (Ángel García Martín). He married a farm girl and worked on the land. He liked to drink and one day he fell off his horse and cart and the wheel went over him and crushed him. He left two young children. That was Zumbo.

Is there any justice in this world? I don't think so. The one who is least to blame always pays. It's the same today as always. One lives better than in those days, of course. But I already have my bag packed to go to the next world. I'm an old crock. They've operated on me three times. I'm buggered. The years don't go by in vain. Sometimes one remembers things, other times one forgets. Your head isn't like it was…

"The battle of the Ebro lasted three months and four days and I was there two months and 20 days. One fought to conquer a strip of land and at night the other side took it back. And the next day the same."

Antonio Ruiz García (Malavista), farmer, born in Frigiliana on July 1, 1910, died on September 28, 2004. Served on the Nationalist side in the Civil War while a brother served with the Republicans.

I was born in the Barribarto (Barrio Alto, the upper quarter) and I grew up there in Calle Alta. I moved down from the Barribarto when I was 32 but I've still a sister there. Mostly the poor live in that quarter, although there were some folk with money. But the rich have always lived here in the main street, Calle Real. I've always said: "I'm not rich, but I live in the rich man's street."

I lost my father when I was no more than 11 and my mother had to open a shop in Calle Alta to feed herself and four children. Life was difficult, but we didn't lack for much as we had our own land and the soil always produces something, whether it's a lot or a little. Others had it harder.

I was at school until I was 12 and then they took me away to go to work in the fields. At that time the basic wage was three pesetas a day, then they raised it to three pesetas fifty. And now see how it is. But we don't know if it will continue like this. Nobody has seen tomorrow's world, that's the truth.

I've always worked on the land. Sometimes I went to work for four or five days with families who asked me to, although I had more than enough work to do on my own account every day, going out from the village at first light. I worked and my wife too, working, working. Hunger never knocked at my door, ever, because I had land and those who have land sow potatoes and get a return.

It's the way it's always been, some have lived well and others badly. The life of the village was the mountains and the land. The de la Torre company had the Ingenio sugar mill and the sierra was theirs too. They bought it in 1929. Some went to collect esparto and they had to walk at least four kilometres because the esparto that was nearer had already been taken. Then they had to come back to the village along the paths and carry it on their backs to Nerja to sell it. Some had mules or donkeys and could load it up but those who had no animal had to go on foot. When they built the road to Nerja, which was like a goat track, I was nine years old.

Then there were the muleteers who loaded up with fish in Nerja and carried it to Granada. They started out at night to arrive at dawn in Granada, in Granada itself. People used to bring wheat over those mountain paths, from Fornes, Jayena and the nearest villages of Granada, to sell it in the village. Some carried sacks of bread over to sell. A loaf was worth two or three pesetas but a worker didn't earn enough to buy one. The people didn't have much to eat.

I remember how they built an electricity station by a big waterfall in the Chíllar river and the workers earned three pesetas. There were folk from Cómpeta working in the plant who had to come from Cómpeta on Monday morning to be at work by eight o'clock. It's a three-hour walk from Cómpeta. They stayed there the week, sleeping on the ground. If it rained, there was some sort of shack. On Saturday evening they would return home and then come back again on the Monday.

You tell all this to people today and they don't believe you. I have three grandchildren here. As I've said to them many a time: "You've been born with the stew ready on the table and a spoon in your hand." Yes, the old ones have seen everything.

When the Civil War started, they drew lots for military service and my number didn't come up. But my turn came later. They called me up in the first days of May when the war had already been going for a while. I had a brother already serving. One brother was with the Republicans and one with the Right. A bad business — that's the Civil War.

Everything to do with war is bad. For a short while things can go well, a couple hours between morning and night with luck. And if you're unlucky… But not everybody in the war dies. Somebody always survives to tell the tale. Five of us went from the village and we all came back except one. They killed him in a village called Celadas, near Teruel. It gets very cold there. It's the coldest place in the whole country.

I belonged to the forces from Africa and I was in the shock troops at the front. There were fellows from the Left and from the Right, there were Moorish soldiers, the Legion, troops of every sort. While the war was on, there was food for us, because you have to win the war and a hungry soldier is useless.

I was in the front line for 18 months and a bit and I was in the battle of the

Ebro*. That lasted three months and four days and I was there two months and 20 days. Everything about it was bad. Most of the soldiers in Spain, on one side or the other, died in that battle. One fought to conquer a strip of land and at night the other side took it back. And the next day the same.

In Frigiliana the Reds entered the church and threw the saints into the street, loaded them on a lorry and burned them over at the Loma de la Ermita. They burned everything, including the documents that were in the church. But some saved the papers because among those who entered the church were folk of all types and some preserved documents in their houses. Later they produced them when all that was over. The church was left empty and they set up a committee there where the workers held meetings. They sold charcoal, soap, lots of stuff. It was a market.

I went off to the war in 1937 and came back in 1939 at the end. My brother who was in the Republican army went to France. He couldn't write or anything. When all was over, an order came to say he could return. But he couldn't come for some time. Finally he came and was here a month but they had operated on his throat because he had cancer. He went back to a hospital in Lourdes. A son of mine and my sister went for him and brought him to the village. He lasted seven or eight days, no more. He went one day to the farm and seven or eight days later he died.

Many folk fled Frigiliana for fear of the war. They went looking for an escape route towards Almería, which was free at that time. Those who had mules loaded them with what they could from their homes. But the houses stayed here. They burned down the houses and everything in them of those who'd acted very badly. If the owners came back, they found nothing more than the walls. All that was a sad affair.

Many of those who went away did so because they'd robbed the rich people and they had to leave at the run. None of the rich went. Rather, they were delighted because it was their side which took over. The rich person has always lived well and the poor badly, since the beginning of time.

There used to be more than 200 mules and donkeys in the village. I had mules for a long time, many of them. Now there are no more than four or five and they're out in the country, where a cortijo may have one horse or mule. In the village there's only one mule left.

I remember when a few went running off to the sierra. They couldn't stay in the village because they'd been stealing. The Civil Guard hunted them and in the end caught up with them all. In those days one didn't know who to fear more: the people of the sierra or the Civil Guard. If you went to work on the land, the Civil Guard believed you were going to take food to them. All you could take was enough for one day's work. And if you met those of the sierra, that was bad too because you had been talking with the guards.

At night there were always *civiles* in the street. They knew that some of those in the sierra were coming to get food. Some folk couldn't go out because they had family in the mountains. But those who didn't could go about with no trouble. He who keeps on the straight and narrow always does so. But he who doesn't... As the saying goes, you get what you deserve.

At that time you had to have a safe-conduct signed by the Civil Guard to go out to the countryside. One morning this fellow was going ahead of me past the Santo Cristo. A pair of Civil Guards were there and they said to him: "Hey, the safe-conduct." It was an important guarantee. He replied: "Here's the papelucho (useless thing)." The guard said: "Worthless is it?" He hit him across the shoulder with a stick. "A guarantee is a useless bit of paper?" The Civil Guard didn't even ask for my safe-conduct because he was too busy hitting the other fellow.

A little further on I met the chap leaning against a wall and complaining. "For Christ's sake," I said to him. "Why did you have to say a papelucho? A safe-conduct is a personal guarantee they've given you." "It's a piece of trash," he kept saying. "It's a useless paper." An ignorant man. If he had just given the paper and said nothing, they would have replied: "Go with God." It was that word that offended them.

Before there used to be many bars, even shops, in Calle Alta and now everything is here in the main street. The upper quarter is almost empty. Many foreigners have bought houses there, paying a pile of cash for rickety places. Many sold their houses because they were excited by the millions they received. But already many are sorry they sold them.

**At the battle of the Ebro in 1938, thousands of men died on both sides, including those of the International Brigades, in what proved to be a cruel war of attrition.*

"Walking up there, from time to time I found bodies buried, but I didn't report them because they would have put me in prison. There are still many buried in the sierra."

Miguel Rodríguez Liranzo, forest guard, born in Frigiliana on September 9, 1922, died May 6, 2003.

My father was a forest guard working for the Duke. The Duke was in Madrid, a lord who had a lot of money. All these mills here were his. Everything was his. The family de la Torre came later.

Although my father was a guard, he didn't wear any uniform, just ordinary clothes. The guards' uniform was given to those who worked for the State. I never got to school, because I used to go to the mountains to look after the goats from the age of 10. I was here at the start of the war and then they fetched me and the whole draft and took us to those yellow plains in Africa in Franco's army. I was three, or four, or five years in Africa, a lifetime in those Africas. Later I was in El Aiún. The Moors, howling they were, howling, killed a lieutenant who was from Málaga. In those parts, if you weren't shot, you died from something else.

Shortly after coming back from the army I began to work as a forest guard. I carried my food in a bag and two slings to throw stones. I wore esparto shoes made by me or my father. Travelling through the sierra, I saw many things, maybe too much, and a lot that I've forgotten.

The people of the sierra were guerrillas. There were others who supported them and the outlaws would come by night and give them fistfuls of banknotes. I've seen up to 50 of them in a group, like a small army, with guns, food, everything. I saw Roberto, the chief of the guerrillas, in the Venta Panaderos. It was a Civil Guard post but manned by Moors. Then they replaced the Moors with guards, because the outlaws were going to eat the Moors alive, they were going to kill them. The Civil Guards were the toughest, tougher than the Moors. They didn't want friendship with the civilians. The Civil Guard wanted to be alone, and it's the same now.

In a place called the Fuente del Esparto, the guards did all sorts of things. They killed four or five outlaws there and, so nobody would know they were responsible, threw them in a chasm called the Poyo del Embudo. Some days later they took out the rotting bodies, in pieces. When they pulled one out of the chasm, his leg came off at the groin and nobody could stand the stench. They took them in sacks on mules to Nerja and there they are, buried by the Civil Guard. But their families don't know where they are. One was an in-law of mine.

When one of the villagers, El Moreno, attacked a Moorish soldier, I saw it. I was coming along with a bit of firewood for the house. There were two or three moros washing in the irrigation channel towards the river. This Moor was in the channel naked. El Moreno whacked him on the head with an axe and left him for dead. Then he ran off to the sierra with two others from the village. They tried to catch them but they couldn't.

They killed Pepe Mocha, one of those who went with El Moreno, over beyond Zafarraya. The Civil Guard ambushed them when they were looking for food and killed six or seven. Pepe Mocha wasn't a bad lad, but neither was he too bright. He only had two teeth because he'd lost the others when he was a little kid. He'd never eaten meat, only sugar cane, and that's why his teeth fell out.

There's a place called El Collaíllo de los Civiles where the outlaws used to camp. The guards caught one and gave him a beating. They thought he was dead and took him on a mule to do an autopsy in the cemetery at Cómpeta. But the next day he came back to life. He resuscitated and they let him go.

Roberto executed several of his group, perhaps a dozen. There wasn't much mercy up there, nothing more than death and discipline. They didn't have trials. I remember that once the people of the sierra threw a shepherd with his hands tied into a pig-sty and the pigs ate him alive, all of him. Nothing was left of him but his sandals, which were of rubber. Pigs will eat anything they come across, including a living person. The shepherd was one of the group, but he had informed on them and for that they killed him. That was in Jayena, over there in Granada.

I was in danger the whole time in the mountains. When you moved along trails by night there was the risk of being shot. Walking up there, from time to time I found bodies buried, but I didn't report them because they would have put me in prison. There are still many buried in the sierra. But I haven't dared to say so. They've been there many years and others have carried some away or have told their relatives.

"Once, all night long, about 20 of us were up on the roof of the Venta Panaderos when Cabo Largo and seven or eight Civil Guards were inside. Somebody suggested throwing a bomb down the chimney."

José López Centurión (Rodolfo), born in Nerja on September 10, 1929, guerrilla in Roberto's group, surrendered, served prison sentence. Deceased.

After the 1936 elections, I remember how my father (Jerónimo López Muñoz) came home when they burned the church and there was a lot of disturbance. He was in the UGT (Unión General de Trabajadores) and worked at the Larios mill. He came home complaining that it was a breakdown of order and a disaster and my mother Adelina was crying and telling him not to get mixed up in anything or they'd kill him. The war broke out on July 18 and in February, 1937, when the Nationalist troops took Málaga, we went to my grandfather's farm in the Río de la Miel and my father fled to the Republican zone.

He left us with my mother, a very strong, hardworking woman. During the early part of the war she used to buy eggs from a farmer and bring them to Nerja to sell, and she performed errands, for sugar and things they ordered, and other times she picked olives. Along the flanks of all these mountains were people who had fled. They were cut off. Guerrillas called the Niños de la Noche (the Boys of the Night) came over from the other zone.

And here begins the tragedy. The man in command when they destroyed the Cantarriján bridge was Julio Ramos Corral, a Communist commander of the Niños de la Noche. He had a list of all those who helped the people who were running away from Franco's regime. He put my mother's name on the list as she had looked for a house for him. Ramos Corral went to see his family in Torre del Mar and they arrested him, with all that documentation. That's when the exodus began.

The first they grabbed on the list was Miguel Moreno González of the Río de la Miel. They gave him a beating and confronted him with others in Vélez Málaga. Then the Civil Guard and the Falangists forced him to go around pointing out the houses of those on the list. It wasn't that he denounced them. As my mother figured on the list, they detained her too and we children were abandoned, with my father in the Republican zone and my mother in prison. The rumour was that

José López holds a photo of his brother Francisco

Miguel Moreno reported my mother and there began a tragedy of lies, because that wasn't true.

We kids were shared out. My little brothers, the twins, were two years old and I was eight. I never went to school because I was raised in the country, alone. And I was the one who had the worst time. I went to live with an uncle. He was separated from his wife and a drunkard. One night he came home drunk at three in the morning, gave me a tremendous beating and kicked me out of the house. It was for this reason at a very early age that I made my own decisions. I had to walk two kilometres over the hills to reach my grandmother's house. I arrived shattered and I suffered depression. He'd hit me in the stomach and I was bringing up everything I ate. I was near to death. Later a doctor told me that I would always have a weak knee. I stayed with my grandmother until I recovered then I returned, willingly, to the aunt I'd been with before, away from my family. I was five years there, until my mother came home in 1943 and I went to her.

When she returned from prison, the first thing I asked her was who had reported her. She said she had had a face-to-face meeting with Julio Ramos Corral in Vélez and he told all that had happened. They sentenced my mother to 12 years and a day for helping a soldier escape, which was an offence then. Five years she spent in jail just because she gave food to those men who came to the farmhouse, when there was nothing else she could do. We aren't people who hate. I have never felt hatred for anybody.

Then, in 1945, my father came out of prison. At the end of the war he'd been sentenced to 30 years for being a member of the UGT and all that. As he couldn't get work, my father decided to rent my grandfather's land in the Río de la Miel and there he went. But I didn't want to go, no, sir. I'd already been through all that and I wanted to get away. All the same, when my elder brother, Francisco, went into the army in 1946, my parents obliged me, as the oldest at home, to go and help them work the land.

Francisco was serving at Jaca. When he came here on leave at the start of

1947, he deserted and went to the sierra. He never came to our house in the Río de la Miel. They kept him far from the family so that he had no contact with us. Although we got on very well together, I never knew why he went off, unless it was related to what I've told about the family. Or because he was tricked, which is what I'm most inclined to believe.

When those from Oran arrived in 1944, they came believing that the Americans were going to liberate us from Franco when the World War ended. And the Russians and, if not the Russians, others. I've heard many conversations on those lines, but I've never believed it. I've always had the misfortune that, like my brother, I didn't go for that.

I also joined the people of the sierra in 1947. They had left with me a man with a sick stomach so that I could bring him a bottle of milk and some eggs. The Civil Guard came searching but they didn't find him as he'd concealed himself very well. Even so, I didn't trust anybody and I took to the hills with another fellow. I met up with my brother in December of that year. As the elder, he rebuffed me, asking why I'd come, it wasn't what we'd thought, it was very different. In other words, he'd become disillusioned.

When 10 of the guerrillas arrived on this coast in 1944, along with the leader, Ramón Vías, they brought some norms: not to kill anybody, not to steal, not to pick on the country people. That's why they were called the Maquis. They went everywhere dressed as we are, like any country person, and he who wanted to go home to see his family could do so. This lasted through 1944 and 1945 until 1946 when Ramón Vías died in Málaga. When Roberto put his men in uniform, a *guerrillero* couldn't go to see his family or anybody else. He was simply a soldier. Nobody could go anywhere alone. Two had to go on guard duty. This wasn't discipline or training. It was distrust of one another. You couldn't trust your own comrade. Then the *contrapartida* (Civil Guards disguised as Maquis) appeared. And in 1947 came the deaths.

At the beginning of 1947 they killed a man who was making charcoal at the Fuente del Esparto in Nerja. The guerrillas had given him 300 pesetas to buy something for them. But this man had been five years in prison and had children dying of hunger and he spent the money on food for his kids, then went to Barcelona to look for work. He couldn't find a job so he returned to make charcoal and they killed him, saying he was an informer. Many people here did not accept that.

In June of 47 they finished off Antonio Sánchez, El Tejerillo, a *guerrillero*. He was born in the Almuñécar area and he was one of five youths who went to the sierra from Río de la Miel, but his own comrades killed him. One of the group escaped and headed home, to give himself up no doubt. His own chums caught him and killed him for not being in agreement with them.

The crime was to disagree. In a democracy if I disagree with them, I think

I have the right to quit. Seizing me and killing me because I think contrary to them, I consider that Communist dictatorship. You felt afraid of your enemies but also of your own comrades. There was no way out for anybody.

The only ones they were supposed to protect were the country folk. If the enemy — the Civil Guard and the Franco regime — are criminals, murderers, I don't have to act the same way. If I behave the same, for those country people I'm just another executioner. That's the reality. It's something that I have never understood.

From time to time they would enter a hamlet, three or four houses together, and Roberto would give a talk. To some peasant in a rural home they talked about politics, about the lands they were going to give him... All that was very pretty. But the peasant was in shock. Because they told him: "If you disregard us, we'll come and kill you." And, as that is what they did, the people were afraid. They feared us. Truly that's what I felt. So, giving protection? Forget it. It was terror. Those of the Communist Party covered themselves with the Republican flag and they fooled us with the flag. They didn't explain what the Communist Party was to the many youngsters in the sierra, country types who couldn't read or write.

From 1947 they created a totally Communist dictatorship. The leaders, who were all Communists, got together in meetings, but not the others.

We wore an armband showing the Republican flag, which you wore like a soldier when you went to some place where there were other people. But there was no discipline. They didn't instruct us in Marxism, nothing of that. I didn't see them give schooling to anybody. Hombre, if somebody asked for a primer, they would buy it for you, yes. But the idea there was a teacher giving lessons, that's a lie. You grabbed what you could and read with a comrade and in that way I was more resourceful than others. It was different from what many of them said.

They said we would receive a wage every month. They offered it to many and sometimes they paid 500 pesetas. Not every month, but when they did a job of some importance then they gave you the 500 pesetas. Perhaps I picked up the 500 pesetas three or four times in the two years I was in the sierra. And this was always for my mother who was the one who suffered most and had the right to have food.

My school was the sierra. I learned thanks to a friend of mine, Carlos, who was a little older. He went to live in Nerja and was in a house there listening to the radio, picking up information. According to the Civil Guard, he was killed in Cázulas, Granada, in 1949. His real name was Francisco Reyes Montes and he was the son of a *carabinero* from Motril. Up there in the sierra of Nerja he used to say: "You have to learn." He did sums with me, helping me. I could put letters together, read, but this was thanks to him, not because the teacher obliged you to do it. I taught myself to read in the two years in the sierra, going in my free time to that man. When I arrived up there, I asked about those I knew. Everybody told me they were in the Sierra Nevada. In fact, they were dead, they'd killed them. When they killed somebody, that was the lie they told, "he was in Sierra Nevada" or "the Civil Guard killed him in an ambush" or stories they made up for those of us in the sierra. They all had a meeting and judged them. It was crazy. It demoralised me and I no longer trusted anybody. I was mistrustful already because of my sufferings as a kid.

Jaimito, a young fellow from Frigiliana, was with me in the sierra but for very little time. They ordered him and another to go from the Venta Panaderos to the Nerja river for some saucepans. The Civil Guard fired at them and he threw away his shotgun and the saucepans and ran away. Another one who was with him also threw away the pans but he kept his shotgun. If I'd thrown away the gun, I wouldn't have returned, knowing what was going on there. What happened impressed me greatly. When he arrived back, the Frailes met as they always did. The chiefs were those who ruled and accused. They accused this youngster of everything. I believe they would have killed him. It was the first time I saw how they acted.

They were always forming patrols to go for supplies or do something by night. Having judged Jaimito, they named him at six in the evening to go on a journey with the younger Fraile. He went off to the tent of Joaquín Centurión, who was then commander in chief of the Sixth Battalion and senior to the Frailes. His nerves were so on edge that he almost threw Joaquín to the ground, telling him: "Joaquín, for god's sake, they're going to kill me, they want to murder me!" That was the most shocking thing I'd seen.

He was so afraid that he seized hold of Joaquín. Then Joaquín told the younger Fraile to get out of his sight and he put me instead of him on the list of those going out that night. It was the first night I went on patrol and we didn't go anywhere, not to pick up food or anything, just to the Venta Panaderos. When we returned at midnight, El Fraile told us to say nothing about where we'd been or what we'd done. I suspected that they'd been going to take Jaimito off to kill him.

Four or five days later, I was put on guard duty with Jaimito. You went out in the morning to the top of a hill where you kept watch and they relieved you at midday. There I put the pressure on Jaimito until he spilled the beans about a person I'd inquired about when I arrived, Edmundo (Miguel Martín López), a lad a bit older than me from Río de la Miel. They'd told me he was in Sierra Nevada. Jaimito told me what had happened on the route from Río de la Miel to the Frigiliana river. In a place called Puerto Umbrales, Fraile the younger shot Edmundo in the head from behind and killed him. They buried him there. He's one of those who disappeared. Edmundo made the mistake of coming down to the coast then returning to the sierra and within 24 hours they killed him. A little later Jaimito gave himself up and he went off to the Legion.

Many times I've been asked if I was a Stalinist. At that time I didn't know what a Stalinist was nor who was Nietsche nor anything. Since the war I've continually heard the words "Communists, Socialists, the Right, the Anarchists, the Republicans", but when they held the democratic elections in 1977 I put my head in my hands. I counted nine Communist and five Socialist parties. So what I see is that the Right has always been well organised.

All the time I was in the sierra, I was a guide. I was always involved in getting supplies and not in killing anybody. They put my brother in charge of that group. I was in the area of the Venta Panaderos in the Frigiliana river where the muleteers passed. They were carrying products from here like molasses to the province of Granada and then bringing back chickpeas, flour, beans, a lot of commodities in a time of hunger. This was the time of the black market. I stopped many muleteers for the food they were carrying. We unloaded it and the chiefs paid them. Sometimes those of the sierra stole but mostly we bought and then carried the stuff away on our backs, loaded like donkeys but we had got the supplies.

I made sure that I was never seen with a farmer or a shepherd because of the danger I and they ran. I had to dodge around the paths to avoid bumping into the Civil Guard. But also I was afraid that in some slip-up my own comrades might kill me. It was plain that you couldn't trust those with you because there was an informer in the group who wanted to find favour with the boss and would denounce others. He eavesdropped so he could tell the chiefs what you had said. I didn't like that. In a dictatorship you feel afraid.

We went hungry up there. We had fleas. We didn't live, like some say, from robberies and kidnappings. We didn't receive money from anybody on the outside. We were isolated. And there were few weapons. For example, in the group of José García Muñoz, Ceferino, he had one of two muskets and a 9mm pistol and 800 bullets. Sergeant Rojas Álvarez, Arturo, had a 9mm pistol. The other seven were armed with shotguns. The leader had a grenade.

All those aiding us in Nerja were given false names and we didn't tell the chiefs who these persons were. When, with 15 or 20 men, we picked up goods, they loaded up and never saw who was supplying us. Only my brother and I knew.

Then arose the matter of the *contrapartida*, false Maquis who dressed the same as us, corduroy trousers and jacket, khaki shirt, a beret and *albarcas* (shoes with rubber soles cut from tyres) which we bought in Granada. From 1947 those of the *contrapartida* would turn up before a Republican farmer or shepherd and demand that he brought them food. If he didn't know the people of the sierra, he fell into the trap. He would provide them with food and another day they would

ON
de
na

nsa de
ry que
que de
de las
prepa-
de los
tras, y
ción y
actúen
ss. La
mpesi-
sr más
ir, por
pueda
grando
spolia-

LAS ACCIONES DE LAS GUERRILLAS DE ANDALUCIA

El combate del Cerro del Lucero

Las fuerzas represivas sufrieron veinticinco muertos y quince heridos

Meses atrás, gran parte de las fuerzas del Sexto Batallón de la Agrupación Guerrillera de Granada, estaban acampadas en el Cerro del Lucero, sito en las proximidades de Cómpeta. El Lucero era punto de concentración y base de partida para toda una serie de operaciones de propaganda política que, en aquellos días, iba a realizar el glorioso batallón de Ramón Vía por los pueblos y aldeas que desde las Sierras de Tejeda y Almijara se extienden hasta la costa.

sivas que disparaban alocadamente, los guerrilleros ahorraban su munición, disparando a tiro hecho, mordiendo repetidamente en la carne de los tricornios y moros.

Desde el puesto de mando enemigo se establecido en la venta Panadero empezaron a salir órdenes perentorias. Había que acabar con la resistencia de los guerrilleros. Pero la cosa no era fácil. Sucesivas olas de asalto fueron quebradas. La moral de las fuerzas atacantes empezó a decaer. Al mediodía

del Sexto se apoderaron de una escopeta, de una pistola y de abundante munición.

¡Justicia!

El día 27 de febrero fuerzas de la 1 a Compañía del Sexto Batallón visitaron el cortijo de « Los Pozos » propiedad de los falangistas conocidos por « los Pavone », situado en el término de Salar (Granada). Iban buscando al guarda

EL INF
DE MU

LEGAN a nu
nuevas infor
canallescas r
das por las autor
contra las mujeres
vía con motivo de
na actitud que é
a raíz de los Incid
enero pasado, de lo
mos sucintamente
lumnas.

Por haberse soli
reclusas con la pro
cía hecha ante un
na que visitaba la
dole las bestialidad
gimen a que están
rector de la Cárc
al exterior. Y los
Prisión provincial .

A violent clash on the Lucero mountain is hailed as a significant guerrilla victory by *Mundo Obrero*, Communist party organ

seize and shoot him. Then the Civil Guard would say some guerrillas had killed him. In December, 1947, the *contrapartida* kidnapped five fellows from Nerja and they killed three at Canillas de Albaida and two in the Barranco del Manu, on the edge of the Frigiliana sierra. There were many of us who proposed to Roberto that when a guard was killed we took away his uniform and we also disguised ourselves, but the chiefs did not go along with this.

In response to those groups, my brother warned the country people that they should report to the authorities anybody they didn't know. But the chiefs would not swallow this manoeuvre of myself and my brother. We were trying to look after the country people so that nothing happened to them and so that nobody knew who were the suppliers. But the bosses told the Communist Party that we made these rules to set ourselves apart so that, if we ourselves didn't go, the farmers would not open their doors to anybody and would report to the authorities. In fact, the farmers had it difficult.

The only confrontation with the Civil Guard occurred on Cerro Lucero. I was involved because it was when all the groups gathered around Christmas every year. There were more than a hundred of us. Those who were in Sierra Nevada came to the Nerja sierra and in December, 1948, the meeting was behind the Venta Panaderos. That day a group of 20 of us who had been to Frigiliana for supplies came in loaded at five in the morning. We must have come through the middle of the Civil Guard because they already had us surrounded. We knew that they were around but we didn't know where. So we went to sleep.

Above the Panaderos inn there are two pine trees and the Civil Guard knew that our guard was in one of those. They knew of two ways out of the encampment but not about a third, which is how we escaped. At eight in the morning the cook went out below to have a shit. The first thing he met was a dog and he began yelling that it was the Guard and then the shootout began. The camp consisted of tents made from strips of canvas, and we all came running out in shirt-sleeves and hid behind the rocks with our shotguns. The shooting went on from eight in the morning until it got dark, but I never fired a shot. From afar in the afternoon I saw them down below, but what are you going to hit with a shotgun at 300 metres or more? Shoot so they see the smoke that has come from the gun? With a shotgun you can repel, which is what happened. All those who came up were pushed back. I think there were many wounded because they were falling down.

We moved upwards and came out on top of the hill so as to protect our backs. That is when they wounded two of us, at nine at night. They were hurt because, as we got away, we had to jump a crevice and the fellow who saw us let off a burst at our backs. I was in the middle. They didn't catch me but the one on my right was hit in the leg and the one on the left in the elbow. He with the bad elbow I had to carry out on my back.

I was in Los Caños farmhouse on July 1, 1948, when Paco Cecilia was killed in a Civil Guard ambush. The same day Joaquín Centurión Centurión, commander of the Sixth Battalion, died too in the Torrox river near Acebuchal. Some countryman had probably given us away as by then you couldn't trust the farmers because we'd terrorised them. At the time that Joaquín died, we were more of his way of thinking than that of the Fraile or Roberto.

We'd set out from Alcóncar on June 30, 20 of us, to pick up two loads of food left for us at Los Caños. Joaquín came with us, also Paco Cecilia and Vicente Vozmediano, from Frigiliana, three of the leaders. My brother came too. As we went past a shrine in the middle of the pines in the afternoon, we could see the Moors on El Fuerte and I told Paco Cecilia: "I don't like this. I'd rather not go on." Joaquín heard me and scolded me, saying: "Superstitious!" I was superstitious — it was a quirk of mine. Paco Cecilia told him: "Don't get at the young lad. He's just joking."

When we reached Cuatro Caminos, Joaquín went with eight others towards the river and Torrox and we picked up a path to Los Caños. We approached from the rear of the farmhouse. When we were by the door, the guide had separated from us and was going down with the others to the water tank at the back of the farm. I went out to the corner of the cortijo and called to Vicente: "You go up. You know where the supplies are."

The Civil Guard must have heard this. I was on my own, as I always was, and I went to the bottom of the *paseros* (beds for sun-drying grapes) where I lay down with my back to the farm. There was a kitchen above the raisin beds where firewood was kept. I was looking up the slope when I heard a pistol-shot. I began turning my head towards the house and they fired a burst at me that ripped up the earth and threw it in my face. I lost my hat and two omelettes which I was carrying in a basket for myself and Paco. After a moment I moved down to where there was a wall and the other fellows. They were blazing away at us and 10 of us out of the 12 made a dash towards some poplars in a small gully, and there we got clear. We didn't fire a shot and there were no wounded. Vicente appeared and we asked him where Paco was. He said he hadn't been with Paco and hadn't seen him, as if you shouldn't question a Communist. One couldn't ask them anything at all because it was dangerous. My brother was there too and he knew that Vicente had gone with Paco. A short while later we left by the same path by which we'd come, without supplies or anything. This would be at one in the morning on the first and we reached Alcóncar in daylight. There we gave Paco up for dead.

At midday the 11 of us that remained left Alcóncar and headed for the Río de la Miel. We passed right across the sierra and the following day at dawn we reached a spot called the Camatocha, in the sierra of Nerja. On the afternoon of the second we reached the Tajos Rodados above the Río de la Miel. That night my brother went with another fellow and Francisco, Joaquín's brother, and — I don't know where — they obtained an *arroba* (11.5 kilos) of potatoes.

On the morning of the next day they bought a baby goat from an uncle of Joaquín. We had cut up the meat and were cooking it with the potatoes in an empty water tank in the gorge when El Tuerto threw a stone at me, as I was the guide. I climbed up from the camp to the guard post and he said: "I can see a lot of little shapes with red heads up there." "It must be a bunch of goldfinches," I said. I looked through the binoculars and there was a fellow leading down a gang of Moors, I don't know how many there were, coming straight for us. At that, I told the guard: "Come on! Head up the hill!" And I called to the others: "Get your packs. We're getting out of here. The Moors are looking for us." I jumped down where they were preparing the meal and told them: "Chuck the food away and get out. We've got the Moors on top of us, and who knows what's coming behind?"

I got them out of there and we moved towards Nerja and dug in at a spot called Los Catalanes. Already we'd gone three days without eating. Nothing at all. When the Civil Guard detained me later and I refused to eat, they didn't know that I had once gone for up to a week without eating.

On July 5 we moved up above our hiding place and then the leaders began arguing, fearing that the whole Río de la Miel was being watched. I told them: "Look, the best thing we can do is, cool as you like, go to Maro, enter a bar, eat a bellyful and die stuffed with food. Or do we just collapse in a dead faint? Better than that, we can go to some farm and eat the little they have."

By chance we ended up at the house of one of my aunts. They were eating and the little they had they gave us that night, but they couldn't satisfy all 11 of us. So we returned to the same spot. Already it was the sixth day.

The next day we went down to another farm and they gave us cheese, milk and other things, but they didn't have much. I didn't go into the farmhouse and I stayed outside with a fellow called El Careto. He said he was going to have a shit and I replied: "Good, but only you know what you've got to shit." We'd gone so many days without food. Well, we'd had something, mostly 10 kilos of raw potatoes shared among us. The others came back bringing a bottle of milk and a piece of cheese for the two of us. They asked: "Where's El Careto?" But El Careto wasn't there, and he hadn't had a shit.

As the Civil Guard was advancing upwards, we had to warn the others. In the area of the Frigiliana river there were at least 30 under the command of Felipillo (Manuel Martín Vargas, from Escúzar, Granada). When we returned, they too had passed five or six days without eating. Previously they'd killed some goats and roasted or fried them and now they were picking up the bones tossed on the ground and boiling them up in pots to drink the broth.

Felipillo wanted to kill me. What provoked him was that, before all those people, I told him it was his fault that they were going hungry. So he tried to kill me, but my brother threatened him and threw his pistol on the ground. Then my brother named five of us to go to Nerja to obtain food. When we got to Nerja, we were dehydrated. In one of the houses they gave us hot bread with olive oil, but we couldn't swallow it. We couldn't taste. Coffee we could drink. But all we could eat was sliced tomatoes.

After two days we'd recovered a little. We loaded up like donkeys with 16 litres of oil, with rice and flour, and at night we left, going up along the Chíllar river. We passed by Puerto Umbrales and then, after walking all day over the sierra, in the morning we reached the upper part of the Frigiliana river, where we'd left the others. And there was nobody there. All we found was a dead man. I don't know who he was. He wasn't one of those of the sierra. Felipillo's lot should have left us a message but there wasn't one. When we realised this, we were just about on our last legs.

Up there and in the Venta Panaderos there were Civil Guards. But we'd been left no signals. The leaders used to leave notes saying approximately where they were in a tube lodged in the trunk of a pine tree. But there was nothing. Because my brother had threatened to kill Felipillo, he'd betrayed us. The five of us had to retrace our steps through the pinewoods back to the Nerja river. From July, all through August and September, we were lost, looking for watering holes. We couldn't make contact.

We didn't find them until the end of September. The general staff and everybody was there — and they received us virtually at gunpoint. Felipillo accused us of having deserted. We'd heard on July 12 that Joaquín had been killed. He was family — his father and my grandfather were first cousins and my mother and Joaquín were second cousins. Yet the general staff received us as though they would shoot us. Just as well that the fellow from Agrón who knew Felipillo wiped the floor with him. But, as it involved a Communist, nothing happened. The Communists covered up each other's errors.

In 1947 and more so in 1948 they (the Civil Guard) ejected all the country folk, from Río de la Miel and Acebuchal, from all the farmhouses. During the Civil War they did the same thing. They pushed them into the village so they had no contacts. That's why we got our supplies in Nerja.

I used to go to the Venta Panaderos. I've been there laughing and chatting. But never drinking any wine. They didn't allow it. As for Roberto having a relationship with a girl from the venta, I wouldn't know.

Up there relations of any type with women were forbidden. We were prohibited from having anything to do with wine or women. So that, when we approached a house, respecting the womenfolk was a priority. One time about 20 of us, including Joaquín, were the whole night on top of the Venta roof when Cabo Largo and seven or eight guards were inside. Somebody wanted to throw bombs down the chimney, but the inn owners were there and we weren't going to do that to the family.

We already had a bad name thanks to the case of Miguel Muelas Callejón, of Río de la Miel. They killed him in 1948. We'd picked him up in Nerja and told him to get out of the area, go to Motril or Málaga, because if others grabbed him they would kill him. But they did catch him and kill him. My brother confronted the general staff and told them they'd committed murder. Up until then we'd had no arguments of any sort with them. As he who committed the murder was Communist, Francisco's opinion was not welcome.

My brother was against informing the chiefs who were our helpers and also against being forbidden to speak about the *contrapartida* with the country people. He defended the peasants because they aided us. We had to warn them that the *contrapartida* members were dressing like us and that, if they did not know them, they should denounce them. It was a way out for the farmers. As it was, if one of the sierra surrendered and reported that a peasant had helped us, the Civil Guard would grab him, beat him up and throw him in jail. Is that protection? Protection would have been to warn them that, whether they helped us or not, they were in danger. But that didn't suit the bosses. What suited them was terror.

On December 1 of 1949 they took us before a court martial in an encampment. The whole general staff, all their lieutenants confronted us. I didn't know what was going on. They accused us of everything, of being traitors, of telling the country people to report them, that we wanted to split our group from the others, that we ordered supplies for ourselves.

My brother demanded that the accusation about separating his group be made in front of the whole group. But there was no escape. They condemned the two of us to death. When he separated from me, Francisco told me: "Don't help these criminals and murderers in any way. Get out of here." That was the last conversation I had with my brother. They took him away and, as it was known that, when someone was moved like that, they were going to finish him... One of them told me that indeed they were going to kill him and me the same. He said that I had to reveal to them all the passwords and the collaborators, tell them all I knew. And then nothing would happen to me.

What could I say at that moment? I had to agree. But the following night they sent me for water. I've always been a bit sharp and I said to the one who accused me, Manuel Martín Rico (mayor of Nerja in the Civil War), the Communist Party's secretary general in the sierra: "Give me a pistol in exchange for the shotgun while I go for the water." To ingratiate himself with me after making those accusations, he gave me the pistol with two magazines. I could have finished off half the group, the four comrades who came with me for the water bottles. It was terrible. I was on the point of killing four innocents so I could escape. If I had, perhaps I wouldn't be here because if the Civil Guard had picked me up they would have tried me and condemned me to death for murder just as if they had been four guards.

I have nothing against the Communist or Socialist Parties. I've had connections with them both, even been a member, and for more than 30 years, until the year 1993, I was in Comisiones Obreras (the Communist trade union).

But today's Communists lie to cover up the murder of my brother. Some have claimed that a Torrox Civil Guard told the Frailes that my brother wanted to escape and that's why they killed him. That's a lie. That guard, nicknamed La Coneja, was responsible for five murders because he belonged to the *contrapartida*. Ten days before the court martial he had incited Francisco to desert, to disarm the three who were with us and run away. But my brother wasn't going to give himself up. He told me that he preferred to be killed rather than desert. As I hadn't seen him for a year, I thought he could have blood on his hands, but in the two years I was with him he didn't commit a crime of any sort.

That night I escaped. Instead of heading for the village, as I knew the sierra well I went up the mountain because I knew they would go looking for me below. I hid in a hollow all night, wide awake. I went all day without eating, but I had water because I'd brought the canteen. I spent my time reading about arrests and all those things in a book the Maquis had stolen from the Civil Guard.

I was up there 11 days. Finally I went down and entered my home and stayed there 15 days. Then I learned that the guards were searching near a relative's house. I thought that those of the sierra had reported that I was in Nerja. I told my mother: "Go and look for the priest and tell him that I'm coming to Nerja tomorrow night at 10. And that I want to go to his house." And so it was. We went into the priest's house. Don Miguel Martínez García was seated there and gave me tobacco. It was all very calm. He went off and, soon after he returned, Lieutenant Reyna with 11 guards armed to the teeth arrived. I wasn't carrying any weapon. He asked me what arms I had. I didn't fool him. I told him that in the sierra I had a shotgun with 25 cartridges and had left them there. I didn't mention the pistol.

The first night when I was arrested I slept at home and the next morning they took me, without handcuffs, to the Vélez headquarters, where a Civil Guard captain took my statement. That was awkward. He produced a big book with all the photos of everybody in the sierra and asked me if I knew them. I said "No." When he showed me neighbours and all those folk from Nerja and Manuel Martín Rico, I couldn't deny that I knew them. But the others, no. I didn't tell him anything about my brother dying. They couldn't get anything out of me.

The colonel and a Lieutenant Rivas went to the next room. I listened at the door and I heard them give the order to Reyna to take me into the sierra and apply the Ley de Fugas, as they weren't going to get any more out of me. When I got back to Nerja, Reyna sent me home but said I had to return at night. I had to take a mattress and blanket to sleep in the barracks, but by day I wasn't a prisoner.

After I was told this, I went to the priest's house and told him what I had heard. The priest put on his cassock and went to the barracks and spoke to Reyna. Then he informed me that they would not take me to the sierra.

My mother had a pig in a stable which had walls of mud and rock. Two or three stones had fallen out, creating a hollow. I got the pig out of there. They were building the Civil Guard barracks in Nerja and I went to the bricklayers and asked for a bucket of cement. I put the pistol in the wall, replaced the stones and covered the lot. When it was dry, I tied the pig up there. When the pig rubbed against the patch, what with the manure and everything, it looked like it had been there 20 years.

The 25th of December Manuel Martín Vargas (Felipillo), who was secretary of finance and organisation in the sierra, gave himself up. He informed on a whole Nerja family, six or seven between children and mother. He denounced men from La Caleta and he denounced Esteban el Panadero. And he denounced me, saying I'd brought a pistol, that I'd come to have a tooth out then go off again to the sierra, and that I knew many people in Nerja who were helping us. I had no idea that he had surrendered and said all this, but on February 12 when I was at our door the Civil Guard arrived, handcuffed me and took me to the barracks.

Reyna had the pistol on his desk and a whip and he said: "So far you've been fooling us. But the tricks are over. You're armed — you have a pistol. And you know a lot of the people here." I told him: "The same as I told you the first day in front of the priest and I told the captain and the colonel, I tell you now: there's nobody in or out of the sierra who will get out of me more than what I have said."

José López Centurión, aged 20

Then he produced Manuel Martín Vargas himself, dressed as a Civil Guard and with a pistol in a holster. When I saw him, I lost my temper. When he came up to the table, I hit him across the face with the whip and yelled: "This son of a whore! Is he going to tell you the truth? This liar! This rogue! He hasn't told you that he wanted to kill me and that, driven by hate, he's come here deliberately so that you kill me, something he hadn't the balls to do up there in the Frigiliana river. If it hadn't been for my brother, he would have murdered me up there." I was trying to wring his neck with the handcuffs, to kill him. "I'm going to jail, but when I get out I'll look for you and kill you and I'll go back to jail." Reyna just said: "Stop it! I'll shoot!"

That night they took me to the famous Cortijo Mora. My feet didn't touch the ground. But they didn't hit me. I went on a hunger strike. They brought food but I went five days without swallowing a crumb. To pump me for information, they put me with a fellow who had been in the sierra and he had to get out, yelling: "This type is crazy. He's going to kill me."

I was close to it. Nobody touched me. They put the food before me and there it stayed, bread and all. Five days. Then the sergeant major had to report and he went to the priest and my mother. My mother brought me a pan of milk and that I did drink, immediately.

Then the priest drew me aside and said: "José, they know very well you have the pistol. Give them the pistol otherwise they're going to go against your mother. They'll accuse her of a cover-up and they can send her to prison. Deliver the pistol and end this martyrdom. You go to jail and that's it." So then I told the priest: "Tell the sergeant I'll hand it over."

They took me to Nerja. We went to the stable and I asked for a pick and that they released the pig. When the pig was let loose, it grunted and I said: "See? He's telling you that he knows where the pistol is." The guard pulled out the rock I indicated and out came the pistol. They knew I had it to avenge myself later, because they knew all that had occurred in the sierra.

They'd already found my brother, hanged — although I didn't know this until later. The day after his comrades took him away they came up with another group in the Sierra de Cázulas. When they were all eating, one went behind him, threw a noose around his neck, kicked him and broke his neck. A nasty death. The Civil Guard knew all about it. The authorities accused a fellow who gave himself up in 1951 of killing my brother and he did not deny it. They shot him in Málaga in 1954. He was lefthanded and from Frigiliana, but I can't say more than that. In the sierra they obliged many to stain their hands because they suspected they were going to surrender.

People ask me about Roberto. He was a man like anybody else. He had charisma, sure, and he was tough. One time I was at the point of his pistol for more than half an hour. One day in summer I was lying down below a pine where I had hung my shotgun. I always go my own way. I've never been a talker. Now I get together with the old-timers and chat more, but I've always been more solitary. Vicente, from Frigiliana, told me to go for water. The water was closer than from here to the corner, in the same pine grove. I left the shotgun and picked up the container. Every day we did the same task, but that day Vicente accused me of having gone unarmed. He went to Roberto and told him. Roberto himself put the pistol at my head and said he was going to kill me and that one did not leave one's weapon. When he called me a traitor, I told him: "You've got here some who are much more traitor than me. If they catch me one day, I'll never inform on anybody." They didn't take away my shotgun and nothing happened to me, but the life there was dangerous.

Stalin may have changed policy in 1948 and Santiago Carrillo may have changed policy and ordered those people, through the Communist Party, to abandon the sierra, but they did not obey Carrillo nor the Party. Stalin's words didn't reach here or — if they did — they weren't accepted by the people of the sierra, not by Roberto nor the Frailes.

In the end Roberto betrayed the others. One betrayal pays back another. The Frailes betrayed Joaquín and the others in favour of Roberto. They were the ones who praised him. I don't know who recommended him to them, but the Frailes had great friendship with Roberto and a lot of confidence in him. The eldest was chief of the general staff and, when Joaquín died, his brother became commander of the Sixth Battalion, so they were in command.

From what I understand, Roberto told them that he was going to Vélez. Before going, he cut in half a note of five *duros* with some scissors and said a Communist would come with the one half, a good man who would prepare their papers. It seems that when Roberto went to seek support he was not going to return. He went off with the half banknote and with as much as 500,000 pesetas to prepare the documentation.

I know, from a reliable source, that he gave himself up to the National Police. He told them that, if they gave him a passport for South America, he would deliver up all the people of the sierra. He said he was the chief. They didn't believe him and called the Civil Guard headquarters in Granada and Málaga to ask if they had anybody who knew Roberto. In prison Vicente said he'd seen Roberto in Madrid when they took him there. By 1951 Vicente was working with the Civil Guard — I have the report of a Civil Guard colonel.

Vicente identified Roberto in Madrid and then they brought him to Málaga. They held him in a small barracks in the Malagueta district. A Civil Guard lieutenant in civilian clothes was the one who showed the half bank note to the Frailes brothers and said he would prepare documentation for four or five of the guerrillas. A covered lorry was prepared (for their escape) but Civil Guards in plain clothes were waiting inside to arrest them.

I went to prison on February 18, 1950, and came out on July 26, 1952. This was due to the pardon ordered by Franco thanks to the Eucharistic Council of Barcelona. They gave me the full pardon for my sentence of six years and a day. When I got back to Nerja, I was claimed by the Navy. I served for 21 months and I was fine. They didn't trouble me and they didn't persecute me. I was appreciated. Afterwards, I went to the Basque Country, found work there and got married. My children have made careers for themselves up there. In summer I usually return to my house in Nerja.

My brother was killed in the Sierra de Cázulas (Granada province) and his remains were found along with those of another person from Motril on January 1, 1950. They were apparently buried in the cemetery of Otívar. But 50 years have gone by and I still can't obtain any official confirmation about where his remains lie.

"What the Civil Guard did was their duty, nothing more: taking care that the village lived as well as possible."

Pedro Pizarro Cruz, retired Civil Guard, born in Monturque (Córdoba) on May 13, 1925, died in Frigiliana on April 21, 2006.

I joined the Civil Guard in 1949 when I was 24 and was posted to Frigiliana. When I signed on, a guard earned 420 pesetas a month. There were 50 of us here, a lieutenant, a sergeant major and two corporals. We came from all parts. My group consisted of eight or nine guards and we ate together and slept in the same dormitory, like in the army. There were also many Regulares (Moorish soldiers), a company of them split between Frigiliana, Cómpeta and Torrox.

Our mission was to maintain order. At that time there were a lot of people in the sierra, fugitives from the war. They were delinquents, all of them. Many, the principal ones, had done a great deal of damage before the war, when Spain was a republic, and they had killed people before the National troops came in. Of course, those who had killed somebody couldn't give themselves up. They were the leaders and they tricked young fellows and lured them away. There were many hardships and a lot of hunger and they fooled the youngsters, telling them they were going to give them money, that they were going to be bosses, that they were going to have everything. But they gave them nothing because there was nothing to give. They didn't have anything. They believed that they were going to change the regime, but there was no chance of that. The war had been won, the war was over. Peace.

There were nine guards and a corporal living in the barracks. Then there was a group in the house up above Lízar, another where the olive oil factory is, and another in a flour mill in the Molineta. When we weren't going up into the sierra, we were manning check points, in the place called Santo Cristo and others in

El Tejar (down the road to Nerja), so as to control the people and see that they didn't carry stuff to the people of the sierra. We in the Civil Guard had no fear. At that age, when you're a youngster, you're never afraid.

There were more than 20 from this village in the sierra, and the families had to be watched so that they did not take them food. A person was allowed to take out very little food to the country, only one meal to eat at midday. At night, from 10pm, nobody could go through the streets. If a child had fallen sick or something similar, that was the only reason one could leave the house.

The whole village was involved with the people of the sierra, 20 families are a lot for a village this size. He who didn't have a cousin up there had a brother or a friend. Naturally, if I had a son in the mountains, I'd try to take him food, any way I could. But this wasn't getting them anywhere. Everything was controlled.

The guerrilla group was under the command of Roberto. He was a hard man — he even killed his own people. If somebody did not suit him, maybe he didn't do what he wanted, he ordered him to be eliminated. They killed two young men down there in the river. They hung them from a pine and they hung a message on them: "Every tree produces its fruit and the fruit belongs to that tree." One of the victims had a brother in the Guardia and the other used to collect esparto —judge for yourself how they were harming the guerrilla. They were two young fellows living from what there was in the sierra, but they killed them because they believed they were our accomplices or were spies, or something like that.

I never had the luck to see Roberto. But a lot of folk knew him, including some Civil Guards. He was a waiter before the war. He was an officer in the Red zone and then, as he'd done a lot of damage — he killed many people — he couldn't give himself up at the end of the war and so he took to the hills. He became a bandit, as they say. And he went about recruiting people, two here, three there. Those like the mayor of Nerja during the Republic, or who had been bad and killed people and couldn't turn themselves in. So they ran off to the mountains.

They were delinquents. Here they grabbed a youngster called Ángel "Bernardo" and asked for money from his father. He had to pay up and then they released his son. That's what they did, kidnapping, killing, that was it. Up there above the Loma de la Cruz they killed a fellow, Miguel Moreno. He hadn't betrayed anybody. It was just that one of them had his reasons and they picked him up and killed him.

Then, they went to Los Almendros cortijo. The owner was a police chief in Málaga, called Ángel Herrero. (Note: in fact, Herrero was deputy chairman of Málaga juvenile court.) They grabbed him and demanded cash, a large amount. Then they sent somebody for the money. The owner thought there were only a couple of the Maquis there and he hit one over the head with a stick. But the others jumped up and, when he tried to run away, they caught him and killed him and also his foreman. Some time later three men were working very near, at Los Caños farm, and they killed them too.

We had a real battle once with a group of hundred and more in the area of Cerro Verde. A corporal who was with me died. They wounded a sergeant major and also killed one of the Moorish troops. That was a very badly organised affair and afterwards a captain who went to the Venta Panaderos to hide was arrested.

Then there was the theft at the flour mill at the Molineta, where they stole 18 sacks, each one holding 100 kilos. They arrived by night, opened up the mill, took away the flour and that was it. Afterwards it was discovered that they had left some sacks on the slope down to the river because they couldn't carry them all. Following that, a detachment was based in the mill.

There were a number of kidnappings. They would ask for a ransom, maybe 20,000 *duros*. At that time 20,000 *duros* was a lot of money, because a man working in the countryside only earned two *duros*. Here they didn't manage more than two or three kidnappings. They did try another against Justo López, a *señorito* who used to live almost opposite the town hall. But his son had a pistol and closed the door. Firing broke out and they couldn't pull it off and had to run away.There was another confrontation one day in 1950. We were coming from the dam in the Chíllar river, where the water falls to make electric power. When we were up high on the Almendrón peak, we were tired and the lieutenant said: "Those who are very tired, come with me. Those who are not, go that way and you'll reach the river first. Wait for us in the river." But just when we were going down those of the sierra were coming up and there was a shootout. Maybe there were seven or eight of them. Two died and we seized two of them alive. The others escaped.

Later we had another skirmish in the Pichirri gorge and four of them fell. And one called Vicentillo surrendered. Then, in Madrid, Fernández Montes de Oca, a lieutenant colonel who was the commander in Málaga province, and a sergeant major arrested Roberto in a cafe. Roberto talked and they made use of letters from him to lure those still in the sierra. They came down thinking they were going abroad and they were picked up. Why did Roberto betray all his comrades? That I don't know. Was there torture? Ha, ha! That's something I don't know either.

We picked up in Frigiliana one of the sierra called Paquillo, a little fellow. One night, when we were at the cinema, he was up at Lízar with two or three guards. Suddenly he grabbed the sub-machinegun off Francisco Altamirano Recio and escaped. Then he was seen wandering about Salar de Loja in Granada province, where he came from. He killed a guard there. But they caught him and killed him, and all those of the sierra. Yes, they all died.

We used to go out on patrol with around 50 men, and we'd be four days or so in the countryside or the sierra. At the exits of the village and where tracks joined we would put check-points. To keep watch on the key points, day and night. By day we would be watching from the high points, the top of El Fuerte, of el Almendrón, on the Pinto, but we had no binoculars. Some men on each hilltop. Many nights, many, I spent at the lookout post on top of Cerro Lucero.

I was armed with a sub-machinegun and a pistol and two bombs. I had 360 bullets. Those who had rifles had 150 rounds and 60 for the pistol, each one with 200 or so. I was involved in two skirmishes when there was shooting. I don't know if I killed anybody. I was never wounded. although on one occasion I was cut by some flying thyme. I was lying flat and aiming my gun and there was a bush of thyme next to me. A shot was fired, hit the thyme and the pieces cut me.

I was here in Frigiliana until April, 1952. Then it was over. Only two from here were still in the sierra and on January 19 we captured El Moreno in his mother's house and the next day Lomas died. Lomas met his end on the Pedregal hill. He tried to run and the lieutenant killed him. He gave him a burst from his rifle and so did another guard, Rafael Requena Zamora, with his submachine-gun. They killed him between them. As for El Moreno, they took him to Málaga and they executed him there.

They say the guards applied the Ley de Fugas (i.e. shot people while trying to escape) when it wasn't necessary. No, no. I've never seen that law applied. All those captured alive went to Málaga and they were put on trial. They were judged. If they received the death penalty, they were shot. That's not applying the Ley de Fugas. Today there's no death penalty but then there was.

Here they killed three fellows because they were committing lots of misdeeds. El Moreno attacked a Moorish soldier with an axe and his mates were enraged and smashed everything belonging to El Moreno, his lands, the trees, everything, they reduced it to dust. Then the Moors killed three relations of those in the sierra. Sure, those three were innocent. It was a lottery. All those with family in the sierra were in the draw and, as chance would have it, they grabbed those three. They didn't look to see who was the prettiest or the ugliest.

When a guard and a corporal died here, nobody went to the funeral. Nobody! And yet, when they killed those three, all the *señoritos* and the whole village went to the funeral. That went down badly. On one side you have the people of the sierra who have killed many persons and on the other the Civil Guard and the military defending the whole village. Nobody goes to the burial of a Civil Guard but when one of the village dies everybody goes. Does that seem right? That's why Captain Fernández Muñoz gave the *señoritos* a hard time — he beat them all. There was no other reason.

If you talk of ill treatment, there was one who stood out, a corporal they called Cabo Largo. Antonio González Bueno was his name. That man was a tough type, but just because one person is bad doesn't mean that all are bad. If a man goes a little beyond his obligations because he believes that in that way

Telegrama codificado
2 Sept 46, Almería-Madrid, Dirección General de la Guardia Civil -
Se tiene noticias que en la mañana de hoy, día 2, han salido dos barcos de Oran y uno de Argel con 100 o 150 hombres cada uno armados fusiles y bombas de mano. Estos barcos vienen hacía litoral sur de España frente costas Africa ignorandose porto desembarco. Extreme vigilancia y deme cuenta.

Civil Guard coded message picked up by
the Communist radio listening service

he can arrange things better, the others are not to blame. He believed that he was going to solve matters in that way. And it couldn't be. But, remember, we couldn't go alone through the streets here. We had to go accompanied, because anything could happen.

When I arrived here, I was lucky. I had a sergeant major from my home town and I had no need to hit anybody, nor to harass anybody. To the contrary, I saved one man's life. One night the guards arrived at the barracks, it would be half an hour after midnight, after the film show, and we wanted to go to the post in the Molineta to sleep. The lieutenant tells us: "Careful on Puerto Blanquillo, the people of the sierra pass by there." We'd left our arms in the Moors' barracks in the Calvario so we went for them and the sergeant orders me to go ahead with the sub-machinegun. Between each one of us there was quite a distance. At Puerto Blanquillo it was drizzling and it was dark with no moon. I took a hundred steps. I had the sub-machinegun, which was loaded with 30 rounds, switched to rapid fire. Then I saw somebody only a short distance away, like from here to the next corner. I called out: "Halt! Don't move!"

The man, a tall fellow, was wearing black because a son of his had died. He was Manuel Nera who lived up above. He was carrying a hat and when I said: "Halt, don't move!" the hat fell from his hand. The sergeant started shouting: "Shoot him! Shoot him! Shoot him!" How could I shoot him? If I had, he would have been like a sieve. The man was frozen to the spot. Then up came two guards and the sergeant. "Didn't I tell you to shoot?" "If I'd shot, I would have killed him." The fellow made a living selling molasses in Córdoba and Jaén. Night had come and he had lingered with the guards in the Molineta where there was a bar run by a woman called Dolores Jaime. It was already one in the morning and they told him: "Take care when you go up the hill as the guards will be coming down. It could be difficult if you stumble into them." And bump into them he did. If it had been another in my place, less responsible, he would have shot and killed him.That man lasted another 30 years, another 30 years.

Hombre, things happen because they have to happen. The innocent die in wars. And, when somebody is killed, a person may be blamed who is not guilty at all but he still goes to prison.

I was in the *contrapartida*s (groups of guards posing as Maquis) as well. I was with a sergeant major and a corporal and eight guards. Our mission was to go to a spot and establish whether the people were collaborating with the outlaws. In the *contrapartida* you went in civilian clothes, camouflaged as though you were those of the sierra, so as to find out who were with them and who were against them.

The unfortunate thing is that here the people lived from the sierra: from the esparto, from the thyme, from the wood for the Ingenio, which used a lot of firewood boiling the molasses. They used to transport long beams for the houses and all those things. It was inevitable that they saw the people of the sierra, but of course they weren't going to say so. Because the next day they would not be able to go to the sierra again. Most of those who went off to Argentina or Barcelona did so because they had cousins or uncles or somebody in the sierra.

I was 33 years in the Guardia Civil, in Barcelona, Cádiz, Córdoba, Ciudad Real and Málaga, everywhere except the Basque Country. I reached the rank of corporal and then sergeant. I married a girl from Frigiliana and when I retired in 1992 we returned here. We live in the Barrio Alto.

Today things are a little more peaceful. In my view, what the Guardia did was their duty, nothing more: taking care that the village lived as well as possible.

"You were, as the saying goes, between the devil and the deep blue sea. You were afraid of those up there and you were afraid of those who were here."

Eduardo Triviño Martín, farm worker, born in Frigiliana November 29, 1929.

I was seven years old when the business of 1936 happened. They held elections and it wasn't a matter of one party or another, just the Left and the Right. Those of the Left won by an overwhelming majority, but they only ruled four or five months, no more. As there was a lack of everything and no money, they took the cow off the rich man, they killed it and they shared it out among the whole village, for those who had nothing. They slaughtered a few that way.

Previously, the rich controlled the economy. They had cows and the poor would take a half share and rear them, but in the end the rich gained almost everything. The rich man would say: "This cow is worth 10 *duros* (50 pesetas) and when she's one or two she'll be worth 20." He would take the 10 *duros* and then the 10 *duros* profit would be split between them. But the rich got all the profit, because though he put the price at 10 *duros* it actually was worth six.

They say that the Reds entered the church and threw out all the images, but that's not so. The people who entered were the Socialists of the village. They made it a storage place and they brought supplies there and shared them out. As this area was surrounded by the invaders, they had to bring supplies, wheat, chick peas, with mules from Granada. They removed the saints. They picked up the images and put them in a room and nailed up the door, and the church was reserved for supplies.

Between Two Fires

Four crazies came from Nerja to burn the saints, but the leftwingers from here who were in charge wouldn't let them. It was three or four Falangistas from Frigiliana who burned the images so as to put the blame on everybody and kill some of them. None of the Left were involved. But, when the Nationalists arrived here, they blamed all those of the Left for burning the saints, whether of the Socialist Party or not, just for being leftwing. They arrested my father for burning them. Here there was no more than one Communist. The others were Socialists and they took them off to Torrox and killed them. They killed a bunch, and they didn't stop killing until recently. Just before he died, Franco killed people.

They called it a "civil war", but it wasn't a civil war at all. A civil war is when those of the same nation fight one against the other. But here came the Germans, here came the Italians. All the big chiefs, the extreme Right, they came to help here.

There were four in my family, three boys and a girl. I was the smallest. I went to school but I left without even knowing how to write my name. It wasn't a good school. I was older when I went because at first the town hall didn't let me go. An uncle of mine said: "How come you're not going to teach him to read!" and he spoke several times to the mayor who said I should go. But then the teacher told him that he would not admit me and others because our fathers were in prison.

My mother's side of the family weren't of the Left or the Right. They didn't involve themselves in anything and nor did my father, but he put his name down for the Socialist Party. That's all he did, but he spent seven or eight years in jail. He was there less time because he was very good at writing and figures and they took him from Málaga to Dos Hermanas, a village in Seville, to do the accounts for a canal they were building. Paco el Gordo, also from the village, was there too, working on the canal. My father came and went as he was accounting for the materials, such as the cement they brought in.

I began working on the land when I was six or seven, with my grandfather. As everybody went to the sierra and there was nobody to work the land, the little ones had to do it. Women work here but not on the farms except when they help their husbands. My grandparents had a few cows and I used to look for grass for them and do other jobs. I knew everything you had to do on the land. My grandfather was already old and my uncles were all in the war. When some young kids of 13 or 14 came to work, I had to tell them how things were done. I was there when my uncle came from the war. He was the youngest of five children, four brothers and a sister who was my mother, and was the only one who could read. In the past everybody here was illiterate.

The Barrio Alto was always the most illiterate quarter, the poorest. Up there the folk didn't want to be taught. During the time of the people of the sierra you couldn't leave your house in the Barrio Alto after midnight. They beat up those they picked up down below after that time. Perhaps somebody was careless. They could be talking, taking a drink in one of the few bars there were. As nobody had a watch, maybe when they realised the hour it was already midnight. They would rush out and by night the street was full of Civil Guards on one side, Moors on the other. When a guard asked a person where he lived, he didn't dare tell him. The guard would say: "Do you live in the Barrio Alto? Don't you know that by 12 you have to be in bed?" And he would whack him with a cudgel.

There's a story about two fellows, one from the Barrio Alto and the other from the Chorruelo, just down from the church. Both of them liked the booze and they had land and enough money to pay for a few drinks. They were talking one night, a bit exalted in their cups. "Let's exchange houses," they said. They haggled over the houses, but finally they didn't swap them and they went homewards. It was well past midnight and, when one was about to head for the Chorruelo and the other to go up the Zacatín to the Barrio Alto, along came the Civil Guard. They stopped them and asked them where they lived. "I'm down in the Chorruelo," said the one. "Then get off to bed. And you, where do you live? In the Barrio Alto, right?" And they cracked him three or four times over the head. When the other chap saw this, he said: "By gosh, Antonio, if we had swapped, it would have been me who suffered the blows." And the joke is that the one they beat up was a rightwinger, very much so.

When the Civil War was still on and the Right had taken over here, those in the Republican army were trying to give themselves up, heading for their home areas where they were known. A lot of soldiers, from Granada, Córdoba, Jaén, all over were coming down this way, when they knew their army had been destroyed. Two of the last ones were coming through the sierra with mules. It was the time of the black market, when they brought bread, flour, chick peas as contraband from Granada. These two were travelling by night so that nobody would pick them up. They were in La Rambla, above the Venta Panaderos, when they bumped into two Falangists from the village.

One, wearing his soldier's uniform, asked for some bread. "You're a soldier, aren't you?" they asked. "Yes, I was called up, I was in the army and I'm trying to get home." They told him: "We're going to give you more than you can digest." Then they fired at both of them and killed one. Afterwards, it's said they dragged his body about, jeering at him.

Nobody in the village liked those two. Many of those on the Right said: "Look at what those rogues have done! They killed a fellow when he asked them for a piece of bread." He may have been a Republican soldier but he could have come from a family on the Right, who knows? When they drafted men for the war, some ended up on the Left and some on the Right. Some changed sides when they could. A few years later the people of the sierra grabbed that Falangist and were going to kill him. Instead, they punished him by forcing him to bring them food. For quite some time he was carrying up food and goods to them, for shooting a man who was just looking for his home.

When the Right took over here, as they were killing folk, those who could went off to the sierra to save themselves. Later more people went because there was so much beating and so much hunger. If those in the sierra did anything, they blamed the people of the Barribarto, as they called those from the upper part of the village.

The priest at that time, Don Miguel — they called him "Eye of the Bull" — what he did was prevent a lot of beating and he stopped people being locked up in the cemetery. He stopped many things. They were shutting up people as a punishment if you entered the village when the sun was gone. Even if the sun had not set and was still shining on the sierra, that was not good enough. You were put in the cemetery after receiving a few blows. It was used as a prison. You were only let out to go to work the next day. Whoever a man was working with had to tell him in time: "Get back to the village while there's still a bit of sun." Some did let the workers return in time, but not the poorest. When the priest learned of this, he stopped it, saying the cemetery was for the dead not for the living.

It was a very bad time. Everybody was intimidated, in shock. Later, when the people of the sierra had gone, all right, he who enjoyed beating still did so, but it wasn't like before when they beat up people just for the hell of it.

After the war there was a good deal of hunger. We all had ration cards to buy food and clothing. Almost everybody in the *pueblo* had a little piece of land and there was always something to eat, sugar cane, wheat, figs, apricots, potatoes, beans. But in other places they had nothing. People from the capital were stealing in the Málaga farmland because they were starving, and the people of Nerja came here, asking for food and also stealing, taking unripe fruit, sucking cane, and not just by night, by day too. It was tougher in the Nerja area because the security guards reported people and they were fined and beaten. Here the guards threatened people but didn't take them to the barracks.

All those who did something and were sent to prison were unbalanced types. Those who had settled down didn't cause trouble or harm anybody, although anybody can get up to mischief, but mischief of little importance. Here at the time of the Civil War they didn't kill anybody. In other places they did, they killed priests. On the contrary, here leftwingers concealed the rich people when they came from elsewhere to finish them off. They protected them all so that nothing happened to them. In Frigiliana they didn't want anybody maltreated and, if a little incident occurred, it was because somebody was not quite right in the head.

Later, many ran off to the sierra, while in other villages few did because here the rightwingers were worse. They dealt out more blows here than in other places. People went off because they were afraid of being beaten and they couldn't work because they were the sons of somebody in prison or already in the sierra. At that time it was intolerable here, intolerable. Of the few that stayed and didn't get beaten, I was one. Luckily I never got beaten up, and I don't know how I escaped.

They called you to the barracks for anything. They'd say: "You're taking food to the people of the sierra" and they called you to the barracks to try to get information out of you. An uncle of mine, Antonio García Martín, had his father in the sierra and another uncle, Francisco Triviño García, had a nephew. Cabo Largo called them to the barracks with another man who didn't have any relative in the sierra. Cabo Largo (Tall Corporal) was Antonio González Bueno and he got his name because he was very big. He was the worst and he had two brothers like him, also Civil Guards. He used to drive people into the sierra. He would almost kill them in the barracks and tell them: "If you don't go to the sierra tomorrow, you're dead. I'll beat you until I kill you."

One evening I was coming down from some work in the sierra and I met Francisco Triviño who was going up and I asked him where he was going. I thought he was going to cut down a pine tree to make a roof beam as they would give three *duros* for one. Many were doing this, stealing from the sierra, cutting pines and making charcoal. If they caught you, they denounced you, but if you got away with it you earned a day's pay.

He replied: "Where am I going? To the sierra. Don't you know what those sons of whores did last night? They called your uncle and Eduardo and me and they hit us and hit us. And the Cabo said he'd call us again tonight if we hadn't gone to the mountains and he'd beat us to death. He's not going to kill me. I'm going." He took off his shirt and he had his whole back and sides full of bruises from the beating. His whole back was bleeding. I felt sick. I wanted to go off too. Any day, I thought, they're going to grab me.

But my uncle didn't go off and that night they called him to the barracks. They gave him such a beating that he had to go to the doctor two or three times a day and have injections. The priest told him: "Come on, let's go to Málaga to show them so they remove the corporal from here. Come with me." But he said: "No, because later you'll go somewhere else and I'll be left here and they'll kill me. I can't report them. I've got a house and family and they would kill me."

He spent many days in bed. The doctor and the priest visited him two or three times. They wanted to take him to Málaga but he wouldn't have it. The third fellow had two sisters in Nerja and they gave him the money to go to Barcelona. It cost 18 or 20 pesetas to go by boat, so he went off to Barcelona, out of the way.

Soldiers were stationed in El Ingenio during the war and later, at the time of the Maquis, they were based in two or three places. Prisoners were put in there and beaten up, but I don't know that the soldiers did anything to anybody. They were forced to be here so what could they do? There were at least a hundred or more Regulares, the Moors. And, apart from those in the barracks, there were several detachments of Civil Guards. Next to the barracks a family had a boarding house and the people of the sierra used to come in by the back door. Six or seven guerrillas would sleep there while the Civil Guard was hunting for them all over the place.

Of course, for many those days meant good business because they managed to get rich and buy farms and houses and land as the people of the sierra were paying them for supplying food.

For a long time nobody was aware of the guerrillas, only those who needed to know, those they trusted who had been many years in prison and had suffered many beatings. They were with them to see if they could change the regime. Everybody heard of Roberto, but nobody knew who he was.

One time I was confronted by one of those of the sierra. I don't know if there were more around, I only saw one, Vicente (Martín Vozmediano). He told me that I had to bring him food, that I should look for two or three others to bring him flour. I told him that I wasn't going to bring flour and that those up there who weren't working should go for it. He called me everything, that I was a fascist, that he was going to hang me from a pine, that I was a traitor. I told him: "In my house in Frigiliana I'm more leftwing than you. You're nothing, neither here nor there." I already counted on his killing me. He pointed at me two or three times with a sub-machinegun that he was carrying. "Go on, shoot!" I said. "Fascist!" he called me over and over. I came away and nothing happened. Well, I got away because he let me, otherwise how could I escape with the gun he had in his hand?

The people of the sierra took a fellow named Paulino from his farm and killed him. They asked for money, but they didn't get any because the wife said: "If I give them the money, they'll just kill me too." Paulino was from Río de la Miel and he'd killed some of the Left during the war, or that's what they said. His own wife said he'd killed a number and for that reason he was afraid to stay there and he'd come this way. A brother of those he killed was in the sierra and was going to kill him. They took him to get rid of him and they asked for money. The woman didn't give them any because they were going to kill him in any case.

Most of those in the sierra didn't go for political reasons. The first, yes, it was about politics, but the others who went later did so because of the beatings and the hunger they suffered. In the case of El Moreno, he wanted to go to the mountains but they wouldn't admit him unless he killed somebody so he couldn't defect later — there were many who were fed up with being in the sierra. They told him to kill a Civil Guard lieutenant and he said he couldn't do it because he was very friendly with the lieutenant.

With another fellow, Mocha, El Moreno went to an irrigation channel where the Moors went to wash themselves. A Moor was there and El Moreno struck him with an axe he had hidden. The two ran off and El Moreno said they should head for the sierra. Mocha was against it, but El Moreno told him: "The moment you go to the *pueblo*, they'll kill you, they'll chop you in little pieces. Let's go!" And they went off to the sierra.

They say that the Moor didn't die, he recovered. But then three youngsters were killed here. They had done nothing, except that one had a brother in the sierra, another also had a brother and the youngest had his father. They (the Civil Guard) picked them up and locked them up for three days without anybody knowing where they were. First they were in the barracks then they took them to an oil mill down in La Molineta. There they were seen. A window looked out on a path and they could speak with somebody. They weren't given water or anything and then they were handed over to the Moors.

The Moors had fun with them, dragging them around all night. They tied them up and they pulled them about, throwing stones at them, smashing them up, dragging them from above the mill to the road, from here to there. There was blood everywhere, pieces of clothing, pieces of bone. Bits of skull, the one's brains, a piece of one's hand were picked up. When I saw them in the cemetery, fingers were missing and their hands mangled from being dragged.

You had to be brave to look at that. Not everybody could do so. I said that I had to see it. My cousin was there, destroyed, and he told me: "Don't go in. They'll catch you and kill you. It will shatter you. You're very young to see these things." I was 20 at the time. I went inside and I saw it. My uncle was there by himself, raging, and crying: "Murderers, criminals..." They had hit him and pulled him away, but the priest said: "He has to be at his son's side." They put him inside the cemetery and the priest told them to leave him alone.

Later, when my uncle put a plaque on the cemetery niche saying "Murdered by the Civil Guard", they took it off. When they saw what he had put there, they ripped the plaque off and destroyed it and another one had to be placed there.

That was the worst that could happen in any village in Spain, how they beat people, how they tortured them. The kids and the adults were intimidated and scared by the Civil Guard. Here there were no rich capitalists. There were folk who had more than enough to eat and could employ a few maids because they paid them nothing. Maybe they gave them two or three pesetas a month and they had four or five to do all the household jobs. Those people were the ones who caused all the mischief. Some who called themselves rich did no damage. Those who did most harm were those who had less money and wanted to be somebody. In those times you were, as the saying goes, between the devil and the deep blue sea. You were afraid of those up there and you were afraid of those who were here. Because any unbalanced type for any little thing could say: "So and so is a Fascist. He's done this and that." Even though you had done nothing and said nothing, they would grab you and give you a hiding.

Once when I was looking for esparto with another, one of the sierra approached us. He chatted with us for a while and said nothing about bringing him food or anything like that. He just asked us if we had seen the guards and we said no, but fearing that some of the sierra would surrender and report that we had given them information. With all these things, one was afraid all the time, of those down here and those up there.

They found two bodies at the Cruz de Napoleón (Cross of Napoleon), the bodies of Paco Bendita and El Terrible, and it was they (of the sierra) who eliminated them. One of them, El Terrible (José López Jurado), was taking food to those of the sierra. He wasn't used to work. He was used to be with the goats, although he didn't have many. He was poor and he had a wife and two or three kids. Things were very bad so he had to earn something. He took food to the people of the sierra and they paid him.

But everything was strictly controlled and also it rained a lot. Every day it was raining, not like now when months go by without rain. Two or three months in summer went by and it was always raining, five or six days at a time. With so much rain he couldn't work in the countryside either. The people of the sierra gave him money and told him that as soon as it cleared up he should bring food to them. But he spent all the money and then told them it was all gone and he couldn't go out because of so many days of rain and so many Civil Guards everywhere. Three times he ate up all the money and also he took some of the money to the barracks, or so I heard.

The people of the sierra hung some sacks containing food up the riverbed and Paco Bendita found them. He cut off a piece of bread. There was tobacco in another sack and he took some of that. And he put on a pair of *alpargatas* (sandals), as he was practically barefoot. Then he hung the sacks up again and left them as they were, but they'd seen him. They didn't say anything to him.

Later he talked about it to his mother. She had another son who was trying to get into the Civil Guard. He didn't know how to read, but then you only needed to sign your name to get in. The mother told Paco Bendita to report what he'd found to the barracks. But he protested: "No, no, they'll kill me." So it was the mother who informed about it. The son had to go to the sierra to earn a living and there they grabbed El Terrible and Paco Bendita, and they hanged both of them. They were hanging there at the Cross of Napoleon quite a few days. People saw them, but nobody dared to say anything, until somebody sent his little boy to put a paper on the barracks door saying where they were. The guards already knew they were missing and, when they saw the message, they went and brought them. That was a big thing. Everybody was shocked, on all sides.

In the end only two from here were left in the sierra, El Moreno and Lomas.

They had no money, nothing. They ate what they could. Then El Moreno came to the village during the San Sebastián fiesta. He was going to buy *turrón* for him and Lomas and he went to his home in El Calvario, not far from the barracks. A married brother of his who lived in the province of Granada was there with his wife. They were trying to get his pistol off him so that there was no shooting in the house, the woman asking questions about the gun as though she didn't know what it was. When he got hold of the pistol, the brother made an excuse to go outside and went to the barracks to tell them they could pick up El Moreno.

El Moreno didn't want to give himself up. He was tough, but they caught him and he told them where Lomas was. He was in a relative's cortijo and there they got him. They brought the body back on a mule, parading it right through the village before all the people at the fiesta. There were some who enjoyed that spectacle, like a woman who shouted: "Fresh meat here! They've caught a mountain goat!"

That day they brought in the last of the sierra. They buried him and that was it. In other provinces, up in the north, there were still people in the sierra. But not here. Lomas was the last.

They dressed El Moreno, the one who hit the Moor with an axe, as a Civil Guard and also my first cousin, Manuel Triviño Cerezo (Valeriano), when he surrendered. They fooled them saying they were going to continue in the Civil Guard. They told them: "You tell us who supplied you with food or helped you and, the more of those people we discover, the more pay you'll get." And they believed it. They put a lot of folk in jail, by saying: "In this farm they brought us food and here we slept one night, or more." In this and other villages, they informed on those who had helped the people of the sierra, those who had sheltered them.

They (the Civil Guard) took El Moreno to Granada province and he informed on many there too. When many had been imprisoned and they saw none were left and they'd got all the information out of them, they got rid of the two of them. They killed them in Málaga. Everybody knew they were going to get rid of them. Their families believed that they were going to be Civil Guards, but everybody knew otherwise.

"I'm neither Communist nor Fascist. Since the Civil Guards killed my brother and his own comrades killed my father, what party do I belong to?"

Virtudes Martín Ruiz, housewife, born in Frigiliana on October 11, 1929, lost her father in the sierra and her brother at La Loma de las Vacas.

My father left me when I was seven to go to the war, to the Red zone, when Franco took over in 1936. He had to go to the Red zone because if he'd stayed here they would have killed him, as many others were. He left me aged seven, my five-year-old brother, whom they killed — may he rest in peace, and a baby of 15 months, who died. And so we have suffered, on account of the village, because those who ran the village were the rich folk.

I remember the day my father went away. I went to the door of the Civil Guard barracks where a lorry was loading all those who were going to the Red side. There were a lot of them. I was crying because my father was going away and he, poor fellow, was crying at the sight of me crying, I was so small. But he said: "If I stay, they'll kill me." He was a Communist and Franco's forces were already all over the place.

My mother's mother, may she rest in peace, had bits of land and there my brother and I went to eat with her while my mother was cleaning houses to buy food. Later she also went to work at the Nerja sugar factory. She was working for Larios for a long time. As kids we suffered a great deal, and when we were big too.

My father was three-and-a-half years in the Red zone before he came back. Things were more peaceful and he believed nothing would happen to him. He wanted very much to return. It was a little before the end of the war, but the blows hadn't stopped.

They told me: "Your father's coming down by Puerto Blanquillo." I was 11-and-a-half and I ran down the road like crazy, looking for my father. He was desperate to see me as so much time had passed, but, when he arrived home, the Civil Guard didn't let him enter, not even to wash or dress himself. They grabbed him in the street, took him to prison and then to Málaga and he was another three-and-a-half years behind bars. We suffered hardship and anxiety. The rich humiliate even little children and we were poor so they humiliated us very much.

When he came out of prison, the poor man went to work at what he could: in the sierra making charcoal, collecting esparto or thyme. That was the life of the poor then. Already when I was 12 I was mopping and cleaning a big house. For lunch they would give me fried fish but no bread and a boiled sweet potato. And what was I earning? One *duro* (five pesetas) for all that cleaning.

At the age of 12, I used to go to Alcóncar to collect olives. We got up at seven in the morning to head up the river at eight, a big gang of girls all the same age. My uncle Blas, who was the foreman for Sebastián Torres, used to say: "Look at them, look at them! They're like baby goats going through the water, skipping across the gaps." Young folk aged 12 and 13. All the children were working, in the olive harvest, collecting thyme, carrying on their backs small loads of esparto, which the Company bought. They put a cauldron in the riverbed to prepare the thyme. That was the life of the poor.

When I was a little girl, before my father went to the Red side, he went once to look for grapes after they'd picked the good ones. He managed to collect a basketful of small grapes. My mother was going to Nerja to sell them and earn something, but a man from the village caught her. He said: "You have two bunches there that I was going to tread for wine." He seized the two bunches and my mother, and for each bunch she spent two nights in prison.

One of the forest rangers as a youngster had been very friendly with my father but when they married the friendship broke up. As a guard he was boss of the sierra, which belongs to the Ingenio, a very big company. One day my father was making charcoal and he said: "They've already picked the carob beans, so I'm going to see what's left. If I can get a load to sell, between the sack of charcoal and the carobs, I'll have had a decent day's work." But that guard arrived and asked him what he was doing. Thinking that they were friends, he tried to explain. Says the guard: "Oh, yes? Those carobs have an owner. Come on, leave them, we're going to the barracks." He took him to the barracks and the corporal we called Cabo Largo gave him a real beating and put a sign on him which read "For being a thief". He was bleeding from the mouth from the beating. After that he couldn't leave the house because they looked for him wherever he went.

When there was movement in the sierra, from the guerrillas, then things got ugly. My father had a brother called José in the sierra and he approached one day and told him: "Sebastián, bring us something to eat, because we're surrounded by Civil Guards and nobody will give us food." My father told him: "Hombre, you're getting me into trouble. I can bring you food any time but I'm in a difficult position."

Well, as he was his brother… We were living over by the Civil Guard barracks, but they stored food to take it to the people of the sierra in a house in the Barrio Alto, where there was a tavern. The men had to take it up by night. One night three went off carrying food and the guards shot and killed them. But my father, instead of going the way they did, sneaked along by the river. A woman who was looking out of her window at three in the morning when she should have been in bed saw him sneaking towards the sierra with the sack on his back. She went out of her house and knocked on the window of the Civil Guard armoury, which showed some nerve. Out came the fellow on duty. "What's going on?" "A man was sneaking down right now to the river with a sack on his back. He's so-and-so." She gave the name and everything.

If you didn't call the Civil Guard, they wouldn't get up because they had no wish to risk their lives. But, as they were alerted, they had to do something. There were Moors here and soldiers and guards. There were military everywhere and the Civil Guard put everybody on alert. Some went one way, some another. When he reached the mountain above the Chíllar river where he had the rendezvous, my father heard the Moors' voices and thought: "That's it. They've got me."

When he saw all of them there, he put out the light he was carrying to see the path and tossed away the sack so they wouldn't catch him with it. The guards and the Moors caught him, then dressed him like a Moor, in a *jellaba*, and brought him back to the village. There was a Moorish barracks at Cuatro Vientos and they had him there one or two days, hitting him to find out where he got the food and he said his brother had forced him. They put my father's hat in his mouth so that nobody heard him cry out from the blows they dealt him with a plank with nails. They hit his feet, then the Moors and guards hung him up and beat him with a whip.

They took him under arrest to Vélez. Then they grabbed my mother and my brother, Antonio, and took them to the prison in Vélez too. He was a little baby, he still couldn't walk, and she had to breast-feed him. He got his first teeth in prison. An aunt of mine was in prison too, and two first cousins and relations from Zacatín street, all those accused of buying food for the people of the sierra.

When they tried my father in Málaga, he denied that his wife had bought the food to take to his brother. "My wife doesn't know what I'm up to. She herself told me not to get involved, that it would cause trouble for the family. But I paid no attention to her, as I should have. My wife was the first in not wanting me to take food to the sierra." In view of this, they released my mother, but my father was another 14 months in prison, after having already served three-and-a-half years. We used to visit my father in prison. My mother went every week, with a box full of food because they didn't give him enough to eat. Every time I would say: "Mama, I want to go with you to see papa." And I saw him: bars here, a wall there, and in the middle wire netting. What a way to see your father.

When they let him out, he carried on making charcoal, bringing back esparto and thyme. But the movement was still going on. The war was hotter and hotter. And the Civil Guards picked up the poor fellow at every opportunity. He had to take a piece of bread or something to eat on the way to give him strength for the work, but they said it was for the people of the sierra and they beat him.

Lieutenant Reyna (Francisco Giménez Reyna), a Civil Guard who was here, a very bad fellow, and Cabo Largo did it, enough to kill him. Cabo Largo would say: "You have to go to the sierra and if you don't go I'll kill you." The poor chap didn't want to go to the sierra but if they were going to beat him to death then he had to go. One morning he went off to work and he never returned.

As a result of beatings they also drove off my uncle Blas (Martín Navas), who died near Motril, and my uncle José. They were Communists. José was Roberto's horse. He was a man of great strength and, as Roberto was lame, he lifted him up and ran all over the sierra with him on his back. When Roberto was arrested, so was José.

But do you know why Cabo Largo said what he did? Because he was eating at the same trough as the people of the sierra. I saw it with these very eyes, from where I used to live. At the back of the Civil Guard are two or three windows and from the window where Cabo Largo lived he was throwing out big white sacks to a villager who was a muleteer and had two animals. The sacks were full of food and the muleteer carried them off. He travelled to Jayena for bread and flour and carried food to where they picked up the sack from Cabo Largo. Then they would put money in the sack and a list, saying: "Don't go tomorrow to such-and-such a spot as we're going there." So that one didn't bump into the other. That was what went on between the guards and the people of the sierra. And the bill went to those who shouldn't have paid.

My family didn't supply food to the people of the sierra, but many people became rich, taking food to them and getting well paid. It was great for Cabo Largo because he earned a lot of cash through this business. He sent them sackfuls of food and they sent him money, more than it was worth.

When my father went up in the sierra, my brother Manolo, a lad of 15 years, followed the same life of getting charcoal, thyme and firewood. Because there was no other way to earn a living in the village. One day my father met my brother in the sierra and said: "Son, we've got nothing, but don't even bring a cigarette paper to smoke yourself because the Civil Guards are going to catch you. The river is surrounded. The guards are stationed behind the bushes to see if you are bringing food." One of his comrades, Vicente, one of the three Artabús brothers, was with him and said: "What are you telling your son?" "Vicente," says my brother, "I'm pursued by the guards. I would love to bring food to my father, but how can I?" Then Vicente tells my father: "You're going to get some esparto and make a noose and you are going to hang your son." My father was crying on one side, my brother on the other.

"Roberto is up there," says Vicente. "Go and tell him about this and ask his forgiveness to see if he'll let you off. Because I'm going to hang you." The two of them went on their knees before Roberto who asked them: "What are you crying for?" "Vicente says that my father should get some esparto to hang me because I said I couldn't bring any food, because I'm persecuted, Roberto." Roberto told him: "Get off home and nothing will happen to you in the village. Don't look for esparto, just get out of here." My brother came home and we saw him closing doors and closing windows. "Manolo, what's going on?" we asked him. "Close the window, they're coming for me, they're coming for me," he said. And when he'd cried himself out and recovered, he related what had happened. He told us about El Artabús wanting my father to hang him and that Roberto had patted him on the shoulder and told him to go home and nothing would happen.

An uncle of mine by marriage, Eduardo Noberto, had land at Los Tablazos and he took my brother to get him away from the sierra. He was doing all right with him, until one day in April Eduardo told him: "Manolo, we're going to cut down a carob tree at the entrance to the cortijo, which isn't producing beans. We're going to get to work and make a kiln and build a fire to make charcoal. And we'll cut cane. We'll have plenty to do."

They were cutting the cane when up came a big bunch of Civil Guards. "Something's going on," says my brother. "Look at this crowd of guards coming." They arrived and said: "Somebody has attacked a Moor with an axe and we've come looking for who did it." Naturally my brother had an axe to cut the cane, to cut the pines and the carob tree. My uncle Eduardo said: "He hasn't been away from here because he's working here." So that day they let it go. But the next day they didn't.

They'd cut the cane and were preparing the kiln as they'd chopped up the carob tree. Afterwards, my uncle left it two or three months without setting fire to it because it made him sad. He said: "It's all prepared but I feel bad about lighting the fire in the kiln." The next day my uncle told his sons: "Go up with Manolo. He has to report." All those who had relatives in the sierra, the whole family, had to report to the barracks three times a day. If you were out in the country at midday, you had to come back to report and before the sun set you had to report again.

On the way up to the village, they met a pair of Civil Guards coming to get my brother for what had happened to the Moor. They didn't ask him any questions or tell him anything. If he had to be taken to prison, they should have done so and put him on trial to see what was what, but... They told him: "Manolo, we're coming for you. Lieutenant Reyna sent us." My cousins asked: "But what's he done? He's working with us. He's harmed nobody."

One of the guards was Alamino, who should have saved my brother's life because he did a lot for Alamino. Alamino used to buy pigs and other things and he would tell Manolo: "I've bought some small fig trees over there to get the fruit." And Manolo would go to pick up the figs for Alamino's pigs without any pay and he did many other things which should have counted in his favour. Manolo, at 18, had never been in trouble with anybody. Ask about that in the *pueblo* — it was turned into a vale of tears due to this affair. From what one sees, Franco gave carte blanche. To end the guerrilla war they had to kill three of the best. And one was mine.

So they took them. My mother was at the end of the street, on the Cuesta del Apero, when she saw him come along in the middle of the guards with his jacket over his shoulder, and she said: "Oh, my boy, he's going with the guards." The neighbours, to calm her, were saying: "No, no. It's not him. It must be another." That night the three they'd picked up slept in the patio of the barracks, Manolo, my daughter-in-law Antonia's father and the Triviño lad. As the whole village said: "They've picked the best three of the *pueblo*."

In the morning, at around nine o'clock, I came out to see if they were taking him somewhere. I was 20 years old and all upset. I saw a Jeep reverse into the barracks and I saw the three of them in it. Crying and shrieking, I went up to our house and told my mother: "They've put them in a car and one said 'Adiós' with his hand. They've taken them away to prison, mama."

They took them to a barracks in the Molineta and they were all day in the mill there. A woman washing plates in the water channel that passes by saw their three faces at a window. They asked for water and she took a pot of water to them. She asked them why they were there and they replied: "That's what we want to know. Why are we here? We've had nothing to eat." She had cooked some rice for the Civil Guards and she gave them her share.

At nine-thirty at night a family that lived in a mill at the Loma de las Vacas was watching to see what they were going to do with them and saw the three taken out to be killed. My daughter-in-law's husband fell to the ground from a gunshot and breathed no more. But my brother and the other were younger and they say they leaped about before falling down and my brother, he didn't want to die, was grabbing the weeds in the ground, dying and uprooting the weeds.

Then they dragged him to the road. In the morning they told a man who had a donkey: "You've got to take these three to the Frigiliana cemetery." They left my brother headless; he was 18, a young lad who was jumping around, and they shot him in the head until he died. The man loaded the three on his donkey, brought them to the cemetery and dumped them there like dogs.

Not aware of this, my mother and Triviño's mother were saying: "Let's go to the Molino and take them a bit of milk in case they're there." They went down, my mother and the other each carrying a glass of milk and an egg in it for them to drink. A guard called Carrasco was on duty down there and, when he saw them, he was shaken up. He turned yellow, all colours, because he knew what had happened.

"Carrasco, give this to our boys," they told him. Carrasco didn't speak. He went in and out, in and out. "But tell us where the boys are." He said: "Antonia, go back up and ask Lieutenant Reyna and he'll tell you where they are, because I can't."

The two came back to the village, weeping. My mother flung the glass away and the other woman the same because they didn't know where to turn next. They noticed blood on the road and my mother said: "This must be from a puppy somebody's killed." There was no way she would accept they would kill her son. It couldn't be, because her son had never harmed anybody in his whole life, not even when he was little. I was a very bad little girl. I'd hit everybody. But he, the little angel, didn't hit anybody. From his birth he was a kid with a sadness about him, a good boy.

When they got to Cuatro Vientos, my mother saw a group of Moors. They went on walking and she saw a group of women. "Something's happening." On Calvario street she fell to the ground and they took her into a house. They gave her something to revive her a little because she was half-dead. The other women knew something had happened but didn't want to say anything.

The two continued walking to the barracks and asked for Lieutenant Reyna. Reyna came out — and he was going to mass. After the deaths he had caused, he was going to mass! "Where's my boy?" asks my mother. "Your boy?" he said. "What had to be done has been done!" That's the way he replied: what had to be done has already been done! They didn't want us to see them. My uncle Eduardo was the one who arranged the burial; they didn't let us see them.

The whole village went to the burial of my brother and the other two, including the rich people. When *"los ricos"* were returning home, they called them to the Civil Guard barracks and gave them all a beating.

Much later, when there was no longer anybody in the sierra, a sergeant told me that a letter asking questions had come from Madrid. The sergeant had three sons, one serving with one of my sons in Zaragoza, and he took the trouble to ask me if he had written home or not. One day, at the end of the feria, he told me: "Virtudes, you should come to the barracks tomorrow. They've sent me a letter from Madrid asking about the death of your brother and who killed him." He didn't tell me who'd sent the letter.

I didn't want to go to the barracks but I did. The sergeant wrote down with a typewriter everything I told him and the guards there didn't know where to look. I said: "Cabo Largo ordered people to the sierra because he was eating out of the same bowl. And so the more who went there the better."

"Look at this," he said and took a very yellow sheet of paper out of a box. "What bad fellows the Civil Guards are and how good is Frigiliana! All of Frigiliana signed this so that they would kill them." They went about asking for signatures in order to kill my brother and the others. And all the rich folk signed. "*Los ricos* signed and then washed their hands of it. They're not to blame. See how fine Frigiliana is and how bad we guards are!" So that the Civil Guards made use of the fact that the rich ones signed. The sergeant told me: "Everybody went to the funeral. If you go to the funeral, don't sign to have them killed. And if you sign for them to be killed…" Even now, after so many years, justice has not been done in this case.

Up in the sierra there used to be the Venta Panaderos and a family lived there. One day the people of the sierra arrived and said: "Ana, make us rice stew for us to eat today. We really need some food. But be careful in case the guards come." Ana Herrero, the mother, began preparing the rice and it was almost ready when she said: "Fellows, I saw Cabo Largo down below. He most likely has seen you." They all began escaping through a window.

Then the *civiles* arrived. "Ana, have the people of the sierra been around here?" She replied: "Yes. All this rice I'm making was for them. As they went off when they saw you, you eat their share." That's how the woman lived. They put her husband in jail and they put the children in jail.

Until one day Don Miguel, a priest who was here, told her: "Ana, you have to leave there. You can't stay there or something really bad is going to happen." So it was she went to Málaga and found a place. The daughter was Roberto's girlfriend. The one he had in Melilla was prettier than her, but as he had one in every place...

Then, when the guerrilla movement was ending, that rogue Vicente of the Artabús brothers surrendered. They dressed him as a Civil Guard and he went with them searching from cave to cave and they killed anybody they found. Before he gave himself up, he threw my father — may he rest in peace — down the mountain.

When my father learned that his son had been killed, it affected his mind. He was shot in the arm when they were being chased by the guards over Granada way and that rogue didn't want to give him the medicine to cure him. Do you know how they were curing one another? By pissing on the wounds. His arm was becoming gangrenous and, in his crazy state, he said: "I'm going with my son that they killed because of me. I'm going with him." And Vicente told him: "Yes, yes, you're going with him." And he took him up to the top of a hill, you can see it from here, and gave him a shove. He rolled down and ended up in the river.

On the death of my brother my mother and I went to Málaga. There were four brothers and sisters in my family, but one died at 15 months. We put my brother Antonio in a children's home and we went working. We learned what had happened to my father because Paco López, Justo López's son, saw us one day in Málaga and said to my mother: "Antonia, you know that your husband has died too? They threw him off a big hillside. He fell face down in the river and after 20 days a patrol from Nerja found him dead."

There was a fellow who had a donkey and carried firewood to Nerja to sell. The Civil Guards told him: "You have to take this man to Frigiliana." He protested: "But I've come for a load of wood to earn a day's pay." So they told him: "We'll pay you. Take this man to Frigiliana." But, when they took my father to the village, Mr Town Hall says: "Don't bring him here. Take him to Nerja." So they took him to Nerja. My mother went to ask the grave-digger if they'd buried him in the cemetery. "No, señora," he says. "They've dug a ditch at the back and all those they bring in dead they're thrown in together."

They were tossing them in mixed up. They didn't bury them separately so that we don't really know if he's there or not. His name is in the Nerja court records. I went for a death certificate and there it was. They told me: "We had our work cut out to identify him because his papers were in a mess, after 20 days there face down." His head was missing — it had been eaten by the animals.

When I went to report to the barracks, they hit me across the shoulders with a gun butt. I had to tell them where my father was, and me, 20 years old, how was I going to know where he was? Now from so much suffering I have trouble with my legs. I've a bad heart and the doctor tells me: "When you were 20, you could put up with all those blows, but now you're 70 you can't." Now I'm suffering from all those blows on my back. I'm in pain and they're giving me injections and tablets.

When they killed my brother, my mother went to work at the house of Don Manuel Pérez Brián, who lived in Calle Larios in Málaga and was director of the Málaga hospital. They put me in a convent of deaf mutes. I cried a lot, thinking about what had happened, and the nuns told me: "Ay, Virtudes, don't cry." I was 10 months with the nuns, in a kitchen for 18 people. I couldn't go on. A woman we knew in Málaga told me about a place looking for a cook where they paid five pesetas more. In the convent they were paying nine *duros* (45 pesetas) a month.

So, for one *duro* more, I went to work with a military doctor, but I got into a row with the other girl working there. In the end I had to come back to Frigiliana because I fell sick. I became depressed, always in black and a black veil on my head. I was 11 years in mourning for my brother. The custom. One also wore mourning for an uncle or other person for a couple of years, or even longer if your mother was obsessive. If you lost a husband, it was for life. My mother was in mourning for her son all her life. Today nobody wears mourning, not for their father or anybody.

I worked for a year-and-a-half for a village family. Then my husband, José Martín Sánchez, was earning enough to marry me. I married at 24 because I couldn't go on living as I was after all that had occurred. When we were engaged, we saw very little of one another. You couldn't be alone with your boyfriend until the day of the wedding. In addition, my husband went off to work in the sugar cane in Motril and Málaga.

My youth was pretty grim. Firstly because my father went off to the Red zone. As a young girl in this village you couldn't do anything. During the time of the guerrillas, nobody went out in the street. We didn't have dances, nor cinema, we had nothing. There were films on Sundays, but we didn't have the six *reales* (about one euro cent) for the cinema. We didn't have fun. We didn't have a radio either, only when I was married.

After the guerrilla war, little by little things improved as the pay was a bit better. My husband has always been a hard worker, on the land, in construction, and we women have been very thrifty. My husband was earning and I knew how to manage. I had a radio and then I bought a television too. And we enjoyed our little children. We'd go to mass, and then into the Casino to take something, and we'd go to the cinema with my little ones. I've got two daughters and two sons.

These days life in the *pueblo* is wonderful. After so much war and other things I've seen, how comfortable we are now. They give each of us a pension. But I'm afraid of how the outside world is now.

I'm Catholic. My father was Communist, but when Holy Week arrived the first to put on his robe was him. Many of the Communists here made use of people and ordered unfortunates to go and steal from the rich: "Take food from Sebastián's house. Go to Federico's place and take whatever he's got in the house." That's the Communism we had here and it was the wretched who paid for it. But my father would hear the church bells and say: "What's going on in church?" And he would go off to see what there was in the church.

Life for women used to be very restricted. It's not that we were frustrated with life, we were disappointed. We lived because we had to. We had no hopes about life, little to look forward to. At that time I didn't know what politics was. I'm neither Communist nor Fascist. Since the Civil Guards killed my brother and his own comrades killed my father, what party do I belong to? None. If I vote for a mayor, it's because the village has to have a mayor. That's all.

Those of the sierra were good people, I don't say they were bad. My husband had relatives there too, good people. They thought they were going to win the war. The innocents! How can you win when you're innocent?

"He didn't come, he didn't come. I was thinking: 'Oh Jesus, he's not coming, oh Jesus!' I went down the street, where Pepe had a bar. 'Pepe, you haven't seen my husband, have you?.'"

Rosario Triviño González (La Pichana), housewife, born in Frigiliana on October 31, 1930, lost her husband in the killings at La Loma de las Vacas.

I've no idea why I have this nickname. They called my mother by it and we're stuck with it. If they call me 'Rosario', I don't respond. But if they call me 'La Pichana', then I reply. In my young days we had nothing to eat. I had two sisters and a brother— now my brother and one sister both live in Barcelona. While my mother used to go off to pick olives, my older sister, who's three years older than me, had to look after us smaller ones.

Rosario Triviño with a picture of her first husband

I only went once to the school. I didn't have a proper dress to wear and I hadn't done my hair. The teacher, an old woman I didn't know, told me: 'Child, you don't come to school like this. You're very dirty. Go and get your mother to comb your hair and dress you.' I told her that my mother wasn't home, she was away working. 'Well, that's it, off with you.' When my mother came home, I told her: 'Mama, the teacher says you should dress me and comb my hair and that she doesn't want me like this in the school.' So she said: 'All right, daughter, don't go again.' And that was it. I never learned to read. I still don't know and I'll die without knowing.

Nobody here knew how to read, so there were no newspapers, nothing. I didn't know anything about politics, nor what a radio was. Why, we didn't even have electricity.

They cut it off because my mother couldn't pay. In the Barribarto (the upper part of the village) there was a fountain where we went to get the water. All we had was a pile of firewood in the street which we sold by the peseta. And little sacks of charcoal. I've sold wood, I've sold palm hearts, I've sold everything.

None of my family was in the sierra. But my father suffered. The corporal, the one known as Cabo Largo ("Big Corporal", of the Civil Guard), called him to the Cuartel (barracks) for no reason at all and gave him a beating. I went to the barracks and saw my father on the ground, covered in blood, and I began to scream. There was a doctor in the Casino bar and I went in search of him. The priest, Don Miguel, came and said no man should be beaten like that. Finally, they brought my father to the house. As soon as he was better, he left for Barcelona. He stayed with my sister there, and my sister's fiancé went to Barcelona too. A lot of people went, because the life here was just beatings and killings.

The house where I live now was my father's. He made a trip back from Barcelona to buy it. Two thousand pesetas it cost him. He was here a few days and he went back to Barcelona because he'd made his life there. He found things better there and he went away. Here it was impossible. Here there was nothing more than the mountains, making charcoal and such things.

There was no bathroom in our house and no water. One night when I was a young girl and I went in the dark to urinate in the stable, somebody called out: 'Rosarico.' It was Miguel Cerezo, who was in the sierra. They'd sent him to steal and he, the little angel, couldn't steal. He was very small and very thin. All he had was a sweet face, a lovely face. He and I were very fond of one another.

'Miguelico, what are you doing here?' I asked, thinking that others (of the guerrilla) were coming. And he said: 'I've come with only one other fellow. They were going to kill me, because I had to go and steal and I don't want to. Some of those in the sierra on guard duty told me: "They're going to kill you tonight. We ourselves are going to kill you. They've already told us to do it."'

He had a bullet wound in the foot, a skin wound, and he was barefoot, just in corduroy breeches. He'd come running from the mountains. So I asked him if they were really going to kill him. 'Yes, they were,' he said. 'The others advised me to run. They said they'd fire some shots but only in the air.' So he and the other youth had escaped.

My mama was sitting in the open. She was a very nervous woman and, when I told her that Miguelico was there, she had an attack of nerves. She went running to my aunt Rosario who lived on Calle Santa Teresa and told her: 'He's here, your Miguel!' Rosario started to cry. She was working for the Plateros so she went and told Ángeles Platero and the family spoke to a brother of Antonio Ruiz, who was an army captain, and he came here with Cabo Largo.

Miguel was lying exhausted, lost to the world, on a bit of mattress on the floor. The big corporal could hardly fit in our house and, when he saw Miguel, he said: 'But he's no more than a stripling.' They took him away. Thanks to the captain, they didn't beat him up or anything. He went away to join the Legion and from there he went to Barcelona. And in Barcelona he got married. He was lucky.

When I got married, I was maybe 15 and my husband had already done his military service. In those days the couples were not like they are now. It was a case of 'Good night', 'Adios', he to his house and you to yours. And no going outside the village like they do now on motorbikes. No dances, nothing. There was a cinema with shows once a week, but I never went. We didn't have a honeymoon or anything like that. Honeymoon? Then there was no such thing. Just getting married and going to bed.

My husband Antonio and I had a son, the one who runs a restaurant now. He wasn't born here but in Málaga. It happened that I went to the river with my mother to do the washing and there was an apricot tree so I climbed it to get some fruit. My mother warned me I could fall but I paid no attention. Up I climbed, I tried to jump and fell. The baby was turned upside down and, when I came home, I felt bad. My husband called the village's medical assistant because there was no doctor here. There was nothing. This was a godforsaken place.

I had to get to the hospital in Málaga, but my husband had no money. He went and talked to the mayor and told him: 'My wife can't have the baby and she is going to die. I've no money to take her to Málaga. Let the Ayuntamiento (town hall) pay for the car.' But the mayor said the town hall had no money. At that my husband told him: 'Then you better look for some because, if my wife dies, I'm going to break out and thump somebody and go off to the sierra.' At that, the mayor arranged for a car, though with bad grace, and I went to Málaga, sitting up for more than two hours along a terrible road.

After my marriage I went to live with my mother-in-law. She had land, she had wine, grapes, rabbits. But the wedding itself was a bad affair because of what happened with Rosario la Caída, my husband's sister. I knew Rosario when her brother was courting me but we weren't particular friends. She had lost her own husband. The Civil Guard took him away and killed him. At the wedding, when the godfathers and everybody came out of the church, my mother-in-law said: 'Let's go and fry up potatoes with rabbit and have wine and raisins.'

We were having refreshments in my mother-in-law's house when Rosario started crying and shrieking. 'What are you crying for?' asked my Antonio. There was a picture in the house of Jesus with a lot of saints and Rosario knelt down before it and cried: 'Lord, Lord, I ask you to see yourself like my husband.' She was sobbing and uttering terrible screams. Then she told Antonio that she was seeing him just like her own husband, killed and dragged about.

And that's just what happened to my husband. They killed him and dragged him about and I was left with a baby of eight months. Three young men of the village, one aged 26, another 18 and my husband who was 22, were called to report to the Civil Guard. Antonio hadn't done anything. He came home from work, from digging with Manuel Díaz, he who lives opposite the priest's house, and he was told to go to the barracks. It was something to do with the brother he had in the sierra, Ángel, Zumbo by nickname.

Our baby boy was already talking, saying to his father: 'Pa, pa, pa.' Antonio said: 'Ay, my boy's calling me.' And he squeezed him and kissed him and said: 'I'm going to report.' I asked him if he wanted to eat and he said: 'I'm hungry, but not now. When I come back.' As I didn't eat until he used to come home, I waited, and waited, and waited…

And he didn't come, he didn't come. I was thinking: 'Oh Jesus, he's not coming, oh Jesus!' I went down the street, down Zacatín where Pepe los Almendros had a bar. 'Pepe, you haven't seen my husband, have you?' He said: 'No.' So I went to the barber's and asked. 'No,' he said. Then I went to the barracks, which I had never in my life entered. There was a Civil Guard there and I asked him: 'Please, señor. Has Antonio García Martín been by here?' 'Nobody's been here. Get out of here.' So I came home. I was very afraid. My mother was there with the baby in her arms and I told her: 'Ay, mama, he's lost, he's lost. But how can he be lost in the village?' 'What a shame!' she said, and began to weep, and so did I.

They backed a covered vehicle into the Cuartel and put the three in it and took them to the Molineta (a group of houses below the village), where Paco López had an olive mill. They put them in there and there they were for three days, three days in that mill. The next morning I left the baby with my mother and, with Antonia, the mother of the youngest of the three, and my cousin Sagrario, I went down to the Molineta. We took a route so that the guards wouldn't see us. We didn't find anybody but we thought: 'They must have them locked up near here because there are guards at the door of that mill.'

The next morning very early, Antonia and I went down below the village again and all along the road there was a stream of blood. 'Antonia!' I yelled. 'Blood! Blood!' She said: 'It must be a dog's.' We continued down the road then came back up and in the Calvario (the main street entering the village) we came across a young girl. She was not very bright, but she knew plenty. She cried: 'What a shame! What a shame! Ay, ay, they've killed Antonio Matutero…' who was my cousin 'and the son of Antonia la Poeta. The other boy I don't know him.' Then I said: 'The other lad was my husband. Antonia, listen to what she says. They've killed them.' Antonia collapsed on the ground. And my mother-in-law came along, in her underclothes, weeping.

They took them to the cemetery, but they didn't let the women see them because we get so emotional. They let through my uncle Matutero who saw his son and took his head in his lap. The Moorish soldiers were guarding the cemetery entrance. They would hit people with their guns — they were the ones who hit out most at that time. So I never even saw my husband's body. From the moment he went out of our door, I never saw him again.

They didn't take him to the church for the funeral. Instead, they put them all in coffins in the cemetery and there they buried them. At that time, when somebody died, the priest in his robes used to come and say the Lord's Prayer in front of the barracks entrance. So they said the prayers that had to be said and took the bodies to the cemetery. Many people went to the funeral. Afterwards, the Civil Guard called some (the richer villagers) to the barracks and gave them a beating because they said 'you're to blame for these deaths and now you go to the funeral to placate the families'.

After that, I left my mother-in-law's and went back to the warmth of my mother. Because my mother-in-law wasn't very affectionate. She wasn't a very good person, the poor thing. Left a widow, I had to go to work. I took the road to the countryside and to Nerja. I brought onions, tomatoes, potatoes and sold them in the street. Two days after my husband's death I went to Rosendo who had potatoes growing in the fields at Santo Cristo. 'Give me two *arrobas* (about 23 kilos) of potatoes,' I begged him. 'When I've sold them, I'll pay you. Then I can buy some milk for my baby.' Because I didn't have the milk to breast-feed him. Rosendo gave me two *arrobas* and I sold them in the streets and thus I earned something to buy milk for the baby and a little bread to eat. A disaster, a disaster! Hunger. And what folk have today! How they raise kids now!

I went to Barcelona, a widow, with my baby. I can't say what year it was. It was a long time ago because my boy Antonio was only a year or so old and now he's 54. My father was doing very badly in Barcelona too because there was no work. I went to work in a factory handling secondhand clothing, a bad job. To avoid paying social security, I was on the payroll as a young girl rather than as a widow. The only day off was Sunday, when I could see my baby who was with my sister.

I was five or six months in Barcelona. It was awful. We were starving there. My baby had diarrhoea and I said: 'He's going to die here. I'm going back to my mother.' My mother was still in the village and said she had no money. So I decided to return. My father took me to the quay in the Barcelona port and I came back as a stowaway with my son, my sister and brother. A cousin also came. He had enough cash to pay his fare and he brought my trunk. We got aboard in mid-afternoon, climbing over the side. Enough to frighten you to death! My father and another man shoved me over, then my brother climbed up and then my little boy, each one pushing and shoving the other. If nobody killed himself it was only because God didn't want it.

It took many days for the boat to reach Málaga. After we'd gone a day without eating, I had to ask the captain for help. I didn't tell him that I'd stowed away. I said I was a widow, there was no work and my father didn't have any money to feed me, and I had a little boy and a sister. The captain replied: 'Why didn't you speak up before? I would have given your baby some milk and food for you and the family.' In that way they gave us food until we reached Málaga. I slept where I could. Nobody knew I was a stowaway. If they had, they would have tossed me out, who knows where?

For at least two days we were far out to sea and it was very rough. The ship was shifting about a lot and I heard the older folk saying: 'This is bad. Where will it end?' I didn't understand anything of all that. I was like a hen dumped at a farm. I had no idea what it was all about.

Finally we reached Málaga and disembarked, but we had no money to get to Frigiliana. Luckily we saw Eugenio with the van belonging to the Ingenio and we asked him for a lift. He was not supposed to carry people in the van or he would be denounced, but he said: 'Get inside and keep down so nobody can see you.' We slipped into the back and crouched down all the way to Frigiliana, I, my sister, my brother and the cousin. And my baby boy whom I carried in my lap.

Later, I married again. What year it was I couldn't tell you but Don Domingo was the priest and my daughter who lives in Nerja is 45 or 46. Altogether I've had five children, but one, a girl, died. My father and one sister died in Barcelona, but I still have there another sister, and a brother, five nephews and a niece. Only two of us have stayed in Frigiliana, I and one sister.

For me the life was bad here and in Barcelona too it was bad. Now is when everything is all right. The world has changed a lot in every way and for everybody. But before…

"My mother remarked once that Roberto could be an infiltrator. Everybody suspected he was an infiltrator."

Antonio Martín Ruiz, builder, born in Frigiliana on October 28, 1946. His brother was killed at La Loma de las Vacas and his father by his comrades in the sierra.

We were a very humble family of farmworkers. At the time of the Civil War my father was a Republican and he went off to fight in the Republican army, leaving my mother and two children here. When the war ended, they put him in prison, for three or four years, for being a Republican.

I was born in 1946, after my father came out of prison, and I'd be a year or so old when he went away to the sierra in 1947. There was a commander here called Cabo Largo who through beatings forced all those Republicans who came out of jail to go to the sierra as guerrillas. Over the course of three days he gave my father 12 beatings, saying: "If you haven't gone by midday, come back here." So my father was obliged to join the guerrillas. Two of his brothers, José el Panzón and Blas, went to the sierra before him.

Cabo Largo did business with the people of the sierra. A Frigiliana man took food to them which was bought by Cabo Largo, so that he knew where they were going next morning and the Civil Guard could go the opposite way and the two wouldn't meet. The corporal did it to make money. That's why it suited him to force into the sierra all those coming out of prison, to make more. The guerrillas paid very well for the loads of food delivered to them.

Later Lieutenant Reyna came to Nerja and apparently he had orders to get rid of the people of the sierra at all cost. And how he got rid of them: picking up three young relatives of those in the sierra. The Civil Guard detained my brother aged 18, and two others. They arrested them in the evening and held them in the barracks and then they took them to the Molineta. And the next day they killed them. One was brought back dead on a donkey.

What the Franco regime made us suffer! Yet there are people who today are rightwing militants when their parents suffered so many calamities but told their children almost nothing about it. That takes some beating.

They killed my brother in 1950. He was already a man of 18 and I just a kid and he did what you do with little kids, joking with me. He loved me so much. I remember very well all the commotion surrounding those deaths as I lived on the Cuesta del Apero (near the barracks). Imagine how bad the Civil Guard were.

My father learned about this in the sierra and, feeling himself to blame, went a bit out of his mind and wanted to give himself up. But some of his comrades, fearing that he would talk too much, grabbed him and threw him over a cliff in the sierra of Nerja and killed him. My mother told me: "Your uncle José was there but he went up the mountain so he wouldn't see him fall over the cliff." José was in prison for many years and, when he came out, which was the only time I saw him, the one thing I asked him was: why did he get out of the way when his brother fell. He denied doing it. He said it wasn't true.

My mother, who died in 1997, bore all this very badly. The poor woman had a cruel life. We had some very disagreeable times. My brother was interred in a very high niche and my mother couldn't climb the ladder to look after the niche, so we bought a lower one so she could tend it properly on All Saints' Day. I don't want to harbour resentment against anybody but I can't help it. All that left a deep mark. When I was 17 or 18, I thought the feeling would go away as I grew older, but it hasn't. If anything, I think it's more accentuated.

Here's an example of what happened in Frigiliana. I don't know if the Civil War had started or was about to start. Sebastián "Lucrecia", who was secretary of the Communist Party in the village, was in bed with Malta fever. Three or four Republicans came from Málaga to take some *señoritos* "for a little walk". That meant to kill them. His mother told Sebastián that four strangers were going for Don Victor. The fellow got out of bed and he found the strangers already heading along the main street to take away the *señoritos*. He confronted them, saying that they were not taking anybody from here, until he convinced them and they left.

But then look what happened. The Nationalists came in here and these same *señoritos* and a few others put on Civil Guard uniforms and killed Sebastián and seven more in the Torrox cemetery. They blindfolded them all but he said: "You may be dressed as Civil Guards but I know you. You're Don Fulano and you are so-and-so… You can shoot me but I can see you." In these cases there's always somebody who hears and within a few days it was known in Frigiliana. Imagine it: that fellow got out of bed to save their lives, then they did for him.

I only went to school for three years, from nine to 12. I learned plenty as I wasn't dull, but it was almost impossible then for those of a poor family to continue their studies. And, for a person related to people who had been in the Republic, it was impossible to enter a government school because the government was Franco, nor could they enter the administration, nor the Civil Guard, nor the town hall, nor the national police.

So I went to work on the land. From 12 to 15 I was on the farm then I got into building. I started as a labourer and now I'm with a good firm as site manager in public works. I've educated my children for careers, paid by me. One has become an engineer, another has a degree in English philology and the other is doing his doctoral thesis in biology. All thanks to effort and work. Nobody has given them anything.

Everything about my family my children know and it's good that they do, so that they know from where they came. If one doesn't explain to them what their father went through, they'll think life has smiled on them in a certain way because that's the way things are.

As for Roberto, I understand that the Franco regime inserted him in the sierra and kept him there making contacts. Roberto wasn't always with the guerrillas. Some days he was elsewhere. It's suspected that he was compiling information to get rid of the people of the sierra later. Afterwards, nobody knew what happened to him. He disappeared from one day to the next. My mother remarked once that Roberto could be an infiltrator. Everybody suspected he was an infiltrator.

"I'll never forget what happened to my father. Not being able to see him, to embrace him. That will stay with me as long as I live. It's the one thing that I miss."

Antonia Triviño Martín, housewife, born in Frigiliana on May 18, 1950, a few weeks after the death of her father, Antonio Triviño Cerezo, one of three young men killed by the Civil Guard.

They killed my father on April 22, 1950, and I was born on May 18. I'll never forget what happened to my father. Not being able to see him, to embrace him. That will stay with me as long as I live. It's the one thing that I miss. People tell me about him. They say he was very good, very loving, very sociable... But I miss him. I miss never having seen him, touched him, embraced him, that he took me in his arms...I don't know, what everybody has. It's the only thing I want: what everybody has.

My mother was left at the age of 21 with a daughter to look after. The only way was by going out to work. She went first to Málaga and from Málaga to Barcelona, while my grandmother stayed with me in the village. My two grandmothers raised me, Dolores la de Andrés and Virtudes.

Of the 1950s in Frigiliana I have some very bad memories. Not one good one. Because the Civil Guard was visiting my grandmother's house all the time. We would be sleeping and, as a kid of two or three, I remember the guards coming at midnight. They knocked at the door and hit it and wrenched it open, looking for my grandfather. How was he going to be in the house? It was impossible. I was in shock. That was no life.

When my mother married the second time, when I was 11, I had to go to Barcelona. When my grandfather José (José Martín Navas, nom de guerre Tomás) came out of prison in 1964, I was 14. He came to live with my parents. He was a very straight man, rebellious and quick-tempered. He talked with us a lot. Often

I didn't want to hear him, but there was no choice but to listen.

When I have more contact with any person, I have more feeling for them. But I knew nothing about my grandfather and he frightened me, put me in a panic. He was mad about my grandmother, but she didn't get on very well with him. She was a very serious, very strict woman, a very difficult woman. She raised me and was always telling me, I'll always remember: "When your grandfather comes out of jail, he'll come to kill me, to kill me." She didn't want to have anything to do with him. In her view he went to prison and got involved in politics when he didn't need to because they had land and possessions. Of course, my grandmother was also somebody you didn't mess with. She was a very strong woman. She and her husband were different types. In those days no man carried clothes to the wash place for a woman, but he did. And he picked up the little children and gave them the feeding bottle. He couldn't have been so bad, could he?

José knew Roberto and many other people during the war when he was fighting in the Republican army, according to what he told me. He knew the sierra because he was up there before they put him in prison the first time. He wasn't in prison long and afterwards he hit a Civil Guard and went to the sierra. Roberto was virtually waiting for him. Apparently they had already talked. There was an understanding between them, a very strong, intimate cooperation.

We, my mother and my grandmother — may she rest in peace — could have been millionaires, because Roberto gave a lot of money. He said to José: "This is so your family isn't in need and doesn't have to work, so your family can stay home." But he gave it to relatives and the relatives didn't give a *duro* to my mother and grandmother. They kept it and afterwards you could see who had the money, who had bought land and built houses.

Many have benefited thanks to José and some others. Also Frigiliana, Cómpeta and the surrounding area gained a lot through José and his connection with Roberto. He saved the lives of a great deal of people. He was sentenced to death three times but in the end they didn't kill him. And he had three sentences of 30 years but he got out of prison much sooner. I understand that he saved the lives of people in the village, of the de la Torre family, by talking to Roberto and at his court-martial the Bishop of Málaga interceded on his behalf.

It was when I asked for documents that I learned all this. Otherwise, I didn't know whether to believe the story of my grandfather or not. It was like another world for me. It didn't fit in my head. I couldn't assimilate all that he told me.

He said that he intervened many times to prevent people being killed in these villages. And it's recorded in the documents. One of the papers shows that, during the time José María Martín Navas was in Cómpeta, there was no bloodletting at all. And the same here. In Frigiliana they wanted to kill all the rich, but José got in the way and none of the rich was touched.

In Barcelona José continued to believe in Communism. All he would say was: "I don't want to like anything which smells of the Right. Because they're all rogues. Not one can be saved." I would tell him: "Papa, you don't want anything to do with the Right, but you saved the lives of many in the village and gave bread to many people." People who would have died of hunger because at that time (in the Civil War) it was forbidden to take them any food, but he slipped bread and scraps of meat beneath their doors.

He wasn't a bloodthirsty man. He wasn't a murderer, killing for the sake of killing. I have investigated and he wasn't, although there were many who were. It's not because he was my grandfather. Everybody spoke well of him. Having breakfast one morning in a bar, I heard a fellow named Tomás. He said his sister owed her life to him. He struck one of his companions and killed him because he was trying to rape a girl. He hit him with a stone, smashed his head and left him there on the ground.

Roberto had a lot of confidence in my grandfather. He'd been in half the country with Roberto, in Madrid, the Basque country, Pontevedra. They were a few months in Galicia. They were checking on people and working with them in the guerrilla. My grandfather, and I believe one other from Granada province, went all over Spain with Roberto.

Because Roberto was lame, he acted as his horse. Many times José carried Roberto on his back, over the mountains, along tracks where not even horses or mules could go. Roberto suffered a paralysis in one leg — the right one I think — and it was much shorter than the other. Because of this he wore a large boot which my grandfather fixed up many times when it broke and he risked his life to find a shoemaker to repair it for him. Roberto always carried a concealed weapon. His boot had a big platform sole and one time, when José was fixing up his boot, it moved. There was a hollow in the boot and a pistol in it.

Roberto was a womanizer, but that's a male thing. All virile men like women. He had various women. One was called Dolores, from the Venta Panaderos. But the last one was the one that went to his head. She was La Tangerina, whom they picked up in Madrid.

Roberto was a tough guy. He had some education. According to my grandfather, he was reliable and straight, but when there was any sort of dispute he became very aggressive.

He didn't trust anybody to cook his food, except José. José had to prepare all his meals, because he was afraid they'd poison him. José tasted the food first and he also didn't touch food prepared by others. He preferred to eat a boiled or fried potato or anything rather than eat something served by others, and the same with Roberto. Roberto always wanted coffee. He drank coffee made with barley, all there was at that time, and José made it.

Roberto was very attached to José. They were a pair. But that didn't make any difference when he switched over and betrayed them all and delivered them up. My grandfather was the last to fall. He fell because he was pigheaded. He didn't want to leave anybody behind. Roberto told him: "José, at a certain time on a certain day, disappear. A boat will be waiting for you at so-and-so. Don't go where the others go but to a different spot." But my grandad wouldn't do it. He fell in the trap with the others, the last ones. He didn't want to defraud his people. He didn't want to leave them behind.

José understood Roberto and his betrayal perfectly. From my point of view, Roberto abandoned all his people. He trapped them one by one. But José found a justification for everything. I told him that he had been a traitor, that he had sold out his cause, and he told that he had to do it and he did it. I told him: "But, papa, give me an explanation that I can understand. How do you justify this man, if what he did was sell you out and sell out all his people." He would reply: "They picked up that man in Madrid, then they beat the hell out of him and he had no choice but to talk."

My grandfather explained that they had picked up his lover, to whom Roberto was very attached. They began to ill-treat her and beat her and through her they succeeded in making him talk. José continued to justify the deal Roberto made with the Civil Guard. I could not accept it, but he did. When he was in prison, he had fought with people who went against Roberto. He defended him up to the last moment. If I said anything against him, he became angry with me and wouldn't speak to me. He didn't speak to me for weeks on end. He told me: "Nobody knows what I have been for him and what he has been for me. Nobody."

He had a lot of respect for Roberto because he said if they had not given Roberto away he would have changed Spain. The leaders of the party in France and Russia betrayed Roberto. From time to time people visited and José met them. They spoke broken Spanish and, what with badly spoken Spanish and worse spoken Andalusian, they hardly understood one another. But he knew almost all of them and spoke with them. In a train right in the Atocha station in Madrid, there was a meeting with various high-ups where they were hatching something to do with Roberto and the Party.

José Martín Navas (centre) pictured in prison

They didn't see themselves as outlaws but as warriors. They were in a war to overturn the government and they believed in it until the last moment. José stuck rigorously to the cause. He didn't even come to see his family. All of them used to get away from time to time, but not him.

They say that in 1948 the Party decided to remove the people from the sierra. Roberto continued with the Party and my grandfather continued with Roberto because he did so. José said that there was hope here because the men were tough and they could have some success in part of Andalusia. The fact is that it was not so. But Roberto didn't give up and for that reason my grandfather had such love for the man. That man continued inspiring courage in us, the Andalusians, to see if something could be achieved in Andalusia. Because Andalusia is very big with many men and some good could have been gained here. But the people aren't united in this zone. If only Andalusia had risen up, it would have been sufficient, but it did not.

If I said anything against Roberto, José would hit me. He said: "You don't know what you're talking about. He died for us. They picked me up in 1951 and in 1948 the Party had already cut off Roberto, but he still went ahead to see if something more could be achieved." The Party gave up but not Roberto. You could not tell José that Roberto was a traitor. There was no way he would accept it.

The Party was the traitor, according to him, because it left them by the way. After so many years and so many sacrifices, so much suffering and illness, so many deaths, so much lack of food and everything, the Party turned its back on them all as if it didn't know them. José could not accept that.

José had killed people but there was no record of it. Actually, after coming out of prison, he tried to kill Vicente El Artabús (Vicente Martín Vozmediano). He went in seach of him and Vicente ran off and hid. He was a traitor and a murderer; he had killed José's brother, Sebastián. Sebastián had been desperate because they (the Civil Guard) killed his son (Manuel Martín Ruiz, who died with Antonia's father and Antonio García Martín at La Loma de las Vacas). He didn't want to eat. All the man wanted to do was die. Nobody touched him because he was José's brother. But Vicente gave him a push when he was on a clifftop and threw him over. All those present saw him do it.

When José heard about it, he went crazy and went looking everywhere for Vicente but he had gone to ground. When José was released from prison and came to live with us in Barcelona, he could not rest. He'd learned in prison where Vicente lived and went in search of him. He was going to kill him with his bare hands because he didn't have a knife or anything. He was a very strong man, short and stocky. I went with José to the area where Vicente was living. If he caught him there, he was going to kill him.

Vicente went everywhere in disguise. He wore a hat and a raincoat. He grew a

Antonia's father, killed at la Loma de las Vacas

moustache, wore a false beard. But, of course, people knew who he was. He didn't live in a community but instead he built a shack away from the rest and on a high point so he could see anybody coming. He was wicked, with his family, the daughters, with everybody. He was a very bad person.

We went into a bar. Vicente was there and, as soon as my grandfather saw him, he recognised him. He picked up a siphon, one of those with the bottle covered in metal so it won't break. He grabbed it from the counter and threw it at Vicente. It hurt him and he tried to run away. The railway passed right next to the bar. He ran across the track. Just then a train came by. I thought my grandfather was going to be killed by the train because he threw himself beneath it. My gosh! I was stunned. I thought: it's crushed him. As it did not have many carriages, the train went past quickly but he couldn't wait. He threw himself down and emerged the other side. He must have done it many times because he escaped unharmed.

Everybody was shrieking when he threw himself down. There was a real hubbub. Some of the folk there were from the the village so they knew the history and what it was all about. So they thought it fair that José should grab that man to get rid of him. Vicente was bleeding. You could see the blood from a wound on his head. Following the bloodstains, my father tried to find him. But he lost track of him. If he'd caught him, he would have killed him and then he would have gone to jail again. Because he was on probation and he'd only come out of prison less than a week before. He didn't end up back there because the police didn't turn up.

Some years ago I tried to ascertain exactly what happened to my father and I'm going to continue moving heaven and earth any way I can. In fact, they are already identifying those who died (during the Franco regime). They were crimes that they committed. What they did with my father, with Manolo and Antonio, it was a crime, picking them up and killing them. And who pays for it? What I have lost nobody can pay back. I don't want money. The only thing that I wanted was to have him. Like the son of the other victim, who was only eight or nine months old, but at least he was taken in his father's arms, he touched him. But I wasn't able to touch him. I'm trying to, because they say that if you take part in a spiritualism session you may be able to touch somebody. I don't know if it's true or not. I don't know. But I'm ready to try anything so that I can touch him.

"The heavy repression of the Maquis was totally unjust. I tell you, 50 per cent of those who fled to the mountains did so because of the Guardia Civil."

Manuel Prieto López, born October 19, 1919. In the Blue Division served alongside the Germans in World War Two. In the Civil Guard took part in the anti-guerrilla struggle, retiring with the rank of general in 1980.

In the end, the Communist Party abandoned the guerrillas. I've talked with Santiago Carrillo many times and he said he had favoured halting the guerrilla campaign and that Stalin said it was finished. By 1949 they were left with nothing.

What is astonishing is that the members of the Maquis were all Communists. There was nobody from the Socialist Workers' Party and very few anarchists. I viewed the people of the sierra as *bandoleros* (bandits). There were eight or nine Maquis or guerrillas and the others were people who had fled from the beatings dealt out by the Civil Guard. Were they fighting against Fascism and Franco? Ha! Ha! Roberto was. He was a real political type and so were his high command, seven or eight of them. But the others. no.

I served for several years in the infantry and I was in the Blue Division (which fought with the Germans on the Russian front). Then, in 1945, I joined the Civil Guard. I was in Granada for a while with the rank of lieutenant. I was promoted to captain and then they told me to go to Málaga to deal with outlaws there. While I was based at Torrox, I was sleeping peacefully when at three one morning there came a bang on the door. A guard told me: "There are bandits coming."

"Bandits here? Bugger me!"

So up I get and there's Vicente come to surrender. He has with him the pamphlet in which I promised to put over the frontier into Gibraltar anybody who offered information. I tell him: "You're going to come with us to show us all the places where they gave you supplies. Come on, we're going to Frigiliana."

Off we go with a sergeant, two guards and a driver in a Land-Rover. Then this fellow tells me: "Captain, I would like to screw my wife." "Screw your woman? Well, ok." We have to get on good terms with this man. So a guard goes to look for his wife and tells her that her brother is outside. She comes along with their little baby girl and this fellow fucks his wife in the ditch. Afterwards, when the woman had left with the girl, I asked him: "But what did you do with the little one?" And he said: "I put her on top of my cart that was there."

When I was in Granada, on April 14, 1946, somebody put a Republican flag and propaganda in a patio there. We began to investigate. People were saying: "I've seen a Communist! A Communist! A Communist!" A lot of nonsense. Then I received a letter from somebody calling himself Carlos which said: "Lieutenant colonel, you have made a mistake. If you want me to tell you the truth, put the following advertisement in the newspaper…"

I placed the advert. As a result, I received many letters from him in which he told me: "Here you can pick up one of them, here another."

Later a Civil Guard colonel was going to review the forces in Almería and passed by Gergal. Near there, the guards picked up a suspicious individual and it turned out to be Tarbes (José Luis Merediz Víctores, chief of the guerrillas in Granada). When Tarbes realised that the guards had found his technical manual for the guerrillas, written in longhand, he feared for his life, so he said to the colonel: "Wait, wait. I want to talk to Lieutenant Prieto." They called me and he said: "I'm Carlos." "Good god!" I said. "Carlos, who's been sending me letters."

I treated him well, meals and everything, and we went looking for "Ramiro". Ramiro was the nickname of Ricardo Beneyto Sapeña, chief of general staff for the Guerrilla Army of Andalusia. He had a double identity. For banditry he called himself Ramiro. For labour affairs he was Argüelles. We went to Seville, we went to Madrid, wherever it was necessary.

Then I told Tarbes: "Now let's wrap this up. You're going to escape back to the guerrillas. Go with a guard on a motorbike with a sidecar and…" So the fellow throws himself down a gully, the Barranco del Ahogado (Drowned Man's Gully), and the guards let fly, bang, bang, bang.

But his comrades caught him out. It was bad luck. Ramiro says to him: "What time is it? But where did you hurt yourself? And you didn't break your watch? Very strange. Very strange."

Tarbes explained how he had escaped and tumbled down, but if you fall on your arm or side it's unlikely that your watch suffers no harm. For this reason they didn't believe him and they executed him. I lost a magnificent informer, and a raincoat which I let him take with him.

Argüelles was arrested in Seville (for organising illegal trade unions). I had him three days in the Albaicín barracks in Granada. I knew that Ramiro was two metres tall and had a set of false teeth. Either the upper set or the lower was of steel. Also I knew he was well-spoken. But the fellow told me: "You know who I am. But you can't prove it."

So it was, until Roberto revealed: "Ramiro is so-and-so and in that place. He's the one detained as Argüelles." Roberto was trying to save himself by giving Ramiro away. He informed on the others to save himself. I know that he was eight or nine months under arrest telling all. So they shot Beneyto Sapeña and later Roberto. Roberto deserved to die because he had killed many people.

I've seen many who were killed by the outlaws. They put something around their necks and dragged them along at a run, pulling them for 200 to 300 metres until they died strangled. I saw one who was just a youngster, a poor little fellow who was born in Agrón (Granada). He didn't betray anybody, but he was unlucky to be in a farmhouse where the outlaws visited.

The heavy repression of the Maquis was totally unjust. I tell you, 50 per cent of those who fled to the mountains did so because of the Guardia Civil. It provoked them to run away in terror. In Agrón, for example, the whole village went off and those who stayed were put in prison. They sent me there and the first thing I did was release those who were in prison. I said to them: "I don't know why you're here." Nobody was left in the village. The poor devils had run away because they said they'd been beaten again and again.

When Fernández Vitorio, a governor who had been a captain in the Blue Division in Russia, came to Granada, the guards put up a list to record the outlaws killed, one, two, three, four, five, six... "How many?" "Twenty." "How many?" "Thirty." And they put 200 more. I said nothing, but to myself I said: "This is ridiculous." Because there were more deaths claimed than there were outlaws. The governor went along with it. It was a hunting party. They killed indiscriminately… All those bandits were killed applying the Ley de Fugas (i.e. shot while trying to escape).

For denouncing all this, I was nearly expelled. I reported these things about my immediate superiors in writing to the Civil Guard chief. They were going to kick me out of the force. Adiós. But then Don Camilo (Alonso Vega, the Director General of the Guardia Civil), behaved well because he investigated and he agreed that I was in the right.

On one occasion the *bandoleros* killed a squad of soldiers in the Sierra de Cázulas (near Almuñécar, Granada). They had stationed them there because there was a sawmill owned by a family whose eldest member was a general. There were soldiers with three machineguns and a rifle and the bandits killed

15 and took away the machineguns and the cartridge belts (note: according to official files, eight were killed and five injured).

At that, a general told me when we were here in Granada in the Hotel Victoria: "That's it. Every day I'm messed about in some way or other by those outlaws. You go to Almuñécar and kill 10. You have four or five days to do it." I told him: "Yes, sir." But nobody could accept that and later I went to the general and told him that a boatful of outlaws from Oran was about to arrive on the Granada coast. So he ordered me to go there to await the boat, a boat which never arrived. But the slaughter occurred all the same. Others did it, not me. Between Motril and Calahonda there was a barracks and they put nine in there and killed them.

I killed nine outlaws, well, not me personally. Rather, I gave orders: "Do this, do this." That's what I did. The only one I had a brush with was Ramiro Fuentes Ochoa, who with Tarbes edited the paper *Por la República* (For the Republic), when I arrested him in Granada.*

**Prieto shot Fuentes Ochoa four times when he tried to escape from a house in Granada. Accused of being a guerrilla leader, Fuentes spent 17 years in prison. A report by the Civil Guard's Granada headquarters stated that Prieto López "succeeded in arresting 51 members of an organisation of the Socorro Rojo (Red Help)." It continued: "He discovered the meeting place of the Andalusian Guerrilla Army's high command, detaining the political commissar. He obtained the arrest of 'Pancho Villa', responsible for more than 40 murders in Motril. Passing himself off as a captain of the Red Army, he managed to make personal contact with several go-betweens... For services rendered: awarded the Cross of Military Merit."*

Note: General Prieto handed to the author a written statement about *"bandolerismo"*: "As is logical, I don't claim to be in possession of the truth, but I am convinced that to date I know of no method to finish with a similar problem as efficient as that which was employed at that time. At the start of the 1960s, when the '*guerrilla*' won in Algeria and Cuba, I felt Spain was the only place where it hadn't triumphed and was proud to have played a part, in the small role that corresponds to a lieutenant and captain. I believe that the operating system was good and appropriate, for you only have to look at the results, and it could be a model to follow in similar circumstances in the future."

"In winter I would sometimes open the doors and find a metre of snow outside. Then I had to round up all the goats and bring them home."

Federico Sánchez Álvarez (El Molinero — The Miller), goatherd, born in Frigiliana on July 18, 1938, lived for a time at the Venta Panaderos.

My nickname comes from my great-grandfather who had a flour mill by the road at the Molineta, below the village. There were nine children in my family, but one of the four boys died. We grew up on the land and with the goats. Thank God, in my house we had food every day, so I couldn't say we were ever in need.

My grandfather, Federico Sánchez Villasclaras, was a muleteer for a long time. Every night he used to load up two mules with fish in Nerja and take them to Granada by night. At six or seven in the evening he would pass by Frigiliana and at dawn he was in Granada, the provincial capital. They called the fastest muleteers, those who really moved, the "corsos".

They would load each mule, if it was a good one, with 10 to 12 *arrobas* of fish (120-138 kilos). There were no roads then, no cars, nothing. Afterwards he said he'd ruined himself and worn out 18 mules on that route. He would go almost at a run, behind the mule. Some mules fell, others gave up, others were injured, and the legs of some collapsed from so much work.

I've been going to the sierra since I was a little kid with hardly a day in school. For a short time I had a go at the "blackboards" but I learned nothing. I don't know how to write. I can only sign my name, but badly. Why should I tell you anything else? My father didn't know how to write either. Later he learned the lottery numbers, that's what he knew. I know the numbers too, the same as my father.

As a kid I was cutting some meat when the knife slipped and hit my eye. My eyeball protruded a bit and later they removed it. Today they could do something but then there were no facilities. I've done a lot of work using just one eye and

I've never needed the other. Now that I'm getting older my sight isn't so good, but before I could see the goats on the highest peaks.

When I was a youngster all these mountains were full of the people of the sierra — they called them bandits — but I never saw or spoke with them. We had no contact with them. The Civil Guards didn't hassle me or take me to prison, nor my father. There were good folk among those who went to the sierra. People used to take food to them and one night, when seven or eight were carrying food near the Lízar reservoir, the Moorish soldiers were there. They threw a bomb. It killed one fellow from the village and the others had to run off to the sierra.

My father couldn't take out the goats so I went, as I was a child. I never saw the people of the sierra — they kept out of the way. But I did see where they passed and where they stopped. Only once did I come across them. I was coming down the river and there was a man filling a pitcher with water. To avoid confronting him, I turned my back. The goats were coming down along the river and I began to yell at them and, when I turned my head, he was gone. The Civil Guards asked me if I had seen any of them on the Fuerte mountain, and where were they, but I never saw them when I was up there.

One night I was at the entrance to the Casino bar and three men with leather jackets came running past. Another lad who was with me said: "Those are people of the sierra! Those are people of the sierra!" It was the night they shot at Justo and Paco López in their house. They tried to kidnap Justo but he jumped out of a window and they ran off. They did take some of my goats, four in one year. They caught one, killed it and ate it. And a bit later another. But after that they didn't harm me.

My father bumped into them two or three times. Once they were at the Fuente del Esparto when he went there to buy some goats. He was wearing a big fur-lined jacket and one of them said to him: "Federico, sell me that jacket." He took it off, saying: "How can I sell it you if you need it?" He was so nervous that he didn't take out his identity card which was in the jacket.

There was a sergeant here who was a friend of my father so he explained to him what had happened. Said the sergeant: "Bloody hell! Now you've got yourself in a mess!" In the end they made him a new card. A long time afterwards my father met that fellow of the sierra and said: "I gave you the jacket and you didn't send me back the card." "I did," he said, "in an envelope with no address on it." That's the only incident we had with the people of the sierra.

The Civil Guard told my father he couldn't go out to the sierra with the goats or they would kill him. "If you go out there every day, you must be with the people of the sierra," they told him. So I went with the goats, because they needed to eat. When I was coming down from the mountains, my father would come and help me, but he himself didn't go to the sierra.

I started going with the goats at about 10 years old. One day I was up above

Lízar when Corporal Trigo, who was very friendly with me, said: "Federico, we're going to fall out with you because you see the people of the sierra and you don't tell us." I told him that I never saw them. "You were up on El Fuerte the other day with them." It was a lie. There was nobody with me. He asked: "When are you going to El Fuerte again?" "In a couple of days," I said. And he said: "Then take a bit of rope because we're going to hang you from a pine." It was so that I didn't go there. But they didn't say any more to me or do anything to me. I've always got on well with the Civil Guard.

Paco Manuela's family lived at the Venta Panaderos, six children and the parents. Those folk went through a lot what with the guards and the people of the sierra. It was a bad time to be there and they had plenty of problems. One lot would come, then the others, and then the others again. What could they do? The guards came to see if the people of the sierra had been there. And they couldn't deny it.

Dolores, one of the four daughters, was Roberto's lover, from what they say. Later they picked up Roberto and put her in prison. After that she married a goatherd from Jayena and they went to Barcelona.

In the 1950s they sold the Venta Panaderos to my father for about 8,000 *duros* (40,000 pesetas). It was already in a bad state. There were four rooms, a kitchen, two bedrooms and a small room. It needed a lot of work to keep up that place because we grew runner beans, potatoes and the rest. We bought the land for the goats because they got rid of the goats from these mountains and made it a hunting area. We had a herd of 200 which roamed on the land around the inn and in the sierra of Cómpeta. But only in winter, as in summer they were in the Sierra Nevada.

We only lived at the inn three or four years but we owned it for another 15 or 16 when we lived in Frigiliana. There was timber all around and we carried down tree trunks, firewood, charcoal with mules. As there were four of us, sometimes my brothers looked after the goats and I transported timber with two mules. We brought down pines cut from our land every two or three days. Going back, one mule carried the provisions for us and the other four *garrafas* (demijohns) of wine.

Many muleteers passed by the inn and we were selling wine there. They carried tomatoes and grapes to Fornes, Jayena and all the villages of Granada. Some days 20 or 30 would pass, others only two or three. There was more coming and going in summer, when they carried straw or flour, and in winter nobody passed. My father and mother and my sisters were all there in summer, but in winter, when I was 18 or so, I was alone with the goats. That's how we lived, slogging away, and I as the oldest boy felt the pressure most.

When I was up there with the goats in winter, I could walk down to the village for the night but by first light I had to be back at the inn. So as to reach the village earlier, I would leave the goats loose and the gate of the pen open. They would enter the pen and stay there, but I had to get back by dawn or they would go off with the little kids and get lost.

I and my father had up to 500 goats. After I married, I added another 500. I bred with them with no more than two or three males. I just had to keep them in order and collect the young ones. I had them in two flocks. Those that were giving birth I brought them to a pen near the village and the others were at pasture in Alcóncar and Los Hoyos. I sold the kids and my wife made cheese.

I had Málaga goats, all red-coloured. Previously there were more colours but it seems they had less appeal for the dealers and I matched all the red males. The malagueños are very good big goats that yield a lot of milk and meat. Up in the sierra, when they didn't eat grain, they used to give a litre of milk a day and some two litres. Mine used to produce kids all winter long. In February and March I started organising them, taking out the male kids.

I spent 40 and more years in the sierra. In the 1960s we paid the Ingenio, that's the de la Torre family, who own this sierra, four pesetas per goat per year for pasture. At that time a baby goat was worth 400 or 500 pesetas, but I'm talking about a grown-up kid weighing 20 kilos with proper horns. Now this area has been made a nature park and they've banned the goats from the sierra.

In March we used to go over the mountains to pass the summer in the Sierra Nevada. We stayed there until Christmas and when the bad weather started I'd come back to Panaderos with the goats to pass the winter there. I went walking, walking five days up there. Coming back it was another five days. I slept wherever I could, with the goats.

I had to go via Lomas Llanas, where there were some other flocks, and then over the Cómpeta pass to stop at Fornes in Granada province and by the sierra of La Mora where there's a military camp. I passed by Dúrcal to go up to the high part of the Sierra Nevada, higher than the Alpujarras. We took the goats there for at least 15 years because there was more pasture and there we were until the snow sent us back down.

Sometimes in winter I'd open the doors of the farm and find a metre of snow, like a step. Then it was time to come down. I had to round up all the goats and bring them back. It was up to me. I put some food in a big skin bag and a blanket in a small sack. The bag went in front and the sack on my back, leaving my hands free to urge along the goats. That's how I came back from there. I didn't have a mule or donkey. I was the mule.

Quite a few times, when my folk were here harvesting the olives, I came down by myself with 400 goats. All that route I walked for at least 15 or 16 years, there and back. There were days when I saw nobody, but it didn't worry me. It's not that I liked the life but I had to do it. Around Cázulas in summer there would be the *resineros*, drawing off resin from the pines, but after the summer there was nobody. In the Sierra Nevada I used to stay at a farm below the snowline. The goats were up high and I went down at night to a farm with a family from Dúrcal. They had loads of work there, growing potatoes and beans, and I asked them to bring food for me. They'd come of an evening, but sometimes they didn't come up for 14 or 15 days.

You didn't see anybody except for a few herdsmen who had cows, horses and some sheep. We cattle folk were the only ones up there. I was by myself for five or six months. Around Christmas, as it would get very cold, I had to bring the herd back. In these mountains there were never any wolves but there were foxes which would grab any new-born left alone. There were eagles too which killed a few in winter when it was very cold.

I've been married for 30 years and when I married I didn't go any more to the Sierra Nevada. The last year I went there, when I brought back 200 goats of mine and those of my family, a really bad cold night caught me by surprise. It was snowing heavily and I made a vow: "I'm not coming again to the Sierra Nevada! I'm selling them." And I went and sold the goats and bought this property in the village. I sold them to a Cómpeta fellow and another young chap and they gave me 60,000 *duros* for more than 200 goats, which was very cheap.

I've a son and a daughter. He helped me when he was small but later he didn't want the goats. With up to 500 in a herd it's a lot of work in the sierra. When the boy began saying that he didn't want the goats and he was going to work in construction, then I began selling them.

Up there in the sierra I fell and banged myself two or three times. Three or four times I broke ribs. But the worst happened when I was 57. I fell backwards and broke my ribs and punctured my spleen. I mounted the mule and he brought me to the village. They took me to Nerja and told me I had four broken ribs. When I told the doctor, Don Juan Maldonaldo, "I'm drowning", he did an X-ray. My insides were full of blood. He called a taxi straight away and they took me to Vélez. I didn't feel any pain, I was just drowning, dying bit by bit. In Vélez they opened me up, took out four litres of blood and removed the spleen. The doctor told me: "Another half hour and you wouldn't be here to tell the tale."

After that, when I returned to the village, I sold all the goats. "Enough!" I said. Now I don't have one, and there are only three or four goatherds left in the village. Now I've got loads of avocadoes. That's what I do, tend avocado trees, irrigate them, prune them and pick them. That's where I'm at.

Have I enjoyed my life? Enjoy? No. Work. I had to work and that's it. When the goats were going to give birth, it was always I who had to go. I was the one who had to take charge of them, always. "Go with the goats, go with the goats..." Always. Of course I felt lonely up there on the mountain for so many years. But what could I do?

"My family was very worried for several years until matters quietened down. And not only my father was alarmed. There were a number of people who were sentenced to death."

Antonio Raya Olalla, retired taxi-driver, born in Frigiliana on April 30, 1936, died May 17, 2008.

When the war ended in 1939, we were living in San Sebastián street and one of the first things I remember was hearing a lot of people singing and shouting in the early morning. Lorries were going by and men in the Falange uniform with red caps. They were going to line the main highway because Francisco Franco was to pass along in his tour of Spain. The war was over and General Francisco Franco was the victor and the men came along the street singing, singing. I was three years old and my mother raised me to the window and I saw the lorries and the men in their caps.

I started work at the age of nine or 10 in the sierra, in many places, with my father and other folk. But really hard work, cutting wood, on the land, picking olives or potatoes. Later the teacher, Don Enrique Ginés Matas, who took the older children, gave classes of two-hours-and-a-half at night and charged very little. That's where I learned a bit more, because he was a very good teacher with very good qualities.

Frankly, Frigiliana has always been privileged because it never had big estates. Instead the land has been shared among many and there were very few people you could really call rich. In the past they called a *cacique* (local overlord) anybody who was a little better off, but generally everybody had a few possessions and a bit of land. They were difficult, tight times but Frigiliana lived much better than many other villages, although the people worked hard.

I was in the sierra for some years because my father was a forest ranger and was always watching over the men working with the timber. I spent almost half my life in Vélez-Málaga but ended up running a taxi in the village for close to 20 years.

A large part of the village depended on the Ingenio. You could also sell the sugar cane in Nerja to the Fossi family, which was another small mill, or to the Larios works, but everybody was already committed to the mill here. At that time, apart from a few potatoes and sweet potatoes, 80 per cent of Frigiliana land was planted with sugar cane. Then there was another commitment: all that came from the sierra was for El Ingenio. Those mountains yielded a lot. They extracted the essence from thyme, there was the esparto season, there was the timber season. Many folk made charcoal from the pines.

Add to that the goats with their milk and cheese and every year the young ones. A goatherd could have 200 animals, for example, many of which would have two kids. Many of the new breed would not be in the best shape because they weren't robust or had ugly ears or horns so they went for meat. So every year 200 goats could produce 350 kids, 100 for breeding and 250 for meat. They didn't have to sell the milk, the cheese or the meat to the Ingenio, but they had to pay a little for the pasture.

Those who ran the Ingenio had a lot of influence, but they weren't bad, just a bit careful with their properties. People say they were class-conscious, but it's not true. They looked after what was theirs.

Many lived from the sugar cane and the sierra, but others made a living from the grapes and olives. Frigiliana produced many thousands of boxes of raisins and tons of olives. Now they just pick a few of the best, then they picked everything. Agriculture has changed totally here. Today it's avocadoes or custard apples, then it was grapes, raisins, wine, olives, by the million.

Then came the Maquis. At the end of the war there were political infiltrators around. Many of those called "the people of the sierra" came to these mountains, which are very rugged and thus favourable to their purpose. Many from Frigiliana joined them.

Things really heated up. They launched a lot of attacks, doing a great deal of damage. There were acts of vengeance and it became very bitter. Then many forces moved in until there were more of them than civilians. There was a good deal of fear and panic, because a lot of village folk were involved with the people of the sierra, taking them food, making contact. But if the forces learned a family was providing food, they would pick them up, beat them and put them in prison.

To my family the people of the sierra weren't delinquents. They were neither good nor bad since my family wasn't affected, either by their politics or their economics, and my relatives were never kidnapped. The idea that Robert wanted to overthrow Franco appealed to some people, but not many. Frigiliana had all types, both Franco's followers and those contrary to him. To tell the truth, long before Franco, all my family, although a humble one, was inclined towards rightwing ideas. We thought the people of the sierra to be poor devils with bad luck, because we knew some of those who went from here, youngsters who, because of their fathers, had been beaten a lot or wouldn't talk. When a person is hungry and, on top of that, is harassed and beaten and those of the Maquis say "Come on, come on", then he goes.

When I was about 12, the Cruz de Napoleón (Cross of Napoleon) incident occurred. It was the time for collecting esparto and two men were out looking for it as they could sell it in the village. They saw a sack of food amid some bushes. It was part of the supplies which the people of the sierra had been carrying. When daylight came, because the Civil Guards might sight them from their observation points, the people of the sierra left the sacks covered up then retired to a place where they could hide all day and keep watch.

These two fellows saw that there were some esparto sandals in a sack. Each of them took a pair and put them on. Something they needed. It seems they didn't take any food, but when they got back to the village they talked about finding the food. The Civil Guard surrounded the place and, when the Maquis returned to pick up the sacks, there was a shootout and they came close to death. They lost their food and they knew who had found it. Those two fellows didn't harm the people of the sierra, but it angered the Maquis that they reported what they had seen and as a result they were nearly killed. So one day the people of the sierra grabbed them and did all manner of things to them.

Somebody from the village saw them at a place called the Cross of Napoleon, up the river. When the Civil Guard went there, they found they'd been hanged. Alongside them were some big strong sticks and they had their arms broken in various places and their legs smashed. Their tongues and their private parts had been cut off and left in a handkerchief attached to their belts. That's what they did to those young chaps. It was ghastly.

At the end those who didn't give themselves up died in battles. Others surrendered to save their lives. When the war in the sierras became difficult, the authorities made an offer to those who had no blood on their hands: surrender and reveal where the others are. In return their punishment would be reduced. Many turned themselves in here. I saw the one who hanged those two youths. They called him *"el de el cordelillo"* (the man of the noose). He was a specialist in hanging.

We weren't in favour of one side or the other and had no problems except towards the end when there were some misunderstandings. My father worked for the de la Torre company as a forest guard. When things got difficult, the rangers didn't go to the sierra. Instead they did duty in the Company's molasses factory where my father weighed the timber. But some of the Civil Guard chiefs came along and asked: "Who are the sierra experts?" "So-and-so is a ranger who's spent many years in the sierra and knows it very well." So the lieutenant turned up with a lorry carrying 50 guards. An informer had reported the location of a guerrilla camp and the guards went out at night and surrounded it.

Two or three times they called on my father. They would arrive at our door at midnight. "Look here, Antonio," the corporal would say. "the lieutenant needs a guide and we've told him that you know the area well." Or he'd say: "Come on, we're leaving in half an hour. Don't say no, Antonio, or you'll be forced to go." Not "we're talking about next week…", but in half an hour. I was listening. At that time the Civil Guard in all this area had — how do you call it? — carte blanche to exterminate the people of the sierra.

The third time my father went there was a confrontation with the Maquis. Twice they escaped but one time they were surrounded, there was a clash and two or three of them died. When the forces of order attacked, my father was down below in the river, but he had to take them to the spot and the people of the sierra got to know. Then we heard that they wanted to harm him. One of the leaders up there told somebody in the village: "We understand that fellow was forced to come, but two comrades died that night and he was one of those to blame." So they didn't forgive him. My family was very worried for several years until matters quietened down. And not only my father was alarmed. There were a number of people who were sentenced to death. One they caught while others escaped because they went into hiding.

After 1950 things went badly for the guerrillas. They began to surrender and lost strength. The last remaining couple, Lomas and El Moreno, who were from Frigiliana, gave themselves up the night before the day of San Sebastián. The father-in-law of Lomas lived in the Cortijo de Ángel Rojas, above a spot known as El Pedregal. He knew they would come there to pass the night and were bringing food and wine.

El Moreno said: "I'm going down to the village to get some nougat and other things and tomorrow we'll head for the sierra." Lomas stayed with his family while El Moreno came at nightfall to his house and told his mother the situation: that he didn't want to continue in the sierra and had come to give himself up. The mother went to the barracks and told a guard: "My son has repented and he wants to surrender." A corporal went along with a guard. El Moreno was lying down with his pistol on a chair at the side of the bed. "Moreno," said the corporal. "have you come to give yourself up?" "Yes," he replied. The corporal informed his superiors of Moreno's surrender and where Lomas was.

Around three in the morning the Civil Guards surrounds the farmhouse with a double cordon. One of the guards, a strong chap, is handcuffed to El Moreno. Then they wait for daylight. As dawn breaks they see that the people are eating and drinking inside the farm. Those inside notice something and Ángel, Lomas's father-in-law, comes out with a plate of scraps. He has arranged with his son-in-law inside to give a countersign if he sees anything. So Ángel comes out and says: "*Pitica, pitica*! Here's your food." Pitica is the hen. The father-in-law sees nothing out of the ordinary as the guards are behind the bushes and olive trees so Lomas emerges intending to go away. But, as he goes around some prickly pear cactus, out come the lieutenant and other guards and order him to halt. "Don't try to run. Give up. You're surrounded," says the lieutenant. I don't know what happened, whether he tried to hide or run, but the lieutenant fired a shot and hit him in the chest and he snuffed it.

From that moment the Maquis was finished and there was peace. He who wanted to go to the farm could go. All that time people couldn't go freely to the land or the sierra. But then they removed the controls and you could leave and return to the village at any time. From 1952 things improved, the agriculture, wages, everything. And from 1957 there began to be much more work and Frigiliana made great progress.

Before we lived very economically. Today, how people live! Everybody has a good house and in each house, if there are three fellows, there are three cars. And at fiesta time how everybody lives it up! It's great. Many people have prospered in Frigiliana, in every sense.

Looking back, sincerely I see the Franco years as a time which had its *razón de ser* (raison d'être). I understand that, for life to advance in a democracy, the Francoist law could not continue. In Franco's shadow, those who had power abused it and exaggerated in the name of Franco. It was not Franco, I believe. Errors were made. There were acts of revenge, and revenge is cowardly… Yes, Franco had his *razón de ser* in Spain, apart from the doubts I've expressed. For me he was a great man.

"They took us to prison in Málaga. They totally shaved our heads and took away our clothing. We were left with only our sandals. Ten days in a blanket, without clothes, in winter and sleeping on the floor."

Antonio Orihuela Herrero (El Zorro), farmer, retired restaurant owner, born in Frigiliana on March 11, 1931, died June 3, 2007.

My family's nickname is El Zorro (the fox). I was born here in the village. They were very bad years but I had grandparents who had land so we lived well. But then my father died when I was 15 or 16 and my grandparents had already passed on. One brother had died of meningitis when he was little. That left four of us children and things went badly for us. I was the oldest and had to work. I used to go into the sierra for firewood, for esparto, thyme, carried on the back, and I would maybe see the people of the sierra and I would keep quiet about it.

Of the war years I remember that, when the Nationalists arrived, they grabbed all those who were said to be Reds and they killed them. We tried to get away, two brothers, an aunt of mine of my age and her sister and my father and mother and another woman from the Barribarto whose husband was called Frasco el Matutero. We all went off in a small truck — they called it La Canaria — along the highway from Nerja to Motril. But a ship called the Cervera stationed itself opposite a spot named the Bridge of the Marías. Shells were hitting the road because they didn't want us to pass.

People were climbing into trucks, but the road was so bad they were overturning. I saw vehicles on their sides and people carrying their children in their arms, people carrying goats. All walking. There were so many people fleeing along the road that we couldn't go on. So, at the Cantarriján river, my family and that of Matutero got off. He carried on, he didn't want to return. Then we went up the Cantarriján, up into the sierra as far as the irrigation channel. I remember that a file of militia with guns was heading upwards and they asked: "Is this the way to the province of Granada? Are we on the right track?" "Yes," my papa told them. They were looking for Maroto's militia column.

At last we reached the village and nothing happened to us, except that the Falangists shaved my mother. They killed the ringleaders, those that hadn't run away. They hadn't done anything, they hadn't hit anybody nor killed anybody, but when the Nationalists arrived they seized them, took them to Torrox and without a trial they killed them, one because he had been the mayor.

They killed one man called Bastián, because he was a Communist. Here in the village there was only one Communist and in Nerja two or three and in Torrox two or three. Two first cousins from Nerja were at the front at Zafarraya and, when they retreated, they came through the sierra. They didn't go via the highway because there were many troops between the coast and the mountains. In Frigiliana they went to see Bastián, who was in bed with Malta fever. "Come with us," they told him. "Those folk are going to kill you." But with his fever he couldn't walk and they had to go on to Almería. How could they carry him? Then the others arrived. They took him and seven more off to Torrox and there they shot them, without even asking for an explanation.

The Falangistas marked a cross on the heads of young lads and gave them a glass of castor oil, which is a purgative, and made them drink it. They said they were Reds. "This is for your papa, for what he or your mama has done..." Castor oil they gave them. There was one fellow here who was sub-normal, Antoñico Jureles, and they forced him to eat a soup of castor oil, awful stuff.

They beat up the men, those that didn't go to jail for three years. And they shaved the heads of the women. They tricked my mother and then they shaved her. We lived up at the top of Zacatín and a couple came to the door. As we knew them, we opened the door and they said: "Go to your uncle." My mother went down the street to my uncle's house opposite the town hall. But my uncle wasn't there and, when she arrived, they seized her and shaved her. That was just because she did a favour for one of the leftwingers. She'd made a cap for a sister's boyfriend. I went looking for her and there she was, tossed out with a handkerchief over her head, weeping, and I took her home.

They shaved 40 people here. I don't know whether I can say this or not, but all the Fascists here today have family shaved by the Fascists, or killed. Almost all those of the Popular Party have relatives who were killed and all have relatives who were shaved.

In 1940 I was already working with my uncle. I was eight or nine and there was hardly ever any school because sometimes there was war, other times there were no teachers. So I was almost never in school. I did know how to write but with lots of spelling mistakes. At that time it was a miracle that anybody could write. All the women would come to an aunt of mine for her to write letters to their sons at the front. I had an uncle in the war too, in Franco's army. I sent him a letter and he showed it to all the soldiers, saying: "Look, he's only seven or eight and already he knows how to write. And we know nothing."

When the business with the people of the sierra began, a cousin of mine, Antonio Lomas, was working at Los Almendros farm with Don Ángel Herrero, who was in charge. The people of the sierra arrived, with Los Frailes, two of the leaders. They wanted to take Don Ángel away to get a ransom. Don Ángel said to my cousin: "Look, we're going to whack this one and I'll lure the other one away." But, when they tried to escape, they were both killed and the people of the sierra ran off.

Behind Los Almendros is the Cortijo de los Caños where the people of the sierra used to pick up food, but somebody informed on them and the Civil Guard killed Cecilia (Francisco Cecilia Cecilia) there. A short time later the people of the sierra were told that two of my cousins and a brother of my father were responsible, so they went to Los Caños and killed the three of them: my uncle Miguel Orihuela Moreno and the others, Rafael Orihuela Lomas and José Lomas Orihuela. They had said nothing but they were blamed. Some of the youngsters here said they had to kill all the Orihuelas.

After that, I didn't go to the sierra. I had lost all trust. But one day when I did go they picked me up and told me they were going to kill me. I was looking for wood to bring a load back. One of them came looking for me and took me uphill at the point of a pistol and there were four or five of them on the Collado de Paulino. They gave me a cigarette to roll, but I was so nervous at first I couldn't do it. Then Vicente told me: "Tell my father that we're here." It was Vicente Vozmediano, a criminal. When I got back to the village, I saw his father and told him: "I've seen your son." He replied: "Yes, I've seen him too. He told me he'd given you this message and that, if you want to come tomorrow, come with me." And I said: "No way. Tomorrow I'm not going, I'm not going."

The next day I went to another spot in the mountains to load firewood and along came the father. "Didn't you say you weren't going to come?" he asked. That was enough; he'd seen me and they hadn't done anything to me, so I started going to the sierra again because I had to make a living.

Once when I went with a colleague, Aurelio, Vicente was there with a group. They gave a message to Aurelio to go to Nerja and tell a certain Antonio Lomas, El Chato Lomas, that he should prepare eight *arrobas* of oil and they were going to pick them up.

I stayed in the background and it was my friend who passed on the message. I didn't play any part in it. Two or three days later Civil Guards dressed like those of the sierra went to the oil mill. Because Vicente was already collaborating. He'd come down from the mountains and gone to the barracks and then the guards put on clothes like his and they went to the mill. Vicente says: "Have you the oil ready?" And Chato replies: "Yes, Aurelio and Orihuela were here and gave me the message. When my brother-in-law comes, he'll probably bring the oil." Then the guards asked him: "Who are Aurelio and Orihuela?" And he tells them: "From Frigiliana, so and so."

At that time a cousin of mine, a first cousin of my mother, Antonio Sánchez Martín, or Lomas, was still in the sierra with a fellow called El Moreno. On the night of January 19, 1952, El Moreno, came to the village and gave himself up. The next morning all the guards went to the Ángel Rojas farm. Lomas was there with his wife and their little daughter. The *civiles* called out: "You're surrounded. Come on out!" He came out with his hands empty and in front of the little girl they killed him. That day, the 20th, I was coming from the San Sebastián fiesta around midday and there he was, stretched out over a mule. They took him right through the village to the cemetery, and all his family was detained.

On the 22nd I went to work on the land, at the Cortijillo del Cavador, which was farmed by a brother-in-law of the son of the digger, Manuel el Mono. That night, when I entered my home, the Civil Guard arrived and took me to the village prison. There was a married couple inside. Everybody was there nearby, including my mother. They didn't tie us up, but next morning Aurelio and I had our hands tied and they took us off to Nerja. When we passed along the street, nobody looked at us. They couldn't. At least 13 or 14 Civil Guards came with us, corporals, sergeants, lieutenants. I recall seeing a woman in a doorway crying, because all those they picked up they killed.

And there, coming from the barracks along El Calvario, up the street were my mother and my aunts, all weeping. They believed they were going to kill me. They took us down to Nerja and the first thing they did was wallop Aurelio a couple of times — I don't know what he'd stirred up. I shit myself. Then they took us to the barracks and left Aurelio and me tied up, sitting outside in the rain all night, without saying anything to us. It was freezing. That night I didn't sleep at all.

At first light they took us back to the jail, but they didn't ask any questions. The jail was behind the Nerja church. It had a big door and a window that gave on to the beach. So there we were all day, the 24th, in prison but tied up. My mother brought us something to eat. When night came, like goats they took us again to the barracks and we were sitting there all night. I dozed off in a pool of water. They wrote up something and on the night of the 26th they gave us a paper to sign, saying that we had been accessories or go-betweens for the guerrillas. But I had nothing to do with that.

Early on the 27th they took us to the prison in Málaga. The same day at least 14 from the Barranco Huit came in with us. Once there, they totally shaved our heads and took away our clothes. We were left with only our sandals. They showered us and gave us a blanket each and injected us here and there. Wrapped in a blanket from one day to the next. Ten days in a blanket, without clothing, and in winter, sleeping on the floor, 10 days in a blanket. El Chato Lomas, the one who made the oil, gave them money and they returned our clothes. Then, every fortnight or month, they took us somewhere to disinfect our clothes. There were about eight to a cell. Just as well that we were sent something to eat (by the families) because there was hardly any food and that was very bad.

That's how it was until July 10, when we were provisionally released until October when they took us before a court martial and sentenced us to four years in jail. At the end of the year they detained us again to serve the four years. However, there was a Vatican council or congress, the Second Vatican Council I think it was called, and they reduced sentences. Those serving under four years had the sentence cut in half, so two years were taken off.

They took us to work in a quarry for a reservoir on the Segura river in Murcia. We loaded rocks for a crusher which ground them up to make material for the walls. We were there from February in the year '53 until the end of the year when they let us out on conditional liberty. I came home. Nothing had changed. Work was the same. The 'haves' still had and the 'havenots' were still without. It continued as before.

Then, after I did military service in Barcelona, we all went there, four brothers and my mother, and ended up in the house of an aunt. It was 1955 and there was plenty of work. Many people went to Barcelona and to Argentina. When the war ended, they imprisoned many people. Then when they came out, those of the sierra were here and the best thing to do was to leave, otherwise you were going to get caught up in it. They'd picked up a good number, given them a beating and put them in jail. So then they got out of the way.

In Barcelona I linked up with a young fellow, Jordi, a good person and we got on fine. He was the boss and we made things for buildings, all sorts, for lamps, for blinds. I worked there most of the time until 1980. Before that, on holiday in the village, I'd bought land for a house. I gave cash to a first cousin to construct half it and then, when I was 18 months unemployed, I returned from Barcelona and worked to finish this house. On March 9, 1981, we opened a bar and restaurant in the village. And things have gone well. Now I'm retired and I go to the countryside when I feel like it.

I filled out the papers to apply for compensation for the years in prison. They have distributed money in proportion to the time you spent there. They paid first those who were in for more than three years. My wife received just over a million pesetas for her father who was more than three years in prison. My turn came and I have also received a certificate from the president of the Junta de Andalucía.

Between Two Fires

In jail you hear a lot of things. Everybody believed that the Civil Guard killed a father and son who disappeared in the sierra. But, while I was behind bars, what I heard from the people of the sierra there was that they were responsible and not the Civil Guard. I heard from them that at a place called Dos Hermanas, when the two were going for esparto, they picked the father up to kill him. Then the son, called Manolillo el Mudilla because he was dumb, began to cry and they said: "He's going to betray us if we let him live." So they had to kill the two. It was a brother-in-law that killed them. I don't know why. It's just what I heard them say in prison.

As for Roberto, the Civil Guard and everybody says they executed him in Granada. But that's a lie. I think Roberto was working with the Civil Guard. I remember going one day to work in the fields and I was carrying a pot with a bit of *migas*. The guards stopped me and poked about to see if I was carrying some paper underneath the *migas*. I had nothing, but how is it that, while we were searched every possible way, the family of Dolores, Roberto's lover, could sleep and work at the Venta Panaderos and buy food to carry up there? How could the husband and children and Roberto and the people of the sierra be there every night and they did nothing to them?

Roberto was there to entrap them, to find out about everything. At first the guerrillas were a resistance group of Republicans, but Roberto converted them into bandits. As I understand it, he went to Madrid with money and his girlfriend. And in the hotel in Madrid he told her: "Stay here while I run an errand. Take this pistol in case somebody comes." Then he went off and warned the police and they nabbed her, but not him.

They didn't kill that fellow in Granada. Instead, they grabbed some unfortunate, any old prisoner, filled him with wine or whatever, dragged him out blindfolded and executed him. It wasn't Roberto. They let him go in America, in Spain, somewhere…

"Everybody was at mass. A guard entered and approached the Civil Guard chief in the front row. Immediately the chief left the church and we all knew that something important had happened."

Reminiscences of a Frigiliana man, born in the 1930s, who prefers not to be identified.

Frigiliana was like any other village, with people on the right and on the left. We've always had a mixture. In 1936, when the war started, they took the images out of the church and afterwards it was like a store place, full of rubbish and bits of the gilded altarpiece, the door wide open, with people going in and out. As a kid I went in and took away a bit of gilt and it was in my house for 20 years.

The ringleaders who formed the committee had meetings in the church. They would say: "We have to kill a cow. So-and-so has cows. Tomorrow two must go to the farm and bring one back." They would bring the cow, kill it at the side-door of the church, hang it up, cut it up and share out the meat with the people.

The Communists were in control. Some were from here but also they were always coming from other parts, including Málaga. The village had seven or eight what we call *señoritos*. There was Don Manuel de la Torre and his sons, the brothers Don Sebastián and Don Federico, and there was the López family, Don Justo, Aurelio and Javier, and there was Don Victor. They stayed in their houses and the ringleaders would visit them, threatening them. They'd arrive and tell them they were going to take them out and give them a *paseíco* (a walk to their execution).

The men needed work and, as there wasn't much and the *señoritos* preferred to do nothing, the leaders organised it. The committee would say: "So-and-so and so-and-so, tomorrow you four go and work where Don Victor has his vines." They went with their tools and worked in Don Victor's vineyard. Then in the evening one of the committee would go to get their pay from Don Victor. The people of the village were very frightened. They stayed home, going out the least possible, and keeping out of the way when there was any rumpus.

Here you had the sierra and the land. There was plenty of work every day in the sierra and all those who had mules went up there. In the village you had the Ingenio and three water-mills. I recall seeing one of the mills working. The other two had stopped working a while back. The Ingenio and the one mill processed sugar cane to make molasses. They were owned by the de la Torre family.

In my home there was nothing, and there were many more like that. There was no bathroom. There was a basin to wash yourself and a wood fire for cooking. And every day you went to the country and brought back firewood. Otherwise you bought it from the men who carried in loads and sold it in the street.

One could only stay at school until Grade Three, one or two years there. Some went to Málaga to study, because there was nowhere nearer, not in Nerja or Torre del Mar. And to go to Málaga you had to have money, as simple as that. You were in school until you were 14, then you had to go and make a living.

My father was a builder but in those days sometimes there was construction work, sometimes not. Most of all there was the land so that we would do building work or farming. My father had his own small piece of land. They grew everything in the countryside, mostly sugar cane but also wheat, barley, sweet potatoes, potatoes, peppers, tomatoes, the land is a big place. As a lad of 14, I earned nine or 10 pesetas a day. After 1950, I was a man and earned 15 or 16 pesetas.

When July came everybody went to the farms and stayed there until October, harvesting the grapes and preparing raisins. At night they would get together in one or other of the farmhouses. Many neighbours would meet when there was a fiesta, including those who were far away and those who lived in the *pueblo*. Most stayed out there until October 15. When the harvest was over and all the work on the land, they'd return to the village.

As for the time of the people of the sierra, I remember one morning — I think it was in the year 1951 — I was going to my farm which is on the border with Torrox and I saw a handkerchief on the ground. Then somebody whispered to me. I stopped and looked and saw two men seated below a small wall. The one who got to his feet I recognised, because he was from Frigiliana, Matutero (Manuel Triviño Cerezo) was his name, and he'd been in the sierra two or three years. The other man stayed sitting down. He had a shotgun resting between his legs. We were close, about 20 metres apart.

I was scared and began to run. I ran off to get out of the way, running, running as far as the Río Seco and making a big detour. When I got home, I told my parents about it and they told me to keep quiet about it. Later I learned that the man only wanted to ask me about some of his family who were going to come with food. Early next morning my mother came to me in bed and told me: "That fellow gave himself up last night."

He was with the Civil Guard in another village and travelled about the countryside until he came to Frigiliana six weeks later. One day I was walking along the street and was about to enter the Casino bar and there was Matutero outside talking to some Frigiliana men. He called to me and asked me why, when he'd called me that day, I'd run away. There was a Civil Guard in the Casino door, listening and watching. So I played innocent and said he was mistaken and that we hadn't seen one another and that I knew nothing about him. They shot that fellow in Málaga. After helping the Civil Guard in and around the villages they put him in jail. After a short time there he was sentenced to death.

It was after El Moreno, from the village, attacked a Moorish soldier with an axe that the Civil Guard picked up three young men. Two had brothers in the sierra and the youngest had his father there. That's all there was against them. After locking them up in a Civil Guard post in the Molineta they killed them on La Loma de las Vacas (the Hill of Cows). They set them walking along a path overlooking the river and then murdered them.

At the funeral of the three the next day I was in the cemetery when the priest led the prayers. Almost everybody went to the funeral because it was a tremendous occurrence for the village. The father of one of the dead was overcome with emotion, on his knees on the ground beside the body of his son. The priest, Don Domingo, stopped the service until he calmed down. It was very emotional... at the age of 17 or 18 you don't forget these things.

When one of the sierra people died, they found a mule, loaded him on its back and paraded him through the village to the cemetery. The town hall were responsible for his burial. I remember the day when they brought back the last of the sierra. It was January 20, 1952, the fiesta of San Sebastián, and everybody was at mass. The Civil Guard chief, the mayor and the judge were sitting in the front row of the church. A guard entered and passed along the side to approach the officer. Immediately the chief left the church and we all knew that something important had happened.

When we went out into the plaza at one o'clock, along came the guards with a mule and on it the body of Lomas (Antonio Sánchez Martín). It went right through the village. That was the end of the guerrilla. Lomas was the last in the sierra.

"My father went away to the sierra in 1947. He told us: 'Go on home. I'll be back soon.' And he still hasn't come back. We never saw him again."

Salomé Pérez Moreno, born on September 30, 1934, in Fornes (Granada), resident in Nerja, daughter of the guerrilla José Pérez Moles (Ranica).

My father was from Fornes where he was born in 1906. He was tall and tough. I think he was about 160 centimetres and a bit. He was a muleteer and brought things from Fornes to the coast. My grandmother ran the Ventorrillo inn near Acebuchal and the muleteers passed by there and stopped to have a drink or whatever. My father fell in love with my mother, the daughter at the inn, who was a year younger than him. They married and went to live in Fornes. They had a son but he died at the age of two. Then my sister, the one who is in Barcelona, was born in 1932, myself in 1934 and my sister Carmen in 1936.

At the start of the war in 1936 my father, who was a Communist, took off. I don't know where he went. My mother with her daughters came to the house of my grandmother and her aunts in Acebuchal, and there we were until we came to Nerja.

My father returned after two years, in 1938. To tell the truth, he didn't know us and we didn't know him. He was a man who came to our house. We didn't have close contact. We little girls were sitting there and he would say: "Come here. Let's see. Which is Carmen and which is Salomé?"

Then somebody from Frigiliana reported seeing him in Acebuchal and the Civil Guard came for him. I remember them knocking at my grandmother's door. "Aurora, Aurora," they said, because they knew her. "We need a rope to tie up a wineskin that's come undone." In those days the muleteers transported wine, oil and other things in skins, but there were no muleteers around. My father went out in a pair of those white underpants they used to wear. "You have to come with us," they said. So he had to go and he was in prison for seven years and three months. I don't know what the charge against him was.

My father was a prisoner in three places, La Coruña, Santander and Bilbao. It would be in 1946 that he returned and was at home two more years. The life he'd had in prison affected him. It was in his blood. He came out rebellious and it stuck to him. He was with us at home about two years. He got a job working on the Cómpeta highway, But, because he'd been in prison, he was considered a dangerous person and he had to report to the Frigiliana barracks three times a day, in the morning, at midday and at night.

So where could he work? As I understand it — as an innocent kid one doesn't find out half of what goes on — a fellow from Frigiliana told him: "You're not a man unless you go to the sierra. This is no life here."

So in 1947 my father did go to the sierra. I remember it because the same day a cousin of mine who was going to do his military service came to say goodbye to my mother. That afternoon, about four o'clock, when we went out to get firewood, we met a man who said to my father: "José, come on, there's a fellow below waiting for you." My father told us: "Go on home. I'll be back soon." And he still hasn't come back. We never saw him again.

We knew no more of him, until just recently. Now we have learned that they killed him in 1948 and he's buried in the cemetery at Lanjarón over by Granada. My mother spent 14 months in prison and for sure, the dates show it clearly, they

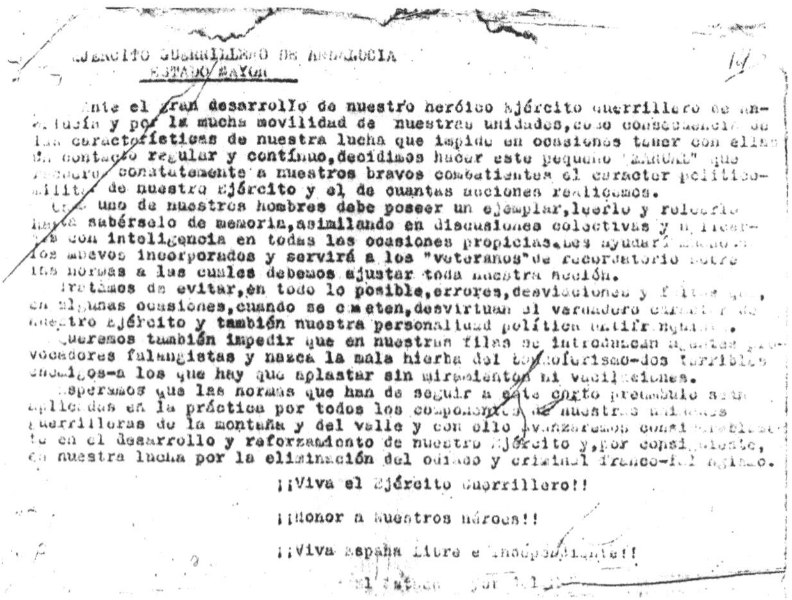

EJERCITO GUERRILLERO DE ANDALUCIA
ESTADO MAYOR

Ante el gran desarrollo de nuestro heróico Ejército guerrillero de Andalucía y por la mucha movilidad de nuestras unidades, como consecuencia de las características de nuestra lucha que impide en ocasiones tener con ellas un contacto regular y contínuo, decidimos hacer este pequeño "MANUAL" que recuerde constantemente a nuestros bravos combatientes el caracter político-militar de nuestro Ejército y el de cuantas acciones realicemos.

Cada uno de nuestros hombres debe poseer un ejemplar, leerlo y releerlo hasta sabérselo de memoria, asimilando en discusiones colectivas y [illegible] con inteligencia en todas las ocasiones propicias. Les ayudará [illegible] los nuevos incorporados y servirá a los "veteranos" de recordatorio [illegible] las normas a las cuales debemos ajustar toda nuestra acción.

Tratamos de evitar, en todo lo posible, errores, desviaciones y [illegible], en algunas ocasiones, cuando se cometen, desvirtuan el verdadero [illegible] de nuestro Ejército y también nuestra personalidad política [illegible].

Queremos también impedir que en nuestras filas se introduzcan [illegible] vocadores falangistas y nazca la mala hierba del [illegible]oferismo–dos terribles enemigos–a los que hay que aplastar sin miramientos ni vacilaciones.

Esperamos que las normas que han de seguir a este corto preámbulo sean aplicadas en la práctica por todos los componentes de nuestras unidades guerrilleras de la montaña y del valle y con ello avanzaremos considerablemente en el desarrollo y reforzamiento de nuestro Ejército y, por consiguiente, en nuestra lucha por la eliminación del odiado y criminal franco-[illegible] régimen.

¡¡Viva el Ejército Guerrillero!!

¡¡Honor a Nuestros héroes!!

¡¡Viva España Libre e Independiente!!

[illegible]

"Long live the guerrilla army!" Pamphlet found in Pérez Moles's possession released her when they killed him. My mother was accused of helping the people of the sierra. The fact is I wanted the people of the sierra to help me because I didn't have anything to eat. When my father went away, he left us without anything. I don't see the sense of it, leaving three little girls and his wife.

More than once I've said that, if my father had been a different person who was closer to us, when he came out of prison he would have picked us up and said: "Right, let's go to Barcelona." Or France. To live. But he left us behind. It was a mistake to have stayed here because, if we'd gone to Barcelona, we would have all made a living. And he would have died when his time came.

I'm not going to say he would have a long life but he would have been at the side of his children and his wife. He left us with nothing more than the four walls, which actually weren't ours. It was to my uncle Baldomero, a brother of my mother, that I used to say: "This is my father." My poor father, may God preserve him, but I felt more warmth for others than for him.

The first time I went to work I earned three *duros* (15 pesetas) a month. Maybe the lady would pay me three months in advance so I could buy a dress for nine *duros*. I've been through much more than you can imagine. In the case of my four daughters, when they finish with some clothing, I make an apron or a bag, anything because it pains me to throw anything away. We never knew any teachers. We didn't know how to read or write, but the truth is that we didn't want to. The years went by and I've never learned. Now, when many older folk are learning, I've realised that it's because I don't have the vocation.

There was a little shop in Acebuchal but little more. We came to Frigiliana on foot. I recall coming when I was 10 and I was barefoot, and my sister too. It wasn't because of some promise (to the Virgin) but because our mother couldn't buy us any shoes. Many times my mother brought charcoal, made by my uncles, to Frigiliana to sell it and took back shopping, and always barefoot. She came to work, to whitewash a ceiling, to pick olives or whatever.

She would say: "I have to wash your dress." But the dress was fit to throw away not to wash. When they came to Frigiliana vaccinating against smallpox, I had no clothes fit to wear in people's company. My older sister wore a dress bought me by Aunt Serafina and the next day she had to take it off and bring it to me so I could be vaccinated. But by the time I went along the fellow doing the vaccinations had gone and I never got one. But I must have already been vaccinated against all illnesses as God hasn't given me one.

I wish I'd been born later, so at least to know more and enjoy a better life than we had. At 10 I was going about barefoot. Mother made us little shoes of esparto and whatever cloth she had. She plaited esparto to make a basket or cover a bottle.

I never saw the people of the sierra around Acebuchal, although I remember people saying one time: "They've killed a man in the sierra." We kids tried to see what was going on. I saw the Civil Guard and the man face down across the back of a mule. He had his trousers pulled up and his legs were very white. White as death. After that I didn't want to sleep alone as I kept remembering the man who had passed by.

The Civil Guard were always asking questions, patrolling around the farmhouses. People told a story about how one night a farmer gave a meal to some strangers and next morning some Civil Guards turned up to question him. "Papa," said the daughter. "Don't say that nobody has come here because this is the man who was here last night." The guards had arrived dressed as civilians the previous night and then come back to see if the farmer would tell the truth.

Finally the Civil Guard removed all the families who had relatives in the sierra. They threw all the people off the land. They didn't want anybody in the farmhouses to stop their having any contact with those of the sierra. And they put a lot of Frigiliana people in prison. When they jailed my mother, we came with my grandmother to Nerja and stayed here. Afterwards my mother worked as a cook and we daughters as cleaners or looking after children. I worked in many houses and I earned three *duros* the first time.

My mother died at 84 without knowing what happened to her husband. She no longer wanted to know. She wasn't bitter. She just adjusted herself to the life she had, which was working to raise her three children. Sometimes we would say: "We're going to see if we can find father." That would throw her into a panic because she thought something was going to happen to her. "Don't move, don't move!" she would say. She was very afraid. In the past one couldn't talk and she still believed that it was a crime.

We never knew what happened to our father until my grandson, Manolo Ortega, began to investigate with Manolo Valero (a Nerja councillor) and José María Azuaga (an historian). Then in February, 2003, Manolo called me and asked me his grandfather's full name. Two days later he called again to say: "We've found grandfather." He is buried in a mass grave in Lanjarón cemetery and they've constructed some niches on top. In the court there they gave us the death certificate and told us we could take away his remains right then. But, when we reached the cemetery, they said: "You can't touch anything because many people are buried here and it's not known under which niche he is." We were walking on top of them. In the town hall they knew nothing. The magistrate sealed it off. We've been left in mid-air. We're disillusioned.

The government hasn't done anything. Each relative has done his bit, searching for a father or a mother. There were nine bodies in Lanjarón, the parents of somebody, the father and brother of another. They killed and buried them there. It happened on June 17 in 1948 and they buried them on the 18th. Why didn't they inform the family? I want to bury the bones where I say, to know where they are. We've always been the orphans of the war, that's all we are.

"Here we call 1948 'the year of hunger'. In August the Civil Guard ejected us. Acebuchal was left with its doors hanging open, deserted."

Aurelio Torres Sánchez (El Obispo), electrician, born March 21, 1946, in El Acebuchal, a hamlet five kilometres from Frigiliana.

I was the last but one to be born in El Acebuchal. The Civil Guard threw us out in August, 1948. We'd been virtually a village, but we were in the line of fire. You had to live with the Civil Guard and with the people of the sierra. They would come by night. They came knocking at your house and saying: "I want food. Do you have any? Here's some money." And if they didn't have any money but they were hungry? You had to live with them.

At one point there were 40 families in Acebuchal de Arriba and Acebuchal de Abajo, about 250 people. There were a lot because married folk had many children. There's a tale about an uncle of my father who was having a drink with friends and said: "Just as well I have so few children, only seven." There were families of 10, 12 and 14.

Our family nickname is Obispo (bishop), coming from my father and my grandfather, Antonio el Obispo, who came from Cómpeta. We're three brothers and a sister. My father died at 81. He was one of those people who have no luck in life.

My grandfather was illiterate but not stupid. Around 1915 he did a deal with the mayor of Cómpeta, presenting a house to the alcalde for a rent or for free, and a schoolmistress was posted here. It's the house where I was born. The school lasted 15 years and there were three or four mistresses. My father and his brothers had to work but my mother went to the school. Before the war, in the time of the Republic, the teacher left. Just the school with the desks was left.

Life's always been hard. I didn't have much fun. We didn't have electricity, nor radio. I used to see men passing by on the way to Fornes. They stopped at my house because Concha, my mother, had a tiny bar and it was on the route of the muleteers, the fish route from Nerja to the Granada market. So I saw the men. They'd sing a bit and drink. Later in the 60s an uncle bought a radio. When I was bigger I used to come to Frigiliana to see a film or during the fiestas.

I remember one fellow came from Monachil in Granada with a flock of good goats. He was a handsome bachelor and he fell for an Acebuchal girl so he went to speak to her father and he sang a copla. It went: "Although the waters of the Monachil river run dry, I will never break my word to you, Dolores." A woman who was there told the girl: "Marry him — he's shown me five *duros*." Five *duros* was a lot of money at that time. He had money that one. Indeed, the house he built in Acebuchal de Abajo cost him 22,000 *duros*, with mosaics and all. But he had to go off to Seville because, when the people of the sierra came, they would have taken everything off him.

Then several things happened and there were deaths. In 1947 they killed Antonio Ortiz Torres, the father of Antonio Federo. They took him off and killed him, on the level ground up above Acebuchal. The why of it is difficult, because there was no reason. Why were they Maquis? There was no reason. Possibly they had it in for him because they asked him for money and he didn't give it them. Or somebody working with him had a grudge against him. They went and killed him and that was it. Shotguns and pistols, that's the way it was then. They also kidnapped a mayor, Baldomero Torres López, my father's uncle who had a food store. He was held a few days until he paid something.

Here we call 1948 "the year of hunger". It was when there was the least food in this area after the war. We were hanging on and I was in the Barranco Moreno between July and August of 48 when the Maquis came, many people with shotguns etc. That August is when the Civil Guard ejected us. Acebuchal was left with the doors hanging open, deserted. There was just a company of Regulares and of soldiers here.

We went to Cómpeta because the villages were completely saturated. In Frigiliana there wasn't a house nor a stable available. So we looked for a house to rent in Cómpeta. My parents and my uncles and aunts went to sleep there. But later I returned to Acebuchal and stayed with my grandfather because they didn't meddle with the old folk and the kids, neither the Civil Guard nor the people of the sierra. My grandfather had a *cortijo* in Los Peñoncillos next to a house by the river and he and all the grandchildren stayed there.

One night when we were there the people of the sierra came to the farm. We were listening and I saw them. My grandfather scolded them: "Please, don't come here. Don't worry us. I have my grandchildren here." "It's all right, Paco Sánchez, we've come to smoke a cigarette. We don't want anything." "No, I don't want you here. Because tomorrow the Civil Guard will come too and then what?" After that, from September 14 to 16, 1949, there occurred the counter-attack at

El Acebuchal in ruins after the inhabitants were ordered out in 1948

Cerro Verde near Acebuchal. The Civil Guard fought the people of the sierra and two guards died, one from Alozaina and a corporal from Guaro. They took prisoner a fellow named Espartero (Miguel Ángel García Platero, from Frigiliana) at the Cerro Verde lime pit, but he didn't die there. They tied him up and dragged him along, beating him, and he died in Acebuchal. My family told me all about it.

I was little, I was only six, but I'll always remember the day the last of the sierra died. It was on January 20, 1952, when we were in our house by the river. They killed the last one, Lomas (Antonio Sánchez Martín), way up on the Pedregal hill, beside the Cortijo del Pino.

There wasn't evil in the people of the sierra, nor did they have political motivation. They were illiterates. What did they know of politics? I'm not a Francoist nor a rightwinger, I can't be. The Civil Guard hit my father. I can't be on the right. My religion forbids it, although they call me "the Bishop". But I can say one thing: Franco didn't order all those people to be killed, for sure. They themselves killed them, just as they abandoned the others that were in the sierra. They found trains, planes and gateways to help la Pasionaria and Carrillo get to France, so why didn't they help those people too?

For them, guns and death. And they had children. Antonio Lomas had two daughters, one a year older than me and one a year younger. He was holding one by the hand when they shot him in the heart. It was the lieutenant. That man must have had kids too. Lomas had a pistol and a hand grenade, but he put them in the kitchen of the farmhouse and surrendered. The lieutenant came up with his rifle and, at one metre away, bang! He killed him. I know this for sure. The lieutenant was accompanied by a guard called Señor Alarcón, who lived in Calle Alcalá in Madrid. He saw that death and, when he went back to Frigiliana, he didn't go out for six or seven days. He applied for leave. They kicked him off to Arenas and after six months he left the Civil Guard and went to work in Madrid as a taxi-driver. More than 20 years ago he called the town hall and asked if my wife's family was still here. He came to Frigiliana to spend three days with the family and then he told me how it happened. It's the truth.

One time they beat up my father, Baldomero, which is as though they beat me too. Antonio Sánchez, my mother's brother, and Pepe Benigno, the boyfriend of my mother's sister, were in the black market. They used to cross from Cómpeta to Fornes, Jayena, Játar, Arenas, taking grapes there and bringing back flour. If the Civil Guard grabbed them, it was bad, and if the people of the sierra caught them they had to sell to them.

One day my father and his two brothers-in-law were caught up in the Frigiliana Pass. The Civil Guard appeared, dressed as civilians as if they were bandits. They took the loads of flour and the mules, then they took off the harness and made them take their clothes off. They forced them to set fire to their clothing and to the harness. Then, when they were left only in white socks, they began shooting at them, but only with blanks or they would have killed them. They chased them off at a run.

When they got to Cómpeta, they hid because they didn't want to enter the village naked. They called out to a man passing: "Hey, tell my wife to bring me clothing and stuff." But the man ran away. They asked another to help and finally they entered Cómpeta. They went to the barracks to report: "The outlaws held us up and they stole our loads and our clothes." They knew who they were, the Civil Guard captain and the others in plain clothes. But they couldn't say anything, or they would have been liquidated. Three or four days later they

El Acebuchal (foreground) has been rebuilt. Cerro Verde, the hillside above the village, was the scene of a pitched battle.

called them to the barracks and told them: "We've found the animals and two or three sacks of flour." The rest they had eaten.

My father had relatives in the Río Seco and every year he made a couple of trips there. He took them flour and brought back watermelons, tomatoes, peppers. One worked just to eat. One day when he was going down the Río Seco, my father was stopped by a Civil Guard who was around here a lot and ended up marrying a Frigiliana girl. "Take off the harness," he ordered. And he burned it. We were waiting and waiting for my father. At last he came, with the mule without any harness, and he told us what had happened.

A short while ago a colleague told me that a retired guard in Nerja had told him an anecdote about a time when he was going along the Barranco Fernández and halted a man. He said: "I took away his harness and burned it and the fellow says 'Hombre, don't burn it. It's the only one I have and I'm going to work.' I told him 'I've burned the harness, but further up they're really going to flatten you.'" Before I learned this I used to speak to that retired guard, but I haven't spoken to him since. He's still alive. But he's got his deserts, even the woman he deserves.

The Civil Guard had four-day tours. They would leave Frigiliana one night, walking to the Venta Panaderos and staying there. Next day they would walk to Calixto, the next to Acebuchal. They'd pass a day around there and sleep again in Acebuchal before returning to Frigiliana. We weren't obliged but if they wanted to they could stay in my house. There were only two beds, one for my father and mother and one for my brother and me. They didn't have proper mattresses. We made them ourselves. When the Civil Guard came, my mother gave our bed to them. I don't know if they had the right and I don't think Franco told them to, but they said nothing and slept in my bed. And we kids slept on the animals' harness. They made us a small bed and the two of us lay there and covered ourselves with the canvas used in the olive harvest.

In 1953 we returned to Acebuchal as there were no more people in the sierra. From my mother's side we had the farm at Los Peñoncillos and from my father's that of El Pino. All those who had land, olives, figs, they could eat. My grandparents had a number of farms with grapes, raisins, peppers, tomatoes, potatoes, maize. We could eat, although it wasn't a good life. But I've no regrets, in fact I'm proud of being from Acebuchal, and why not? There are humble people who didn't go to college and had a different way of life but still know enough to scrap it out with other folk.

Few of us went back, just those who didn't have a house elsewhere. Only one house in Acebuchal had collapsed. The others had their roofs. All the doors were open from the Moors kicking them open and people going inside, but they weren't in ruins. There were plenty of rats, bats and insects. We were there until the summer of '67, six or seven families, more in summer. In those days we didn't have insurance, we didn't have a doctor. But we did have Don José. Don José Maldonado, the Torrox doctor, was very keen on hunting and, when he came to hunt, I went with him. When I was 14, I went for 16 days hunting the mountain goats. My parents, my brothers and friends went hunting with Don José and we didn't charge him anything. Then, when we needed him, we went with a mule and told him that our father or somebody was sick. He went for his horse, came and didn't charge us anything either. He gave us medicine too. "This for this, this for that. No, no charge." He was the insurance we had.

In my youth there was only one way to reach Frigiliana, on a mule or walking. I would be picking olives up above, in the Calixto *cortijo* in a big olive grove, but later it got burned. I would come running, wash myself in Acebuchal and go to Frigiliana or Nerja for a fiesta, and that same night walk back to Acebuchal. Then, after sleeping a little, back to Calixto, walking. I had a girlfriend in Frigiliana and, when I was 17 and she 15, I took her on muleback to the fiesta in Acebuchal. But I didn't continue with that because later I got fed up with that girl. And I went to do my military service.

But then something else occurred. In Acebuchal we always had work in the sierra, but the government produced something called "ICONA", and then "IARA" (forestry commissions), and afterwards came the Greens and the ecologists. They forbade us to work in the sierra, to collect esparto, make charcoal, build lime pits, cut pine trees and collect firewood to sell and to be able to eat. So one day my father said to my mother: "We shall have to go because we can't provide for the youngsters." We left in '67 and little by little Acebuchal was abandoned until everything was collapsing.

Now I'm glad to have been born in that time. I didn't have the enjoyment they have now, but that's not the fault of the young ones. The only thing that I'm sorry about is that, as a result of the customs and family background, we didn't have the opportunities others had. Also we were a bit denigrated. We were a little separated from the people of the village and they had names for us like "blockheads". They might say you were "a stupid" or an *"acebuchaleño"*. It was looking down on you. The same way that in Nerja they call folk from Río de la Miel *"los follesques"*. This has always caused me problems and I used to say to myself: "I have to demonstrate that I am better than you." Nobody has ever been able to take this pride away from me and they never will. I've worked 30 years for the Nerja town hall as an electrician. I got my schooling in the forces so as to take the course for corporals. I signed up and learned electricity.

Thanks to God, thanks to the people, Acebuchal has been restored. I hope it's going to be a holiday village. We brought the images from the chapel to the Cortijo del Pino and every year in June, since 1982, we hold a fiesta when all the families get together. They come from Málaga and all over.

"I don't feel bitter. Because we fought for liberty and for an ideal. We struggled for the Republic, because they wrenched it away from us."

Miguel Padial Martín (Campañito), member of Roberto's guerrilla group, born December 14, 1922, in Alhama de Granada, died October 16, 2007, in Madrid. He met his wife, Amada, a member of the Levante guerrilla group, in prison.

Many people joined the Maquis because of the hardships and heavy repression they were suffering. Others were in prison or in concentration camps, those they didn't shoot, because they shot people right, left and centre. They murdered anybody who might be leftwing.

In every town and village the rich folk would denounce those who had been in the Republican zone: "So-and-so has done this, so-and-so has done that." They would put you in jail or, if you stood out in any way, they'd shoot you. If you were accused of something unimportant, you'd get a beating and spend several years in prison.

They jailed my father as soon as he came back from the Republican zone after the war. He didn't even set foot in his house. He was sentenced to death because he was a Socialist. He was transferred from Granada to Guadix and then back again, and then to Burgos. They revised the sentences and commuted the death penalty to 12 years, then there was another revision and he was released after five or six years. My mother was left at home with four girls under 14 and myself aged 17. We had to struggle to raise my four sisters and my mother had to put them to work in a school.

I went to work on the land and afterwards, from 1943, I did military service in an engineers' regiment which was fortifying the Cádiz coast. Three more years of hunger and hardship. Also there were men of various drafts from the Republican zone, called up from 1936 onwards, all as naked as the day they were born. All they had to wear was a strip of blanket, tied with a belt so you couldn't see their private parts. The war had finished in 1939 but in 1943 they were still there, working as prisoners of war. Those of us in the 1942 and 1943 drafts had military uniforms and did the fortifying work. All those who were prisoners performed the services of cooking, cleaning and mechanics.

They couldn't be discharged until their families sent them some sort of clothing. To some they sent overalls and to others a poor sort of suit, whatever they could so they could be discharged. That was criminal. I was two years in Cádiz province, in Zahara de los Atunes and the area around Tarifa and Algeciras. There were two regiments building fortifications, along with some battalions of convicts, prisoners of war and political prisoners. They were doing all that because they expected that, when the Allies had finished with the world war, they would turn on Spain.

I joined the guerrillas in 1947 with some comrades from Salar and Alhama. I went because life wasn't very good what with all the hunger and misery. As a youngster I'd been in the Juventudes Socialistas Unificadas (young Socialists) and afterwards I joined the Communist Party. The Civil Guard in Alhama didn't know I was a Communist but they did know I'd been in the Republican zone.

Those who went off to the sierra didn't do so because they were delinquents. It was due to the repression, or they had escaped from jail or had been persecuted by the Civil Guard, or they'd suffered so many calamities. Or they had been supporting the guerrilla and they had been discovered. One fellow from Loja who was with me was a shepherd who had been liaising with us but joined us in the sierra when he was discovered.

At the time of the invasion of the Arán valley we expected that all the exiles in France, who'd been in the Republican army, would come over to liberate Spain. But it failed. Even so, I thought that the Allies would one day enter Spain and finish off Franco's regime because the guerrilla movement was very strong. We gave them a headache all over the place. It's not that we were very numerous. If we had been, we would have gained power. We were a few here, a few there and that disconcerted them. They couldn't handle us because it wasn't like a front where you could send in a division and liquidate the enemy.

I first went with my comrades to the Loja mountains. We were a small group in the Sierra Tejeda and towards Ronda, isolated and independent of Roberto. After a while we bumped into them and joined together. That lasted a while but then things didn't go as they ought. Guerrilla war is not like one imagines. It's very hard. There are days when you have food and days when you don't, days when it rains or snows, when you suffer heat or cold. Every day you have to put up with the changes in weather.

We had small tents sleeping two or three which protected you from rain and cold but the harshness of the weather was hard to take. On top of that, you had to march by night, moving from one place to another and spreading propaganda in the villages, showing why you were fighting and trying to convince the people.

But, as the repression was so great, those who weren't in prison were in concentration camps and the others couldn't move. As a result the guerrilla campaign wasn't making any progress.

Fear and hunger are tremendous things. The Civil Guard were on the lookout all the time around the village. You had to earn something to eat and, if you didn't have a day's labour, you had to fetch a load of firewood from the countryside to sell. You needed money to buy the miserable ration of food they gave you. There were ration cards and maybe they would give you a quarter litre of oil, half a kilo of flour or chick peas, a few crumbs of bread, or whatever. If you didn't work, you earned nothing. If you earned nothing, you couldn't eat. The people would go begging around the farms. That was real misery.

There were kidnappings when it was necessary. In the guerrilla war you took advantage of the fact that there were rich folk with money and you dealt them an economic blow. You took as much money from them as you could and with that you had to buy food, clothing, footwear and all those things.

I took part in one or two kidnappings. We would pick up some individual and take him away up the mountain, then send a message to his family, saying: "We want this amount of cash." There was one for 10 or 15,000 pesetas but there were some "economic blows" by the group of 200 and 300,000 pesetas. They always paid. In my group they didn't kill anybody, although of course there were cases. There were also many cases when the Civil Guard, disguised as guerrillas, committed holdups and blamed us.

Roberto arrived as chief of the guerrillas. He was from Madrid and had been a commissar in the Republican zone. There were many people in the sierra in small groups, men from all the villages of Granada and Málaga provinces, and they joined together in one big group. There were up to 150, but we were never together in one unit. Some groups would go one way, others another, organised to carry out missions.

There was always one big group, until they discovered them and there was a real skirmish. We were at a spot called Cerro Lucero. One fellow deserted and surrendered to the Civil Guard in the Frigiliana area. He it was who brought the Civil Guard and the Moors. They made him a temporary Civil Guard, complete with uniform and weapon, to lead them to where we were. Two companies of guards and two squads of Moors came to Cerro Lucero with him as guide.

From the one side they couldn't enter the encampment because it was too steep, but they could enter from the front and two flanks. In the night one of the sentries heard stones rolling. Up comes the captain and asks: "What's going on?" "I heard stones rolling." "Bah!" he says. "That'll be the wild goats." The previous day they had killed two goats. Off goes the captain, but at dawn the sentry again hears noises and sees through his binoculars that they aren't caused by goats. He advises the others: "Those goats have two legs. Look around."

Miguel Padial, second left, and fellow *guerrilleros* display the Republican flag

The whole camp jumped up and manned their posts and a battle began with the guards and Moors that lasted from dawn until dusk.

You knew they weren't coming to offer you pieces of candy. They were coming to shoot you. You always feel fear. It's free of charge and everybody grabs his share. But, when the enemy comes looking for you, you have to confront him. You're not going to wait with your arms crossed for him to kill you.

The battle went on all day and, when it got dark, we were all ready to beat a retreat. We only suffered one wounded, nothing serious, because we were in a good position, a little below the summit, where we dominated the terrain. In that situation the enemy is exposed when he comes in search of you. Many of the guards were killed and we marched off in the darkness.

We had another scrape on Cerro Verde with a group of soldiers. I don't know how the soldiers got into it. According to them, they were going to protect some workers but I don't believe they were protecting any worker because there were none involved. The soldiers arrived, confronted one of our groups and killed a captain of the guerrillas. As a result our group had to face up to them and we wiped out three corporals and several soldiers. We seized a machine gun and all the arms and ammunition they had.

We didn't want to confront the soldiers, but you have to defend yourself. They killed a captain because that corporal was hoping to rise in the ranks and be promoted to sergeant. Well, rise he did, by his death. When they put us on trial, a military officer claimed we had killed his sons. "But whom did your sons kill first?" we asked. After the captain was killed, the rest of us weren't going to quietly wait to be killed too. We reacted and eliminated almost all of them. We weren't the captain's sons.

We used to pass by Frigiliana, but mostly I was in the province of Granada. Several groups were operating in different places, each one in an area they knew. We would go with perhaps two or three guides acquainted with the terrain. Those who were from Loja, for example, moved through Granada. Several comrades would examine the stretch you were going to pass through. We travelled by night with a knapsack containing a bit of food, ammunition and clothing.

We received pay of 500 pesetas a month to buy tobacco or for necessary expenditure. You couldn't visit your family. Mainly this was because if they caught you visiting the family — and there's always somebody who sees — your family would suffer the consequences. They would arrest them, put them in jail, torture them. So you had to say goodbye to your family. You had to grin and bear it and keep going.

As for Roberto, everybody has given their opinion about him. When people live together, there are always frictions. There are those who accept a discipline and those who don't like it. Some take off because they can't take it or they speak out and they are punished in one way or another.

The informers were traitors. Several were killed but one didn't know anything about it, because any execution for a crime committed was carried out by a special group. I was just a normal guerrilla, defending himself when the enemy attacked and nothing more. I never saw anybody executed. Roberto's general staff were responsible. If you order somebody's execution and you have three or four whom you trust, you say: "Go with this group to that place." Then, if you say that on the journey so-and-so died or went away, who is going to check what did or didn't happen to him?

Finally, things weren't going well, life was bad and we decided to quit. Morale went down, naturally. All those years weigh heavily. The party changed its tactics. My feeling was that it had to happen and things could not go on the same. Without moral and personal support, there was no future, while the party said we had to give up armed struggle and talked of reconciliation and all that. Without any support and armed struggle all over, the moment arrives when you have to save yourself. What are you going to do? You can't go back to your village nor anywhere else, because you've no papers and nobody to shelter you. You lay down your arms or go to jail, they shoot you or you rot behind bars.

I escaped with my life because when it was going badly a group of us decided to head for France. On occasions we travelled by train, maybe on the buffers of a freight train, other times we walked, sometimes at night. But the police picked us up in Barcelona and, as we belonged to Granada, sent us back there.

We were lucky. A fellow countryman of mine was shot in the back by the Civil Guard and they took him to a barracks for a medical check. The idea was to see if they had hit him when he was confronting the Civil Guard or if he had been hit when he was running away. Captain Caballero of the Granada Civil Guard asked him: "Were you a long time in the sierra?" "Seven years, from '42 to '49." The captain told him: "Well, I wish I'd seen you there. You've had the luck to fall in the hands of the police. If you fell into my hands, after a good beating, you would have been shot while escaping." That was Captain Caballero of the Civil Guard.

After a year or so they tried us and sentenced us to 30 years. Of those I served 11, from 1949 to 1960, thanks to pardons proclaimed when two Popes died and four years or so redeemed through work. I was on probation for five years, reporting every month and unable to go anywhere without asking permission. I came to live in Madrid because they had it in for me in Granada and in the city there was more freedom.

Here I made contact with the Communist Party and my partner, who had also been involved in the guerrilla movement. We married shortly after and now have three children. In 1968 near May 1 and the events in France that month I was in trouble again. They detained me for distributing party propaganda and conspiracy and sentenced me to six years. Apart from that I suffered the torture dealt out by four or five worthies of the secret police, the Brigada Político-Social. They ask you a question and you answer them, thinking it has no importance. But it does and they start punching you, one on one side, one on the other, until you lose consciousness. When you're left lying on the floor like a rag, they throw a bucket of water over you. Then they tell the *"grises"* (grey-uniformed National Police) to take you down to your cell. After a while, when you've got cold, they take you up again and ask who gave you the propaganda. If you refuse to say, because you have to, they launch into you again. And that goes on until they're tired. Torture is always the same, to see if they can get more out of you.

They arrested Roberto in 1952 and the Civil Guard say he betrayed everybody, but torture is a heavy business and the human body has its limits. The torturers are criminals. I wasn't in Roberto's skin so I don't know what he could resist. But then the Civil Guard do whatever they please, saying: "You sit at that typewriter and write what I tell you. Write it!" They lay into you and lay into you and you write, putting down things you haven't done. You do what they tell you.

When they began arresting all the families, they didn't go for my close relatives and my father had already been in prison before I joined the guerrillas. But they detained a female cousin of mine, as they couldn't catch her husband who was in the sierra, and she was a little over two years in prison. He gave himself up and then they released her. They did that sort of thing very often.

Those who joined the Maquis from Alhama were almost all killed, although they didn't kill anybody from my group. Well, they did kill one who was proved to have caused a death and two brothers-in-law who instead of supporting the guerrillas committed holdups on their own account. They killed a boy they were going to kidnap. When we fell, they also arrested them and executed them.

At the end of course the guerrillas felt disillusioned. When there's no force supporting you, disillusion and demoralisation take over. What happened in the Civil War? It was one army against another and after three years of war everybody was sick of it. They wanted peace, because nobody wants war. And we didn't want to be in a guerrilla war either. We wanted peace and freedom but, if you have neither bread nor freedom, you have to fight. The immense majority of those who were fighting were left by the wayside.

I wouldn't say I feel bitter about all that. We went to fight for liberty and for an ideal. We struggled for the Republic because they wrenched it away from us, a republic constituted by the people and won in elections. Franco rebelled against the Republic and that set off the war, with the people struggling against a very powerful army supported by various nations, by Germany, England, France, the United States. They had a trained, professional army while in the Republican zone the workers formed the army.

I've been taking part in campaigns by the association Archivo, Guerra y Exilio (Archives of War and Exile) to retrieve our memories of the past. There are a lot of things that are being discovered and we're carrying on the fight: to uncover and recognise the crimes committed by Francoism. Imagine it, my wife's father died in the Maquis and a brother-in-law of hers too, and yet we don't even know where their bodies are.

The guerrillas of Frigiliana

Names are followed by village nicknames
and, in brackets, noms de guerre

Shot in clashes with the Civil Guard:
Bautista Acosta Urdiales – Tomarroque (Máximo)
José Castillo Moreno – Pepe Mocha (Mocha)
Miguel Ángel García Platero – Espartero (Julián)
Blas Martín Navas – Panzón (Gonzalo)
Blas Martín Vozmediano – Artabús (Blas)
José Pérez Moles – Ranica (Jorge)
Antonio Sánchez Martín – Lomas (Manuel)
José Sánchez Martín – Lomas (Domingo)
Antonio Rojas Álvarez – Miserere (Carlillos)
José Rojas Álvarez – Miserere (Arturo)

Committed suicide:
Antonio García Martín – Antoñico Virtudes (Gaspar)

Tried by court martial and executed:
Sebastián Martín Vozmediano – Artabús (Sebastián)
Antonio Platero Martín – El Moreno (Silverio)
Manuel Triviño Cerezo – Matutero (Valeriano)

Killed by their comrades:
Sebastián Martín Navas – Panzón (Federo)
Antonio Platero Ayllón – Chispa (Ricardo)

Served jail sentences:
Ángel García Martín – Zumbo (Marcelo)
José Martín Navas – Panzón (Tomás)
Vicente Martín Vozmediano – Artabús (Vicente)
Antonio Ruiz Cerezo (Yelo)

Miguel Cerezo González, El Canijo (Jaimito in the sierra), was in 2008 the sole survivor of the 21 men who went from Frigiliana to the sierra.

They went to the sierra

Acosta Urdiales, Bautista - Tomarroque (Máximo). Born in Frigiliana in 1905. Married. Farmworker. Fled to the mountains on December 16, 1946. Formed part of the Third Group, Sixth Battalion. Took part in the theft of flour from La Molineta in February, 1948. Accused of having killed Miguel Moreno González with a knife when he was kidnapped near Frigiliana in April, 1949. He died on August 26, 1951, during a 13-hour battle at Cerro Gitano (Gipsy Mountain), Sierra de Cázulas (Granada), when a Maquis group was surprised by a contrapartida (Civil Guards posing as guerrillas). Manuel Fajardo (Senciales), leader of the group, from Otívar, José Cecilia Márquez and Miguel Martín also died. Their bodies were put on public display before their burial in the cemetery of the Almuñécar fortress. Remains from the cemetery were removed some years ago, destination unclear. Senciales was shot by Corporal Eladio Ledesma, who was rewarded with promotion. Three guards received the Cross of Military Merit.

Castillo Moreno, José - Pepe Mocha (Mocha). Born in Frigiliana on October 12, 1929. Bachelor. Goat-herd. Fled to the sierra on April 20, 1950, with El Moreno (Antonio Platero Martín), who had wounded a Moorish soldier with an axe. His mother Josefa was jailed for helping the guerrillas. She confessed that her son had been buying food for those of the sierra during two years and had received 1,500 pesetas. He could not adapt to life in the sierra and wanted to return home.

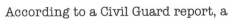

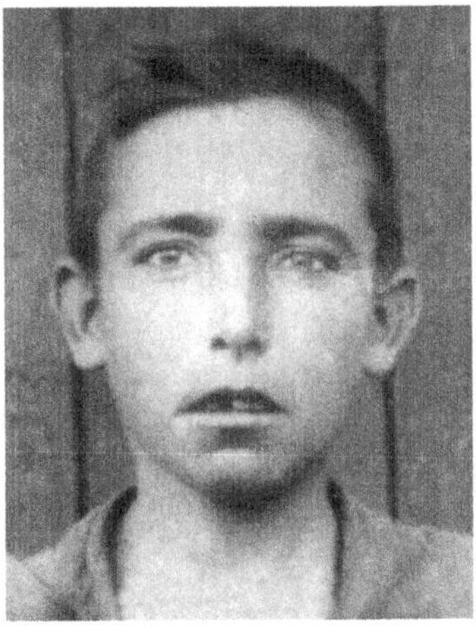

According to a Civil Guard report, a

corporal and 10 guards hid for 20 days at the Cortijo Pozo Húrtiga, near Alhama de Granada. At two in the morning on July 17, 1950, six armed bandits entered the farm to eat. The guards, hiding in a barn, opened fire, killing all six, including Mocha and Juan Alaminos Palacios (Teodoro), leader of the group. The bodies were displayed in Alhama.

Cerezo González, Miguel - El Canijo (Jaimito). Born in Frigiliana on June 2, 1927. Charcoal maker and esparto collector. Ignorant of politics but attracted by promises of money, on March 19, 1947, he ran off to the sierra with Antonio Platero Aylón (Chispa). He fell out with the leaders of Roberto's guerrilla group when he lost a shotgun. Suspecting that he might give himself up, they intended sending him to the sierra of Granada (euphemism for a death sentence). In fear, he fled back to Frigiliana in September, 1947, and hid in a stable where a neighbour, Rosario Triviño González (La Pichana), found him. As his life was in danger from his former comrades, he joined the Spanish Legion and was posted to North Africa. From there he went to work in Barcelona where he married and raised a family. In 2008 he was the only survivor of those who went to the sierra from Frigiliana.

García Martín, Ángel - Zumbo (Marcelo). Born in Frigiliana on November 3, 1927. Bachelor. Farmworker. Fled to the sierra on December 17, 1948, fearing he was about to be detained for aiding the guerrillas. Joined the Third Group, Sixth Battalion. He was called "The Hangman" because of the suspicion that he took part in the torture and death of two men from the village, El Bendita y El Terrible, at the Cruz de Napoleón in the Frigiliana riverbed. He was mistakenly declared dead in a shootout near Alfarnate in December, 1950. He surrendered in 1951 and collaborated with the Civil Guard. After some years in prison, he went to Barcelona where he married. He died in Barcelona.

García Martín, Antonio - Antoñico Virtudes (Gaspar). Born in Frigiliana on July 21, 1928. Bachelor. Charcoal maker. His father, Francisco García Ramírez, was arrested in 1942 accused of being secretary of the Frigiliana Communist network. He fled to the sierra on October 7, 1947, and held a senior position in the general staff. Present at the kidnapping of Ángel Sánchez García, carrying a machinegun, and allegedly took part in the murder at the Cortijo de Los Caños of three farmers accused of betrayal. He was finally trapped by the Civil Guard on July 5, 1951. Seeing he had no chance of escape, he destroyed any possessions of value and killed himself with his last bullet.

García Platero, Miguel Ángel - Espartero (Julián). Born in Frigiliana on August 4, 1901. Married, with six children. Farmer. According to a fellow guerrilla, he was condemned to death for some offence but Vicente Martín Vozmediano refused to carry out the sentence. He died on September 17, 1949, in one of the longest and fiercest encounters with the Civil Guard at Cerro Verde, near Acebuchal. According to the authorities, Espartero wounded the guard Antonio Román Ojeda with a machinegun and was found dead after the battle. Other versions indicate he surrendered and Captain Quilis, annoyed by his answer to a question, shot him. The Civil Register records only that he died from bullet wounds in the sierra.

Martín Navas, Blas - Panzón (Gonzalo). Born in Frigiliana on February 13, 1911. Married. Farmer. One of three brothers nicknamed Panzón. Went to the sierra in December, 1948, and joined the Third Group, Sixth Battalion. Allegedly helped another guerrilla in the execution of a shepherd. Died in February, 1951, when El Polopero's group clashed with the Civil Guard near the Haza del Lino farmhouse, in the Polopos area of Granada province. After a shootout, the Civil Guard pursued a group for several days. Finally they identified three bodies, Blas Martín, José Sánchez Martín (Domingo), also from Frigiliana, and Daniel Villena Ruiz (Gregorio) of Algarrobo.

Martín Navas, José - Panzón (Tomás). Born in Frigiliana on March 21, 1901. Married. Charcoal maker. In 1936 he was the local leader of leftwing militia. While he did not commit any act of violence during "the Marxist domination", he was accused of joining in the sacking of Frigiliana's Civil Guard barracks, of dressing with three others in guards' uniforms and tricorn hats, and of demanding money with menaces from local people. In defence, he claimed to have helped leading citizens, "taking them bread concealed under my jacket". He was jailed for life in 1938, but freed on January 23, 1944. He fled to the sierra on February 5, 1947. Joining the liaison group and armed with rifle and pistol, he became Roberto's closest aide and bodyguard. He was known as "Roberto's horse" because he often carried his chief, who was lame, on his back. Accused of taking part in at least two shootouts where

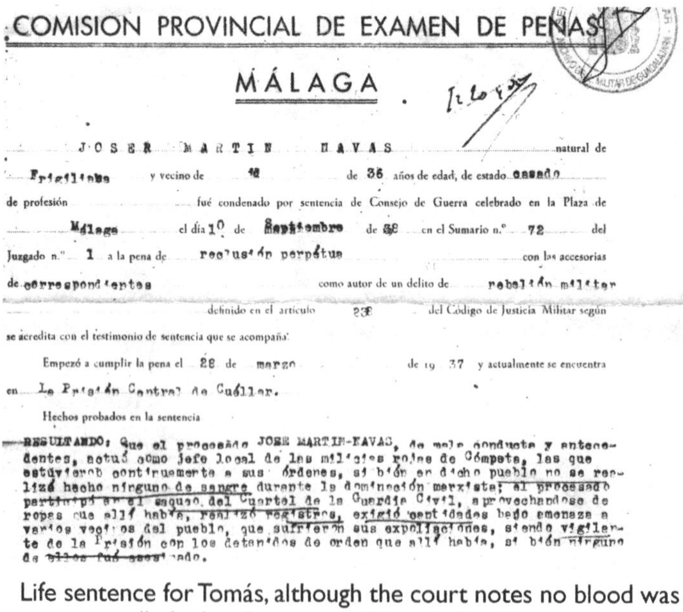

COMISION PROVINCIAL DE EXAMEN DE PENAS

MÁLAGA

JOSER MARTIN NAVAS natural de Frigiliana y vecino de id de 36 años de edad, de estado casado de profesión fué condenado por sentencia de Consejo de Guerra celebrado en la Plaza de Málaga el día 1º de Septiembre de 38 en el Sumario n.º 72 del Juzgado n.º 1 a la pena de reclusión perpétua con las accesorias de correspondientes como autor de un delito de rebelión militar definido en el artículo 238 del Código de Justicia Militar según se acredita con el testimonio de sentencia que se acompaña.

Empezó a cumplir la pena el 28 de marzo de 19 37 y actualmente se encuentra en La Prisión Central de Cuéllar.

Hechos probados en la sentencia

RESULTANDO: Que el procesado JOSE MARTIN-NAVAS, de mala conducta y antecedentes, actuó como jefe local de las milicias rojas de Cómpeta, las que estuvieron continuamente a sus órdenes, si bién en dicho pueblo no se realizó hecho ninguno de sangre durante la dominación marxista; el procesado participó en el saqueo del Cuartel de la Guardia Civil, aprovechandose de ropas que allí había, realizó registros, exigió cantidades bajo amenaza a varios vecinos del pueblo, que sufrieron sus expoliaciones, siendo vigilante de la Prisión con los detenidos de orden que allí había, si bién ninguno de ellos fué asesinado.

Life sentence for Tomás, although the court notes no blood was spilled when he was a militia chief in Cómpeta three guards died and also in a kidnapping in Nerja. Detained in December, 1951, following Roberto's betrayal. He was condemned to death, apparently because he was confused with another guerrilla, Andrés (José Martín García, de Escúzar, Granada), executioner of several guerrillas. Andrés was executed in Granada in April, 1953, but the Bishop of Málaga interceded on Tomás's behalf on the grounds he saved the lives of some rich Frigiliana inhabitants during the Civil War. The sentence was commuted to 30 years' prison. He was freed in 1964 in an amnesty. Died December 5, 1969, in Barcelona.

Martín Navas, Sebastián - Panzón (Federo). Born in Frigiliana January 16, 1903. Married, with three children. Charcoal maker. Communist, fought in the Republican zone in the Civil War, later spending more than three years in jail. Again imprisoned, for 14 months, in 1947 for taking food to his brother José in the sierra. Joined the guerrillas, Third Group, Sixth Battalion. In 1950 he was unhinged by the death of his son Manuel, aged 18, one of three young men murdered by the Civil Guard, and talked of surrendering. His comrades killed him, throwing his body off a cliff. It was discovered on June 17, 1951, by the Civil Guard and was taken to the Nerja cemetery where it was buried in a mass grave.

Martín Vozmediano, Blas - Artabús (Blas). Born in Frigiliana June 5, 1919. Bachelor. Farmworker. One of the three Artabús brothers who fled to the sierra on June 1, 1947, abandoning the charcoal they had been preparing. Branded an extremist by the Civil Guard, he had the rank of sergeant in the Third Group, Sixth Battalion. Rumours suggested he was killed by his brother Vicente because he was sick, but official files show he met his end in a shootout in the Barranco Cordero in the Higuerón river on January 17, 1951. His body was carried to Frigiliana on the back of a mule. The official record indicates he "died as a result of gunshot wounds".

Martín Vozmediano, Sebastián - Artabús (Sebastián). Born in Frigiliana April 9, 1917. Bachelor. Farmworker. Accused of being the chief instigator of the sacking of the village church in 1936 and of arresting local authorities. He fled to the Republican zone and later spent some years in jail. Detained in 1946 for being part of a Communist cell. One of the Sixth Battalion commanders, with the rank of lieutenant in the First Group. Took part in the kidnapping of Ángel Sánchez García, possibly in the killing of three men at Los Caños farm, and in the death of fellow guerrilla Antonio Platero Ayllón (Chispa), thrown into a well. "Very self-sacrificing. You didn't meddle with him," according to a comrade. Arrested December 17, 1951, in a trap set by the Civil Guard in Málaga, he was executed in Granada on May 6, 1953.

Martín Vozmediano, Vicente - Artabús (Vicente). Born in Frigiliana February 13, 1915. Married. Farmworker. Lieutenant in the Third Group, Sixth Battalion. One of the most notorious guerrillas from Frigiliana and the most feared due to his violent character. Sentenced to 12 years' prison in 1939 for helping "the rebellion". Took part in kidnapping of Ángel Sánchez García (freed) and Antonio Ortiz Torres (killed), from Acebuchal. Also in the kidnapping and death of Miguel Moreno González and the villagers El Bendita y El Terrible, all accused of being traitors. In March, 1951, he disarmed another guerrilla, El Jacinto (Francisco Bonilla Arrebola, from Salar, Granada), and surrendered with him to the Civil Guard. Jacinto later ran off from a Frigiliana barracks, taking a sub-machinegun, but was soon killed in a clash at Alhama de Granada. Vicente "put himself resolutely at the service of the Civil Guard in repentance for his past life", wore a guard's uniform and gave away many of his comrades, pointing out their hideaways. It appears he was taken to Madrid to identify Roberto and help in his detention. Thanks to his collaboration, he avoided the death penalty but spent some time in prison. Hated in the village, he went to Barcelona where he died on April 22, 1996.

Pérez Moles, José - Ranica (Jorge). Born in 1906 in Fornes (Granada). Muleteer, married to a woman from Acebuchal. Militant in the Spanish Socialist Party, he fled from Fornes to the Republican side. On returning he was accused of being a member of the Federación Anarquista Ibérica and of various crimes, including carrying petrol to burn farmhouses and taking part in attacks on Civil Guard barracks. Sentenced to seven years' jail, then banished from Granada to Acebuchal. On January 2, 1947, he joined Roberto's guerrillas. His family knew no more of him until 2002 when they learned he died June 17, 1948. Following a betrayal, a battle of several hours occurred near Soportújar, in the Alpujarras region of Granada. Ranica, Juan Romero Arellano (Juanillo) and another unidentified man were killed and buried in a mass grave in Lanjarón cemetery. Civil Guard Emilio Oliva Martín, who was seriously wounded in the right leg, received the Cross of Military Merit and a reward of 3,000 pesetas.

Platero Ayllón, Antonio - Chispa (Ricardo). Born in Frigiliana October 8, 1927. Bachelor. Charcoal maker. He carried food to the group which kidnapped Ángel Sánchez García in February, 1947, and in March ran off to the sierra with Miguel Cerezo González. Was in Roberto's liaison group. A first cousin, Sebastián Platero Navas, disappeared in the sierra, apparently killed by the Guardia Civil. Accused of being involved in the kidnapping and murder of Paulino Fernández Ortega in August, 1947. Three comrades, allegedly Felipe, Guillermo and Jaime, killed him because of his indiscretions with women, including apparently a widow from Algarrobo. He left a pregnant girlfriend in Frigiliana. In July, 1951, a goatherd noticed a bad smell from a well near Algarrobo and Chispa's decomposed body was found there.

Platero Martín, Antonio - El Moreno (Silverio). Born in Frigiliana June 23, 1929. Bachelor. Farmworker. The Civil Guard learned he was supplying food to the Maquis and pressured him to inform on them. Trapped between the two forces, on April 20, 1950, he attacked a Moorish soldier, Mohamed Ben Abdela, with an axe and then fled to the sierra. His mother, Florencia, admitted delivering tobacco and shotgun cartridges to the guerrillas. El Moreno and

P L A T E R O
A N T O N I O
A Y L L O N

(a) Chispa.- Natural y vecino de Frigiliana Provincia de Màlaga de 19 años en 1.947, hijo de Blas y Dolores estado soltero, de profesiòn carbonero con residencia en calle Franco s/n.

SEÑAS PERSONALES.- Estatura 1.750, pelo castaño, cejas al pelo, ojos melados, nariz recta, barba poca y boca grande.

ANTECEDENTES.- No se le conoce haya participado en hechos delictivos de ninguna clase ni haber pertenecido a partidos politicos debido a su corta edad, pero ya mayor se dedicaba a la rapiña de toda clase y simpatizante a las izquierdas. El dia 19 de Marzo de 1.947, saliò de su domicilio al objeto de confeccionar carbòn a la sierra y hasta la fecha no ha aparecido ignorandose su paradero, pero según rumores publicos se encuentra con los bandoleros.

R O J A S
A N T O N I O
A L V A R E Z

12

(a) Miserere.- Natural de Frigiliana Provincia de Màlaga, de 23 años en 1.947, Hijo de Josè y de Ana, estado soltero, profesiòn del campo, con residencia en el Acebuchal.
SEÑAS PERSONALES.- Estatura 1.705, color moreno, pelo negro, ojos al pelo, nariz recta, barba naciente, padece del corazòn y motivado a su enfermedad dà èl color palido.
ANTECEDENTES.- No se le reconoce haya cometido hechos delictivos alguno ni haber pertenecido a partidos politicos debido asu corta edad, pero mayor se dedicaba a la vagancia y simpatizante a las izquierdas.- El dia 2 de Enero de 1.94[illegible] saliò de su domicilio ignorando su paradero, pero si, por confidencias se sabequ[illegible] este sujeto se encuentra en la sierra con los bandoleros.

HECHOS DELICTIVOS EN LOS QUE SE SUPONE HAYA TOMADO PARTE.-

En los tres asesinatos del cortijo de Los Baños el 14-9-48

SANCHEZ
ANTONIO
MARTIN

Apodo: Lomas.-Natural de Cómpeta y vecino de Frigiliana, provincia de Málaga, de 31 años de edad en el 1950,-Hijo de Antonio y Virtudes, de estado casado, profesión campo, domiciliado en calle Alta s/n.
SEÑAS PERSONALES: Estatura 1'650, ojos pardos claros, barba poblada, color moreno, nariz recta, boca pequeña y cerrada.
ANTECEDENTES: Antes y durante el G.M.N. no observó mala conducta, perteneciendo a la U.G.T. sin significarse.-El dia 9 de Agosto de 1947, fué detenido, sufriendo condena un año, por habersele encontrado en su domicilio cortijo "El Iman", ropa de bandoleros.-El dia 20 de Abril de 1950, desapareció de su domicilio, suponiendose tuviera cumplicidad en la agresión y heridas graves a un Soldado de Regulares de Alhucemas Nº 5.-El fichado tiene su hermano José de bandolero en la partida del Roberto, desde el año 1947, por lo que es de suponer que éste sujeto se haya unido a la referida partida.-La esposa del fichado se encuentra en la Carcel por ser enlace de bandoleros.

HECHOS DELICITIVOS DE LOS QUE SE SUPONE HAYA TOMADO PARTE
Se ignora.

Civil Guard reports on three Frigiliana guerrillas, Antonio Platero Ayllón (Chispa), Antonio Rojas Álvarez (Carlillos) and Antonio Sánchez Martín (Lomas). Often the information was incorrect.

Lomas were the last Frigiliana men in the sierra. In January, 1952, El Moreno visited his family during the San Sebastián fiesta and they persuaded him to surrender. He revealed the whereabouts of Lomas. Although he collaborated, informing on those who had given aid, he was executed in Málaga on April 3, 1954.

Rojas Álvarez, Antonio - Miserere (Carlillos). Born in Frigiliana October 11, 1924. Bachelor. Farmworker. Lived in Acebuchal before taking to the sierra on January 2, 1947. Said to have heart problems. One of the liaison group, alleged to have participated in kidnapping of Paulino Fernández Ortega and three killings at Cortijo Los Caños. Apparently was among those who in October, 1947, killed three Civil Guards "in error", the intended target being a hated corporal based at the paper mill in the Río de la Miel. Reported dead by the Civil Guard at Cerro Verde in 1949, but the body was actually that of Rafael Jurado Martín (Nico). He allegedly killed a kidnap hostage in the Alhama de Granada area in 1951 after the family tipped off the authorities. Died in a clash near the Alhama cemetery on August 16, 1951.

Rojas Álvarez, José - Miserere (Arturo). Born in Frigiliana January 26, 1921. Bachelor. Goatherd. Known as The Barber. Worked at the Venta Panaderos. When the owner, Paco Manuela, was arrested in 1947, decided to join the guerrillas. Sergeant in the First Group, Sixth Battalion, he led a group responsible for several kidnappings. According to a Civil Guard report, he died in a battle with the contrapartida at Cerro del Cisne on April 16, 1951, due to the betrayal of Vicente, another Frigiliana guerrilla. His nom de guerre led to a confusion of identities. Another "Arturo", Arturo Moreira, from Galicia, who arrived on the Granada coast from Oran with the Ramón Vías expedition, died on August 17, 1947, in a shootout at a farm used by the Maquis. Moreira killed a guard, suffered a broken leg and, finding himself surrounded, shot himself. The farm's owner, La Cascaja (María Martín Godoy, from Torrox), was arrested and later, reportedly, informed on Roberto.

Ruiz Cerezo, Antonio (Yelo). Born in Frigiliana December 4, 1912. Widower. Farmworker. Nicknamed "Robapera" (literally "pear thief"), apparently because he fled to the sierra after stealing some carob beans in 1945. Took part in several kidnappings. Allegedly took part in a raid on the San Modesto power station near Nerja when four armed men threatened the operator and stole a shotgun. According to one guerrilla, he stole cash from his group leader, then fled to Nerja where he hid in his lover's house. He was believed dead. He was betrayed and sentenced to 10 years in jail. Later he went to Barcelona.

Sánchez Martín, Antonio - Lomas (Manuel). Born in Frigiliana May 14, 1920. Married. Farmworker. The last guerrilla in the Sierra Almijara. After "outlaws' clothing" was found at his farm, he was sentenced to one year in jail. Later, on April 20, 1950, he fled to the sierra, suspected of having participated in an attack on a Moorish soldier (actually the work of El Moreno). He became part of Roberto's personal guard. When El Moreno gave himself up, he revealed Lomas's whereabouts. Early on January 20, 1952, Civil Guards surrounded the Ángel Rojas farmhouse. Witnesses claim Lomas was shot after surrendering. His body was carried on muleback through the village during the San Sebastián fiesta. His wife, Ana Santisteban Gutiérrez, was imprisoned in Málaga for taking clothing and food to the Maquis. Two daughters, Ana and Virtudes, went to live in Barcelona.

Sánchez Martín, José - Lomas (Domingo). Born in Frigiliana on March 4, 1923. Brother of Antonio (Lomas). Bachelor. Charcoal maker. After his parents died, an aunt cared for him in Acebuchal. Suspected of supporting the Maquis and with an uncle imprisoned for helping them, he fled to the sierra on January 2, 1947, joining the Third Group, Sixth Battalion. Among those who kidnapped Frigiliana youth Ángel Sánchez García. In February, 1951, the Civil Guard reported a patrol had repelled "with magnificent spirit" an attack by "a party of bandits commanded by the criminal outlaw Paco El Polopero" in a mountainous area near the village of Polopos (Granada). On February 8 a cable announced the death of "the outlaw José Martín Sánchez (sic), alias Domingo," and the capture of another "bandit". Blas Martín Navas, also of Frigiliana, died in the same encounter.

Triviño Cerezo, Manuel - Matutero (Valeriano). Born in Frigiliana May 17, 1929. Farmworker. Suffered from deafness. Arrested in 1946 with eight other villagers accused of being part of a Communist cell, following a shooting attack on the house of Justo López Navas in the main street. Also detained in 1947, accused of demanding money from a Nerja farmer. Joined the Third Group, Sixth Battalion. After giving himself up on June 30, 1951, his information led to the detention of many supporters of the Maquis. He was accused of several violent crimes. He admitted that, on the orders of Clemente (one of the Frailes brothers), he took part in the killing of Francisco López Centurión (Lucas), from Nerja, a guerrilla suspected of planning to surrender. Tried and executed at Málaga's San Rafael cemetery on April 3, 1954.

SOURCES

BIBLIOGRAPHY

Guerrilla war in the Axarquía

Azuaga Rico, José María: *La guerrilla antifranquista en Nerja*, Izquierda Unida, Nerja, 1996.

Heine, Hartmut & José María Azuaga Rico: *La oposición al franquismo en Andalucía Oriental*, Fundación Salvador Seguí, Madrid, 2005.

Olmo, Juan Fernández: *Episodios del maquis en la Axarquía*, Vélez-Málaga, 1999.

Romero Navas, José Aurelio: *La guerrilla en 1945 - Proceso a dos jefes guerrilleros*, Diputación de Málaga, 1999; *Recuperando la memoria - entrevistas orales a los protagonistas de la época guerrillera antifranquista*, Diputación de Málaga, 1997; *Censo de guerrilleros y colaboradores de la agrupación guerrillera de Málaga-Granada*, Diputación de Málaga, 2004.

Axarquía history

Caro Baroja, Julio: *Los moriscos del reino de Granada*, Ediciones Istmo, Madrid, 1985.

Hurtado de Mendoza, Diego: *Guerra de Granada*, Castalia, Madrid, 1970.

Montoro Fernández, Francisco: *Bandoleros de la Axarquía*, Acento Andaluz, Málaga, 2001.

Navas Acosta, Antonio: *Vida y diáspora morisca en la Axarquía veleña,* Málaga, 1995.

Rojo Platero, Pablo: *Cien años de Nerja y Frigiliana en fotos*, Nerja, 2004.

Ruiz García, Purificación: *La taha de Frigiliana después de la Conquista*, Arte y Cultura, Vélez-Málaga, 1994.

Sánchez Sánchez, Antonio: *Cronología de Frigiliana* and other historical data, unpublished.

General

Acosta Bono, Gonzalo, José L. Gutiérrez Molina, Lola Martínez Macías y Ángel del Río Sánchez: *El canal de los presos 1940-1962*, Crítica, Barcelona, 2004.

Aguado Sánchez, Francisco: *El maquis en España*, Editorial San Martín, Madrid, 1975; *El maquis en sus documentos*. Editorial San Martín. Madrid, 1976; *Historia de la Guardia Civil (1936-1952)*, Planeta, Barcelona, 1984.

Allan, Ted & Sydney Gordon: *The scalpel, the sword - The story of Dr Norman Bethune*, McClelland & Stewart, Toronto, 1989.

Barranquero Texeira, Encarnación: *Málaga entre la guerra y la posguerra*, Editorial Arguval, Málaga, 1994.

Blaye, Edouard de Blaye: *Franco and the politics of Spain*, Penguin, London, 1976.

Boyle, Andrew: *The climate of treason*, Hutchinson, London, 1979.

Brenan, Gerald: *The Spanish labyrinth*, Cambridge University Press, Cambridge, 1943.

Bristow, Desmond: *A game of moles – The deceptions of an MI6 officer*, Warner Books, London, 1994.

Brown, Anthony Cave: *Bodyguard of lies*, W.H.Allen, London, 1976; *The last hero – Wild Bill Donovan*, Vintage Books, New York,1984.

Burgos, Antonio: *Andalucía, ¿Tercer mundo?*, Ediciones 29, Barcelona, 1971.

Carrillo, Santiago: *Memorias*, Editorial Planeta,1993.

Collective authorship: *Andalucía – Historia de los Pueblos de España*, Argos Vergara, Barcelona, 1984.

Coon, Carleton S.: *Adventures and discoveries*, Prentice-Hall, New Jersey, 1981; *A North African story — The anthropologist as OSS agent 1941-43*, Gambit, Ipswich (Mass.), 1980.

Debray, Regis y Gallo, Max: *Y mañana España*, interview with Santiago Carrillo, Editorial Laia, Barcelona, 1977.

Díaz Carmona, Antonio: *Bandolerismo contemporáneo*, CBC, Madrid, 1969.

Domingo, Alfonso: *El canto del búho*, Editorial Oberon, Madrid, 2002.

Estruch Tobella, Joan: *Historia oculta del PCE*, Ediciones Temas de Hoy, Madrid, 2000.

Fernández Vargas, Valentina: *La resistencia interior en la España de Franco*, Ediciones Istmo, Madrid, 1981.

Gibson, Ian: *Paracuellos — cómo fue*, Temas de Hoy, Madrid, 2005.

Hayes, Carlton J.H.: *Wartime mission in Spain*, Macmillan, New York, 1945.

Heine, Hartmut: *La oposición política al franquismo*, Editorial Crítica, Barcelona, 1983.

Ibárruri, Dolores: *Memorias de La Pasionaria 1939-1977*, Editorial Planeta, Barcelona, 1984.

Kaiser, Carlos J.: *La guerrilla antifranquista*, Editorial Crítica, Madrid, 1976.

Lafuente, Isaías: *Esclavos por la patria*, Temas de Hoy, Madrid, 2004.

Líster, Enrique: *Así destruyó Carrillo el PCE*, Editorial Planeta, Barcelona, 1983; *Basta!!*, Editorial Guillermo Del Toro, Madrid 1981.

Morán, Gregorio: *Grandeza y miseria del PCE 1939-85*, Editorial Planeta, Barcelona, 1986.

Moreno Gómez, Francisco: *La resistencia armada contra Franco*, Editorial Crítica, Barcelona, 2001.

Nadal Sánchez, Antonio: *Guerra Civil en Málaga*, Editorial Arguval, Málaga, 1984.

Pons Prades, Eduardo: *Guerrillas españolas 1939-1960*, Editorial Planeta, Barcelona, 1977.

Preston, Paul: *Franco – a biography*, HarperCollins, London 1993. (Spanish edition: *Franco, Caudillo de España*, Mondadori, Barcelona, 1994.)

Serrano, Secundino: *Maquis*, Temas de Hoy, Madrid, 2001.

Sorel, Andrés: *La guerrilla antifranquista - La historia del maquis contada por sus protagonistas*, Editorial Txalaparta, Tafalla, 2002.

Thomas, Hugh: *The Spanish Civil War*, Penguin, London, 1965.

Confidential reports of the Civil Guard

Limia Pérez, Eulogio: *Resumen del problema del bandolerismo en la provincia de Granada*, Granada, 1951; *Reseña general del problema del bandolerismo en España después de la guerra de liberación*, prepared for directors of the Civil Guard, Madrid, 1957.

Newspapers

Sur de Málaga

Ideal de Granada

Patria (Granada)

Other publications

Por La República, organ of the Andalusian guerrilla army.

Mundo Obrero, 1944-1952, and *Nuestra Bandera*, 1945-1952, organs of the

PCE (Spanish Communist Party).

Studies published by La Gavilla Verde in connection with conferences on the Maquis in Santa Cruz de Moya.

Television documentaries

La guerrilla de la memoria, Oria Films.

Las fosas del olvido, Argonauta Producciones, TVE.

Movimiento guerrillero en Andalucía – El maquis, Cibeles TV, Canal Sur.

Archives

Archivo General Militar de Ávila.

Archivo Histórico Provincial de Málaga.

Archivo Histórico, Partido Comunista de España, Madrid.

Archivos Históricos de la Capitanía General de Granada (in Almería and Málaga).

Asociación de Antiguos Militares de La República, Barcelona.

Estudios Históricos, Dirección General de la Guardia Civil, Madrid.

Granada municipal newspaper library, Casa de los Tiros.

Málaga Civil Government files.

Málaga municipal newspaper library.

National Archives of the United States, Maryland.

Parish registry, San Antonio de Padua, Frigiliana.

Registry offices: Frigiliana, Torrox, Vélez-Málaga, Arenas, Fornes.

Spanish National Library, Madrid.

Town hall archives, Frigiliana.

Web pages

Asociación Archivo, Guerra y Exilio: www.galeon.com/agenoticias/

Asociación Recuperación de la Memoria Histórica: www.memoriahistorica.org

Foro por la Memoria: www.foroporlamemoria.info

International Brigades: www.brigadasinternacionales.org

http://es.geocities.com/paisajes_guerrilla/

www.lagavillaverde.org

INDEX

MORE BOOKS BY DAVID BAIRD FROM MAROMA PRESS

Sunny Side Up — The 21st century hits a Spanish village
Documentary. Nostalgic, witty, insightful. What goes on behind those white walls as 'progress' comes to a rural community. "Baird's ironic glance back over the past 30 years is recommended reading for anybody who wondered what happened to 'the real Spain' " — *Sunday Times*

Typhoon Season
Fiction. A fast-paced thriller set in Hong Kong. A body floating in the South China Sea, a missing heroin stash, corruption in high places...in the fading days of empire the British colony is living on borrowed time. And anything can happen in the typhoon season.

Don't Miss The Fiesta!
Fiction. Beneath the placid surface of a remote village in the Spanish sierras sinister forces are at work. Fleeing from his scandalous past, an expatriate finds himself caught up in a whirlwind of primitive passions, leading to a chilling climax.

On sale at English bookshops in Spain and by direct order from the publishers. Or from Amazon and other websites.

For more information, contact:

Maroma Press
Calle Real, 76
29788 Frigiliana
(Málaga) Spain
http://maromapress.wordpress.com/
email: maroma.press@gmail.com

Maroma Press

Lightning Source UK Ltd.
Milton Keynes UK
UKOW06f0405010316

269361UK00009B/91/P

9 788461 220533